Praise for the Fir[...]
The Option Trade[...]

M000277929

"Unlike most books that oversimplify trading situations, Augen's approach forces you to learn by solving real-world problems where stock prices spike up and down and volatility changes constantly. Learning by doing is a distinct advantage for both novice and expert."

—Sean Sztern, Alternative Strategies Group, Desjardins Securities

"This workbook represents a unique and effective learning tool. It will broaden your understanding of options and raise your trading skills to a higher level."

—Dr. W. Edward Olmstead, Northwestern University, author of *Options for the Beginner and Beyond*

"Serious options trading requires skills that can only be learned through practice. Augen's progressively more challenging problems definitely provide that real-world practice. There are lessons here for everyone, from beginner to sophisticated professional."

—James Marcus, Partner, CMG Holdings, LLC

THE
OPTION
TRADER'S
WORKBOOK

SECOND EDITION

THE
OPTION
TRADER'S
WORKBOOK

A Problem-Solving Approach

Second Edition

Jeff Augen

Vice President, Publisher: Tim Moore
Associate Publisher and Director of Marketing: Amy Neidlinger
Executive Editor: Jim Boyd
Editorial Assistant: Pamela Boland
Senior Marketing Manager: Julie Phifer
Assistant Marketing Manager: Megan Graue
Cover Designer: Chuti Prasertsith
Cover Photograph: GlowImages, GettyImages, Inc.
Managing Editor: Kristy Hart
Project Editor: Betsy Harris
Copy Editor: Cheri Clark
Proofreader: Kathy Ruiz
Senior Indexer: Cheryl Lenser
Senior Compositor: Gloria Schurick
Manufacturing Buyer: Dan Uhrig

First Printing October 2011

ISBN-10: 0-13-210135-1
ISBN-13: 978-0-13-210135-6

Pearson Education LTD.
Pearson Education Australia PTY, Limited.
Pearson Education Singapore, Pte. Ltd.
Pearson Education North Asia, Ltd.
Pearson Education Canada, Ltd.
Pearson Educación de Mexico, S.A. de C.V.
Pearson Education—Japan
Pearson Education Malaysia, Pte. Ltd.

Library of Congress Cataloging-in-Publication Data

Augen, Jeffrey.
  The option trader's workbook : a problem-solving approach / Jeff Augen. — 2nd ed.
    p. cm.
  ISBN 978-0-13-210135-6 (pbk. : alk. paper)
  1. Options (Finance) 2. Investment analysis. 3. Stock price forecasting. I. Title.
  HG6024.A3A922 2012
  332.63'2283—dc23
                                2011030802

To Lisa and our little friends
both past and present—
Spokes, Hobie, Einstein, Regis, Rocky, Stella, Skooch,
Rugby, and Bonzo.

Contents

Preface

There are two kinds of successful investors: those who admit to occasionally losing money and those who don't. Despite claims to the contrary, every investor loses money because risk always scales in proportion to reward. Long-term winners don't succeed by never losing; they succeed because their trades are well thought out and carefully structured. That said, very few investors recognize the impact of their own trading mistakes.

These mistakes can be subtle. The classic example goes something like this:

1. "I bought calls."
2. "The stock went up, but I still lost money!"

This frustrating scenario in which an investor correctly predicts a stock's direction but loses money is incredibly common in the option trading world. Leverage is almost always the culprit. More precisely, it is the misuse of leverage that stems from a fundamental misunderstanding of risk that so often turns investing into gambling with the simple click of a mouse. Option traders are famous for this mistake. They know, for example, that a sharp rise in the price of a stock can generate tremendous profit from nearly worthless far out-of-the-money calls. But lead is not so easily transmuted into gold. The problem is entangled with complex issues like collapsing volatility, accelerating time decay, and regression toward the mean. Institutional traders understand these issues and they rarely make these mistakes. Thousands of trades have taught them that not losing money is the very best way to generate a profit.

It's the thousands of trades, winners and losers both, that separate professionals from amateurs. Option trading is just like playing chess: It requires study and practice. The comparison is more valid than you might think. Both chess and option trading are governed by a complex set of rules. Risk analysis is at the center of both games; so is positional judgment and the ability to react quickly. Chess players learn to identify patterns; option traders, in their own way, must learn to do the same.

This book is constructed around these themes. It is designed to let investors explore a vast array of rules and trade structures by solving real-life problems. This approach differs markedly from the catalog of structured trades that seems to have become the contemporary standard for option trading books. Many fine texts have been written on the subject, but most build on this design with slightly different organization or a few novel trading ideas. Collectively they miss the point. Learning to trade options is an active process, best accomplished through doing rather than reading and memorizing. In this regard we have avoided the familiar but bewildering list that includes names like "reverse diagonal calendar spread," "condor," and "short strangle." In their place you will find more descriptive phrases like "sell the near-dated option and buy the far-dated option." But, more importantly, these descriptions appear in the context of trading situations in which the reader is asked to make a choice, predict an outcome, or design a correction. Moreover, the problems build on each other with each section progressing from basic to advanced.

Our goal was to challenge option traders at all levels. So take your time, work through the problems at a comfortable pace, and, most important of all, make your trading mistakes here instead of in your brokerage account.

Acknowledgments

I would like to thank the team who helped pull the book together. First and foremost is Jim Boyd who was willing to take the risk of publishing a new type of options book built around the problem-solving concept. His guidance and sound advice have added much clarity and organization to the text. Authors create only rough drafts—finished books are created by project editors. In that regard Betsy Harris was responsible for turning the original text into a publication-quality document. Without that effort the book would be nothing more than a collection of interesting math problems. I would also like to thank Cheri Clark who carefully read and edited the text.

It is always difficult for an author to be objective about his own work. That job fell to Arthur Schwartz who patiently checked all my calculations and made suggestions about new problems and examples.

Finally, I would like to acknowledge the excellent work of the Pearson marketing team. I've certainly learned a great deal about web-based digital marketing from working with Julie Phifer.

In these historic times of financial unrest, options have taken their rightful place as sophisticated investment vehicles. Making them accessible to a wider audience has been our principal goal.

About the Author

Jeff Augen, currently a private investor and writer, has spent more than a decade building a unique intellectual property portfolio of databases, algorithms, and associated software for technical analysis of derivatives prices. His work, which includes more than a million lines of computer code, is particularly focused on the identification of subtle anomalies and price distortions.

Augen has a 25-year history in information technology. As cofounding executive of IBM's Life Sciences Computing business, he defined a growth strategy that resulted in $1.2 billion of new revenue and managed a large portfolio of venture capital investments. From 2002 to 2005, Augen was President and CEO of TurboWorx Inc., a technical computing software company founded by the chairman of the Department of Computer Science at Yale University. His books include *Microsoft Excel for Stock and Option Traders*, *Trading Realities*, *Day Trading Options*, *Trading Options at Expiration*, *The Option Trader's Workbook*, and *The Volatility Edge in Options Trading*. He currently teaches option trading classes at the New York Institute of Finance and writes a weekly column for *Stocks, Futures and Options* magazine.

Notes

The following abbreviations will occasionally be used:

ATM = at-the-money (underlying security trades close to the strike price)

OTM = out-of-the-money (underlying security trades below the strike price of a call or above the strike price of a put)

ITM = in-the-money (underlying security trades above the strike price of a call or below the strike price of a put)

DITM = deep in-the-money (underlying security trades far above the strike price of a call or far below the strike price of a put)

DOTM = deep out-of-the-money (underlying security trades far below the strike price of a call or far above the strike price of a put)

Sqrt = Square root

StdDev = Standard deviations

1

Pricing Basics

The financial markets are a zero sum game where every dollar won by one investor is lost by another. Knowledge and trading tools are the differentiating factors that determine whether an investor lands on the winning or losing side. This book is designed to help investors expand their knowledge of pricing and trading dynamics. The problems are designed to be solved using basic principles and simple tools such as paper, pencil, and a calculator or spreadsheet program. Although you are strongly encouraged to become familiar with the use of an option pricing calculator, that skill will not be required to complete the problems in this book. However, it is always advantageous to explore different pricing scenarios with an option calculator and, in this context, you are encouraged to expand the problems and concepts that appear throughout the book.

That said, such calculators are the most basic and essential tool for an option trader. Their function is normally based on the Black-Scholes equations that describe the relationship between time remaining in an option contract, implied volatility, the distance between the strike and stock prices, and short-term risk-free interest rates. Suitable versions are included in virtually every online trading package offered by a broker in addition to dozens of examples that can be found on the web. For example, the Chicago Board Options Exchange (CBOE) has an excellent set of educational tools that includes a fully functional options calculator. Readers are encouraged to visit this and other option trading sites and become familiar with such tools. More sophisticated calculators are available in the form of position modeling tools sold by a number of software vendors.

Many traders would argue that they don't need to understand option pricing theory because the markets are efficient, and options, if they are relatively liquid, are always fairly priced. That view is flawed—there are many reasons to understand pricing. Suppose, for example, that you are faced with the choice of buying one of two identically priced call options that differ in strike price, volatility, and time remaining before expiration. A logical choice can only be made by a trader who understands the impact on price of each of these components. Structured positions composed of multiple options have more complex dynamics that bring pricing theory even more sharply into focus. Moreover, implied volatility, a principal component in the price of every option contract, varies considerably over time. It normally rises in anticipation of an earnings announcement or other planned event and falls when the market is stable. Successful option traders spend much of their time studying these changes and using them to make informed decisions. Generally speaking, they try to sell volatility that is overpriced and purchase options that are underpriced. Sophisticated institutional investors extend this approach by constructing refined models called "volatility surfaces" that map a variety of parameters to a three-dimensional structure that can be used to predict options implied volatility. Custom surfaces can be constructed for earnings season, rising and falling interest rate environments, bull or bear markets, strong or weak dollar environments, or any other set of conditions that affects volatility in a time or price-specific way. Regardless of the complexity of the approach, pricing theory is always the foundation.

Options are enormously popular derivatives, and many strategy-specific subscription services have sprung up on the web. This approach raises an important question: Is it better to choose a strategy and search for trade candidates, or to select stocks to trade and be flexible about the right strategy? Surprisingly, most option traders gain expertise trading a small number of position structures and search for candidates that fit. This search typically involves the use of charting software and a variety of tools for filtering stocks according to selectable criteria. Today's online brokers compete for active traders by continually upgrading the quality of their tools. Readers of this book are strongly encouraged to compare the offerings of different brokers to find those that best fit their needs. These tools combined with web-based services that provide historical stock and option prices can be used to construct a comprehensive trading and analysis platform.

Regardless of the approach—strategy or stock specific—pricing is the core issue. Buying or selling options without thoroughly understanding the subtle issues that impact their price throughout the expiration cycle is a mistake. We therefore begin with a chapter on pricing. Our approach is practical with a focus on trading. The concepts presented will form the basis for everything that is to follow, from basic put and call buying to complex multipart positions.

Unless otherwise stated, all examples for this chapter assume a risk-free interest rate of 3.5%.

1. A call option with a strike price of $100 trades for $3.00 with 14 days remaining before expiration. What must the stock price be at expiration for the option to still be worth at least $3.00?

   Answer: The stock price must be at or above $103 at expiration.

2. A put option with a strike price of $100 trades for $3.00 with 14 days remaining before expiration. What must the stock price be at expiration for the option to still be worth at least $3.00?

   Answer: The stock price must be at or below $97.

3. Suppose in each of the two examples described previously, the stock was $15 out-of-the-money when the option traded for $3.00 with 14 days remaining. What can we conclude about the volatility of the underlying stock?

Answer: The volatility must be very high for the option to be this expensive with only 14 days remaining before expiration and the stock 15% out-of-the-money. (Actual implied volatility is greater than 100% for each of these examples.)

4. A stock must continually move in the direction of the strike price to offset the effect of time decay. Assume the following:

Stock Price	Call Price	Days Remaining
$90	$2.22	100
$95	$2.22	50

Can you determine the strike price without knowing the implied volatility or risk-free interest rate?

Answer: $100. For the call price to remain constant, the stock must trace a nearly straight path from its initial price to a point equal to the strike price plus the initial value of the call (in this case, $100 + $2.22). If the stock price climbs above this line at any point in the expiration cycle, the call option will rise above its initial value. Conversely, if the stock fails to keep pace and falls below the line, the call price will fall below its initial value. Figure 1.1 plots the number of days remaining on the y-axis and the stock price on the x-axis for this scenario.

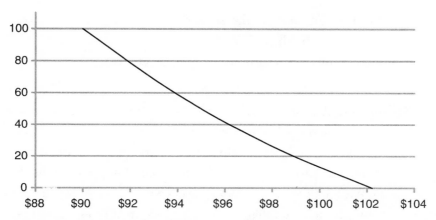

Figure 1.1   Stock prices required to offset time decay in question #4. (Days remaining on the y-axis.)

5. Implied volatility for the call option in question #4 was 28.5%. In general terms, what would be the effect of doubling or tripling the implied volatility?

Answer: Increasing the volatility priced into the option contract would raise the value of the midpoint ($95 with 50 days remaining in problem #4), and endpoint ($102.22 at expiration in problem #4). The new initial option price would be much higher; the stock price would need to climb much faster; and the expiration price would need to be much further in-the-money for the option to maintain its value. For example, in an extreme case where 200% implied volatility is priced into the same option, the initial price with 100 days remaining would be $33.37. To sustain this option price with 50 days remaining, the stock would have to trade at $106.52. At expiration the stock would need to trade $33.37 in-the-money—that is, the stock would need to close the expiration cycle at a price of $133.37.

6. Risk-free interest for the scenario in question #4 was 3.5%. What would be the effect of significantly increasing the rate of risk-free interest priced into the option contracts?

Answer: Raising the value of risk-free interest also increases the option price. As a result, the initial value with 100 days remaining would be higher, the midpoint stock price that would have to be reached to maintain this price would be higher, and the stock would have to expire further into-the-money to maintain that price. However, the interest rate effect is much more subtle. If, for example, we used an extraordinary rate ten times larger than that of the original scenario—that is, 35%—then the table in question #4 would contain the values in the following table:

Stock Price	Call Price	Days Remaining
$90.00	$4.96	100
$97.03	$4.96	50

The midpoint with 50 days remaining has climbed to $97.03, and the stock would need to climb to $104.96 at expiration for the option to maintain its price. The subtle nature of the interest rate effect is apparent when one considers that this relatively small distortion required a hyperinflation value of 35%. However, the linear relationship between offsetting stock price and time decay is preserved despite the extreme nature of the example. As always, the stock price must follow a linear trajectory that ends at a point equal to the strike price plus the initial option value for the call option price to remain constant.

7. You might have noticed that the line displayed in the chart accompanying question #4 is not perfectly straight. Can you explain the subtle distortion?

Answer: Time decay, also referred to as "theta," accelerates as expiration approaches. To maintain the option price, accelerating time decay must be offset by larger moves of the underlying stock. Some of the time decay acceleration is offset by increased sensitivity of the option price to underlying stock moves (delta rises as the stock approaches the strike price). However, the two forces do not exactly cancel. The difference gives rise to the subtle distortion and the line becomes a slight curve. Accelerating time decay similarly affects puts and calls. Figure 1.2 displays the same curve for a put option with a $90 strike price and the same implied volatility (28.5%). The constant price is $1.78. As before, the y-axis displays the number of days remaining and the x-axis the stock price.

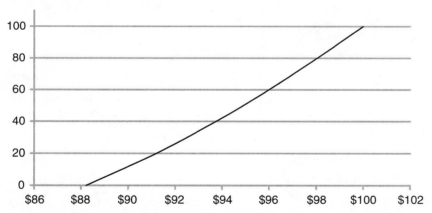

Figure 1.2   Stock prices required to offset time decay for a $90 put with 28.5% implied volatility. (Days remaining on the y-axis.)

8. For a stock trading at $100, which option is more expensive—
   $105 call or $95 put? (Assume implied volatility, expiration
   date, and so on, are all equal.)

   Answer: $105 call. Option pricing models assign more value to
   the call side. This asymmetry of price is related to the lognor-
   mal distribution that underlies all pricing calculations. In simple terms, if a $100 stock loses 50% of its value twice, the stock
   will trade at $25. However, if the same stock experiences two
   50% increases, it will rise $125 to $225. This effect causes calls
   to be more expensive than corresponding puts at the same
   strike price. Thus, a sequence of price changes that generates a
   75% loss can be reversed to yield a 125% gain. These results
   imply that calls should be priced higher than puts at the same
   strike price.

9. If XYZ is trading at $102.50 and the $100 strike price call is
   worth $3.00, would it be better to exercise or sell the option?

   Answer: It rarely makes sense to exercise an option because all
   remaining time premium is lost. In this case we are told that
   the option is worth $3.00 but only $2.50 would be realized by
   calling the stock (we would buy the stock for $100 and sell for
   $102.50). This dynamic holds until the final minutes of trading
   when all premium disappears from the contracts. In practice,
   the final trade of an option contract usually lands in the hands
   of a broker who can exercise in-the-money contracts for very
   little cost.

10. Suppose you are short the calls mentioned in problem #9 (stock is $2.50 in-the-money and calls are trading for $3.00). How much money would be saved if the stock is called away from you?

    Answer: 50¢.

11. Assume that it is expiration day and you are short at-the-money calls on a $100 stock—that is, the stock is trading right at the strike price. What are the risks associated with letting the option be exercised? If you already own the stock (covered calls), does it make sense to let it be called away?

    Answer: All remaining time premium will disappear during the final few hours of trading. If, for example, the option is worth 70¢ at the open and the stock remains at the strike price, the option price will decline to just a few cents by the close. However, the option price is very sensitive to changes that might occur in the underlying stock; this effect is enhanced as the day progresses and the option price approaches zero. Consider, for example, how the stock price will affect the option price near the close when the option might be worth as little as a few cents. Furthermore, the risk increases after the market closes if the stock trades in the after-hours session. The risk disappears for covered calls because the stock has already been purchased. Buying back inexpensive calls on the final day makes sense when it is undesirable to have the shares called away for other reasons such as tax consequences or an expectation that they might trade higher when the market reopens. With regard to trading costs, it is less expensive to allow the stock to be called away than to buy back short calls.

12. Delta represents the expected change in an option's price for a
1-point change in the underlying security. If a $3.00 call option
has a delta of 0.35, what will the new option price be if the
stock suddenly rises $1.00?

Answer: $3.35.

13. Suppose in question #12 the stock climbed $2.00. Would the
new option price be more or less than $3.70?

Answer: The new price will be higher because the call delta
increases continuously as the stock rises. When the stock has
risen $1.00, the new delta will be higher. Gamma is used to
describe the rate of change of delta.

14. Why is gamma always positive while delta is negative for puts
and positive for calls?

Answer: Gamma represents the predicted change in delta for a
1-point move in the underlying stock or index. When the stock
price rises, put and call deltas must both increase. The put
delta becomes less negative and the call delta becomes more
positive. In both cases gamma adds to the value of the delta.
The opposite is true when a stock falls: The put delta becomes
more negative and the call delta becomes less positive.

15. How is gamma affected by time and distance to the strike price? When does gamma have the highest value?

Answer: Gamma is highest when the underlying security trades near the strike price. Deep in-the-money and out-of-the-money options have the lowest gamma. These differences become more extreme as expiration approaches—gamma for at-the-money options rises sharply, and out-of-the-money gamma falls to 0. This behavior makes intuitive sense because at-the-money option delta rises very quickly as the stock moves beyond the strike price when expiration is near. Suppose, for example, that expiration is just 1 day away and the stock trades at the strike price of a call option. If the stock price climbs several dollars, delta will jump from 0.5 to 1.0 and gamma will fall to nearly 0. Conversely, if many months remain before expiration and the stock price climbs several dollars, delta will increase a substantially smaller amount and gamma will remain very small. These effects are illustrated in the table that follows, which depicts delta and gamma for a call option with a strike price of $110 when the underlying stock rises from at-the-money to $10 in-the-money. (Implied volatility of 50% was used for these calculations.)

Stock Price	Strike	Days Remaining	Delta	Gamma
$110	$110	1	0.51	0.136
$120	$110	1	1.00	0.001
$110	$110	366	0.63	0.007
$120	$110	366	0.69	0.006

16. How is gamma affected by volatility?

Answer: Gamma falls as volatility rises for at-the-money options. Conversely, out-of-the-money options sometimes experience rising gamma when volatility rises. Every stock and strike price combination has a gamma peak at a specific implied volatility.

17. How is delta affected by volatility? How does this behavior vary with time?

Answer: Near-dated, out-of-the-money options have substantial delta only if the underlying security is very volatile. At-the-money option delta is virtually unaffected by volatility changes, and delta falls sharply as volatility rises for in-the-money options. These effects make sense when they are recast in the context of risk management. A low volatility stock trading far from the strike price has little chance of ending up in-the-money; it has a characteristically low delta. Conversely, a highly volatile stock has a much greater chance of moving into-the-money and its delta is higher in proportion to this risk. Deep in-the-money call options have a small chance of falling below the strike if the stock has low volatility. The delta on these options will be close to 1.0. If the same stock displayed very high volatility, the price would have a reasonable chance of falling below the strike and the calls would display a significantly lower delta.

These effects can be extended to explain the delta for options that have many months left before expiration. Out-of-the-money options have higher deltas than their near-expiration counterparts because they have much more time left to cross the strike price. Deep in-the-money long-dated call options have a lower delta than their near-expiration counterparts because they have much more time to fall below the strike price.

The following table summarizes this behavior. The left side displays delta values for call options on two different stocks with 18 days remaining before expiration, one with high volatility and one with low volatility. The right side repeats these parameters for calls that have one year left before expiration.

18 Days Remaining/$110 Strike			365 Days Remaining/$110 Strike		
Stock Price	**Volatility**	**Delta**	**Stock Price**	**Volatility**	**Delta**
$100	0.20	0.02	$100	0.20	0.42
$100	0.50	0.22	$100	0.50	0.55
$110	0.20	0.52	$110	0.20	0.61
$110	0.50	0.53	$110	0.50	0.63
$120	0.20	0.98	$120	0.20	0.76
$120	0.50	0.80	$120	0.50	0.69

18. Question #17 related delta to risk. How can the value of an option delta be used as a guide for structuring a hedge?

Answer: The delta value is approximately equal to the chance that an option will end up in-the-money. A call option with a delta of 0.35 should be expected to have a 35% chance of expiring in-the-money. At expiration, deep in-the-money calls have a delta of 1.0 and deep in-the-money puts have a delta of –1.0 because each is almost guaranteed to expire in-the-money. These options behave like long and short stock respectively— that is, their prices change dollar-for-dollar with the stock price.

Stock hedges can be constructed to protect short positions using these parameters. To fully hedge 10 naked calls having a delta of 0.35, a short seller would need to purchase 350 shares of the underlying security. The number of shares would need to vary as the stock rose and fell because the option delta would constantly change. It would also need to change to accommodate time decay and volatility swings in the underlying security.

19. What would you expect the call option delta to be for a stock that trades exactly at the strike price in the final few hours before expiration?

   Answer: 0.50 because there is approximately a 50% chance that the stock will close in-the-money.

20. For every straddle there is an underlying price point where the call and put deltas are each exactly equal to 0.5. This parameter, known as the "delta neutral point," depends on several factors, including implied volatility, time remaining before expiration, and price of the underlying stock or index. When is the delta neutral point exactly equal to the strike price? Why is it not always equal to the strike price?

   Answer: The delta neutral point of a straddle begins below the strike price and rises at a constant rate until it equals the strike price at expiration. The same distortion that causes calls to be more expensive than puts sets the delta neutral point below the strike price (see question #8). Consequently, if a stock trades at the strike price of a straddle prior to expiration, the price and delta of the put will both be higher than those of the corresponding call.

21. Suppose with 300 days remaining before expiration, a put-call option pair with a strike price of $100 is exactly delta neutral with the stock trading at $87.66. When the new delta neutral point is $93.83, how many days will be left before expiration? At $96.92 how many days will be left?

Answer: 150 days at $93.83 and 75 days at $96.92. The steady movement of the delta neutral point is displayed in Figure 1.3. Days remaining before expiration are displayed on the y-axis, and the delta neutral stock price is displayed on the x-axis.

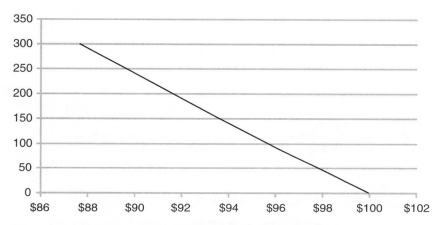

Figure 1.3   Migration of the delta neutral point for $100 strike price straddle beginning 300 days before expiration. Options for this example were priced with 50% implied volatility.

22. How would the slope of the line displayed in the answer to question #21 be affected if the implied volatility for both the put and the call were reduced by half?

Answer: The slope of the line becomes steeper because the starting price is closer to the strike. As volatility approaches zero, the slope of the line becomes vertical. If volatility vanished entirely, the line would be vertical and the delta neutral point would always be the strike price. The difference between 50% volatility and 25% volatility is displayed in Figure 1.4. As before, the number of days remaining is measured on the y-axis and the delta neutral stock price appears on the x-axis.

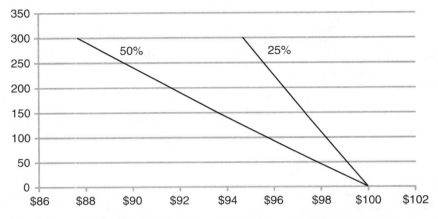

Figure 1.4   Delta neutral point migration measured using 50% and 25% volatility for a $100 strike price option beginning 300 days before expiration.

23. Consider a position composed of long deep in-the-money calls and short deep in-the-money puts for a stock trading at $100, as shown in the following table:

    Stock Price $100

    $90 call (long)   delta = 0.79

    $110 put (short)   delta = –0.70

    What will the delta of each side be if the stock remains at $100 until expiration?

    Answer: $90 call delta = 1.0 and $110 put delta = –1.0 at expiration with the underlying stock trading at $100.

24. Suppose that in question #23 the $90 call originally cost $12.30 and the $110 put sold for $12.05—that is, the total position had a net cost of only 25¢. What was the final gain or loss?

Answer: At expiration the call and put were each worth $10.00, so the final position was long $10.00 (call) and short $10.00 (put) with a net value of $0.00. Therefore, the trade lost $0.25.

25. Assume that the trade in questions #23 and #24 was long 10 calls and short 10 puts. Can you calculate the collateral requirement for the trade? What was the total cost of owning the position?[1]

Answer: It is necessary to set aside 20% of the value of the underlying stock for the short side of the trade. Since we sold 10 put contracts for a $100 stock, the cost would be $0.20 \times \$100$ per share × 10 contracts × 100 shares per contract = $20,000. We must add the value realized from the sale of the put ($12,050 + $20,000 = $32,050).

On the long side we would need to have enough cash on hand to purchase the calls = $12.30 × 10 contracts × 100 shares per contract = $12,300. Therefore, the account must have $44,350 to execute the initial trade. At expiration $0.25 was lost = $0.25 × 10 contracts × 100 shares per contract = $250. The total cost of holding the trade was $250 plus opportunity cost on $44,350 during the lifetime of the trade.

[1] Collateral and margin requirements for option traders can vary by broker. Furthermore, recent changes allow customers whose accounts exceed certain minimum thresholds to take advantage of portfolio margining rules which more precisely align collateral requirements with overall portfolio risk. Readers wishing to further explore margin and collateral requirements are encouraged to visit the Chicago Board Options Exchange website and to contact their broker.

26. Consider a position composed of long out-of-the-money calls and long out-of-the-money puts for a stock trading at $100, as shown in the following table:

Stock Price $100

$110 call (long)   delta = 0.30

$90 put (long)   delta = –0.21

What will the delta of each side be if the stock remains at $100 until expiration? What will the options be worth?

Answer: $110 call delta = 0 and $90 put delta = 0 at expiration with the underlying stock trading at $100. Both options lose all their value.

27. Over what range of stock prices will the loss at expiration be 100%?

Answer: Both options will expire worthless with the stock between $90 and $110. The total range for a return of $0.00 is $20.00. Outside this range, one of the options will have some value.

28. Assume that the calls in question #26 cost $2.56 and the puts cost $1.86. At expiration, what underlying stock prices are break-even points for the trade? Is any collateral required for this position?

Answer: The total cost was $4.42. Break-even points are $114.42 on the upside and $85.58 on the downside. These values are determined by adding $4.42 to the $110 call strike and subtracting $4.42 from the $90 put strike. No collateral was required because both sides were long. The trade would have originally cost $442 for each pair of contracts.

29. Assume that the trade originally described in question #26 decays to $0.00 with the stock at $100 and 1 day left before expiration. An unsubstantiated rumor surfaces that the stock in question might be acquired, and implied volatility soars to very high levels. Is there a level of implied volatility that could restore the price of each option to its original value despite being $10 out-of-the-money with only 1 day left? Would put and call deltas also be restored?

Answer: Yes, as long as there is time left in the contracts, it is possible for volatility to rise high enough to restore the original prices and deltas. If, for example, the original implied volatility was 40% and 50 days remained before expiration, a new implied volatility around 280% would restore the original values. Option prices on both sides of the trade would regain their original sensitivity to underlying price changes. However, because the delta-neutral point of the position would have shifted slightly over the 50 days that the trade was open, the new call price would be a few cents lower and the put price a few cents higher to achieve the same overall position value. These distortions are very slight for options that are 10% out-of-the-money. Actual values are listed in the following table.

Days Remaining	Put ($)	Call ($)	Volatility	Delta
50	1.86		0.40	−0.21
50		2.56	0.40	0.30
1	1.98		2.78	−0.22
1		2.45	2.78	0.29

30. Which of the following call options suffers the greatest time decay (highest theta)?

Stock Price ($)	Strike	Days Remaining	Call ($)	Volatility
95	100	70	4.84	0.4
100	100	5	1.90	0.4

Answer: The second entry in the table suffers from much greater time decay. In broad terms, if the underlying stock remains at $100, this option will lose $1.90 of value over 5 days (an average of 38¢ per day). Conversely, the first entry in the table will lose $4.84 of value over 70 days (an average of only 7¢ per day). These numbers, although useful for quick comparisons, are average values across the entire timeframe. In the first entry with 70 days remaining, actual theta is equal to 5¢ per day; in the second entry with only 5 days left, theta is equal to 19¢. Figure 1.5 displays theta values for a $100 strike price call with the stock price at $95 and implied volatility of 40% (first row of the table). Theta is measured on the y-axis and the number of days remaining before expiration on the x-axis. Note that theta increases on a steeply accelerating curve as expiration approaches. The shape of this curve can be described using a third-degree polynomial.

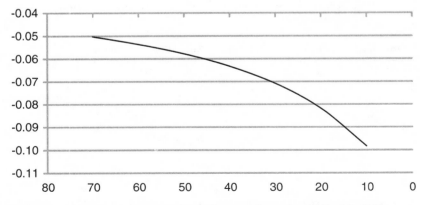

Figure 1.5   Time decay profile for a $100 strike price call with 40% implied volatility and the underlying stock trading continuously at $95.

31. Given the trading price of a call option, can the fair value of a put at the same strike price be determined? What information is needed?

    Answer: Yes—the put price can be calculated using the formula for put-call parity. This formula is derived from the Black-Scholes equations that are used to price puts and calls. For non-dividend-paying stocks:

    $$C + Xe^{-rt} = P + S_0$$

    C = call price   X = strike price

    P = put price   t = time remaining as

    r = risk-free interest rate   % of a year

    S_0 = stock price   e = base of the natural logarithm (2.718)

32. Suppose you were to discover a mispriced set of options for which the call was relatively more expensive than the put. Is there a way to exploit this situation?

    Answer: Put-call parity violations create arbitrage opportunities that normally disappear very quickly. Bid-ask spreads and trading costs make it nearly impossible for a public customer to exploit the arbitrage. Furthermore, the correct method for trading such an arbitrage is complex. It involves selling the overpriced calls, purchasing puts, and balancing the position with a stock-bond portfolio composed of long stock and short bonds. The trade is unwound at expiration for a small profit. In essence we would be long the right side of the equation and short the overpriced left side.

33. What is the primary difference between European- and American-style options?

    Answer: European options can be exercised only at expiration. American-style options can be exercised at any time. Index options are often European and equity options are almost invariably American. Option pricing models are designed around the European expiration and it is always assumed that the option will be bought and sold but not exercised before expiration.

34. Suppose an investor is long calls on an index with European expiration rules. Can you envision issues related to the European-style expiration that could affect liquidity or bid-ask spreads?

    Answer: When investors anticipate that a sudden large move will be short-lived, bid-ask spreads and liquidity issues can surface, making it difficult to close an option position. This problem is well-known to investors who trade options on the CBOE Volatility Index (VIX). The VIX tends to rise sharply in a market decline and fall when the market stabilizes. In principle out-of-the-money calls should gain in value during a market drawdown. However, the anticipation of a sharp decline in the index as the market regains stability after a sudden drop can create price distortions for options that cannot be exercised. Consider, for example, the thought process of an investor who is short calls that suddenly move in-the-money as the index rises during a market crash. Knowing that the VIX is likely to decline as the market stabilizes, and that implied volatilities of VIX options will ultimately fall, the investor will likely hesitate before closing the position at a loss. This approach could not be taken if the calls were immediately exercisable. Unfortunately, because they are not, bid-ask spreads tend to widen by a surprising amount and liquidity becomes an issue. These factors ultimately limit the value of out-of-the-money VIX calls as a hedge against a market crash. Some of the same effect can be seen with thinly traded equity options. Holders of long puts often find it difficult to sell their options for a fair price during a rapid market decline because short sellers of the same puts are unwilling to overpay to buy them back until volatility stabilizes. However, unlike European options that cannot be exercised before expiration, American options can never be worth less than the amount that they are in-the-money. This fact limits the size of the distortion.

35. What is the value of a 1 standard deviation daily price change for a $100 stock having 30% implied volatility? What would be the value of a 1 standard deviation monthly change for the same stock?

Answer: Annual volatility is equal to the expected 1 year, 1 standard deviation price change. Because volatility is proportional to the square root of time, we can derive the value for a shorter timeframe by dividing the annual value by the square root of the number of shorter timeframes contained in 1 year. To calculate monthly volatility we would divide annual volatility by the square root of 12; weekly volatility would be equal to annual volatility divided by the square root of 52. There is some disagreement about the adjustment factor for daily volatility because a calendar year contains approximately 252 trading days. Using this number we would divide by 15.87 to obtain daily volatility which is also equal to the value of a close-to-close 1 standard deviation price change.

Assuming 252 trading days per year, the value of a daily 1 standard deviation price change for a $100 stock with 30% implied volatility would be $100 × 0.30 / Sqrt (252) = $1.89.

The value of a 1 month, 1 standard deviation change would be given by $100 × 0.30 / Sqrt(12) = $8.66.

In each case, multiplying by the annualization factor would return the value of a 1 year, 1 standard deviation price change.

$1.89 × Sqrt(252) = $30

$8.66 × Sqrt(12) = $30

36. For the stock in question #35, what is the probability that the stock will trade between $70 and $130 at the end of 1 year?

Answer: According to the normal distribution, the chance that the stock will trade in an interval that is bounded by 1 standard deviation above and below the current price is approximately 68%. Extending this calculation to the 1 day, 1 standard deviation change of question #35 sets the probability that the stock will rise or fall less than $1.89 in a single day at 68%.

37. For a $100 strike price call with 2 days left before expiration, what stock price would result in the largest time decay (most negative theta)?

Answer: Theta is highest at-the-money and lowest when the stock is deep in-the-money or deep out-of-the-money. As a result, time decay would be greatest if the stock traded at $100. Figure 1.6 provides a view of theta with respect to stock price for this example. Stock price is displayed on the x-axis and theta on the y-axis.

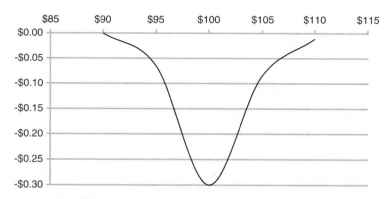

Figure 1.6   Time decay versus stock price for $100 strike price calls with two days remaining before expiration. Prices are calculated with 40% implied volatility.

38. Equity and index options expire at 11:59 PM on the Saturday following the third Friday of each month. As a result, risk does not vanish when the market closes on Friday because many stocks continue to trade in the after-hours session and option values can be affected by breaking news. Despite these dynamics, most option values collapse to just a few cents if the underlying stock is at-the-money and $0.00 if it is out-of-the-money. If there are 32 hours left before expiration, what pricing parameters must exist to erase all time premium?

Answer: Implied volatility collapses to nearly zero at the close on expiration Friday. This dynamic can change if the market anticipates an event that could affect the stock after the close on Friday. It is generally dangerous to leave open naked short positions that are near-the-money because they can be exercised in response to a surprise news event. Even if the stock does not trade in the after-hours session, negative news that is guaranteed to collapse the share price will cause puts to be exercised in anticipation of a sharp decline at the open on Monday.

39. Is it possible for the price of a call to rise or remain the same when the underlying stock or index falls?

Answer: Yes, because volatility tends to rise when prices fall. In the event of very damaging news, a stock can plunge and volatility can rise sharply. For example, consider the following scenario:

Acme stock trading at $100 and $105 strike price calls priced with 30% implied volatility and 90 days remaining before expiration are worth $4.23. Just after the market opens, Acme reports disappointing earnings and the stock falls 25%, with options implied volatility rising sharply to 120%. Put-call parity will raise implied volatility for the calls in concert with the puts. Despite the 25% drop in stock price, $105 strike price calls will rise from $4.23 to $9.41. The stock would need to fall below $60—a 40% loss—to offset this rise in volatility. The following table summarizes this behavior.

Stock ($)	Call ($)	Volatility	Strike ($)	Days Remaining
100	4.23	0.30	105	90
75	9.41	1.20	105	90
60	4.40	1.20	105	90

This scenario played out in early 2008 when large investment banks suffered billions of dollars in "write downs" during a credit crisis precipitated by subprime lending. For example, call options on Bear Stearns stock that previously traded with implied volatility in the 25% range spiked to more than 120% in early March. While the stock declined more than 35% during 10 trading sessions, rising volatility often caused call prices to also rise. The effect was most prominent on March 14 when the stock suddenly plunged 48% in the first 30 minutes of trading, and implied volatility skyrocketed to more than 450% for at-the-money calls.

Modest changes in volatility can have similar effects. In our example, if Acme stock fell $8.00 and volatility climbed from 30% to 50%, call prices would increase slightly despite the 8% underlying price decline. Details are outlined in the following table.

Stock ($)	Call ($)	Volatility	Strike ($)	Days Remaining
100	4.23	0.30	105	90
92	4.81	0.50	105	90

40. With regard to question #39, can you think of a reverse scenario in which the stock price falls rapidly and puts also lose value?

Answer: When an uncertain situation resolves itself, volatility can fall rapidly. This effect is often tied to earnings releases. For stocks that have a history of large earnings-associated price spikes, the market tends to overprice options by setting implied volatility inappropriately high prior to the event. The distortion is especially large when an earnings release coincides with options expiration. For these stocks, implied volatility rises sharply to offset the rapid time decay of the final few days of the expiration cycle. Implied volatility normally returns to normal levels immediately after earnings are announced. Even if the stock price declines sharply, collapsing volatility can reduce the value of put options. This effect is most pronounced for out-of-the-money puts. The following table outlines a simple example of a stock trading at $105 and $100 strike price puts with 15 days remaining before expiration. Despite a $5.00 underlying price decline, out-of-the-money put values fall more than 45% as volatility shrinks from 80% to 30%. Had the event occurred in the final few days of the expiration cycle, the initial volatility would have been much higher and the collapse would have been much more pronounced.

Stock ($)	Put ($)	Volatility	Strike ($)	Days Remaining
105	4.37	0.80	100	15
100	2.36	0.30	100	15

41. Vega measures the expected change in the value of an option for a 1% change in volatility. Suppose an option trading for $2.50 has a vega of $0.30. What will the new option price be if implied volatility rises 1%?

    Answer: $2.50 + $0.30 = $2.80.

42. How does time impact vega?

    Answer: Vega rises as time remaining before expiration increases. Figure 1.7 displays vega for $105 strike price calls valued with 30% implied volatility on a stock trading at $100. The number of days remaining before expiration is measured on the x-axis and vega on the y-axis.

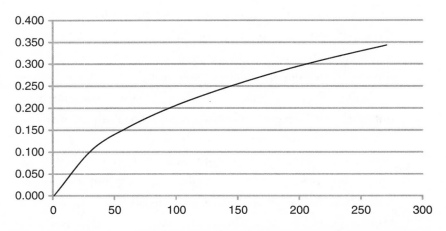

Figure 1.7   Vega versus time remaining before expiration for call options priced with 30% implied volatility on a $100 stock. Days remaining is measured on the x-axis and vega on the y-axis.

43. Rho measures the expected change in the price of an option for a 1% increase in the risk-free interest rate. Suppose a call option trades for $2.50 with rho of $0.10. What will the new option price be if the risk-free interest rate suddenly increases 1%.

Answer: $2.50 + $0.10 = $2.60.

44. The "volatility smile" causes certain option prices to be inflated to accommodate the risk of a large downward price spike. Which of the following options would you expect to be most affected?

   A.   Out-of-the-money puts/in-the-money calls

   B.   Out-of-the-money calls/in-the-money puts

   C.   Far-dated puts

   D.   Far-dated calls

Answer: A—out-of-the-money puts/in-the-money calls. The volatility smile became much more pronounced after the stock market crash of October 1987 when out-of-the-money puts climbed steeply in value. Since then, implied volatility profiles for equity and index options have taken on a distinctly negative skew—that is, volatility tends to rise as the strike price decreases. This effect causes out-of-the-money puts to be relatively more expensive than Black-Scholes theory predicts. Additionally, since put-call parity dictates that the relationship between strike price and implied volatility is the same for both types of contracts, in-the-money calls should also be more expensive.

45. Option traders often substitute deep-in-the-money calls for stock because the delta is close to 1.0 and the option price changes point-for-point with the stock price. Suppose we purchase 10 contracts of a $50 strike price call with a delta of 1.0 on a stock that trades for $75. If the stock were to fall $20, which of the following would be true?

    A. The option trade would lose more value than 1,000 shares of stock.

    B. The option trade would lose less value than 1,000 shares of stock.

    C. Both trades would lose $20,000.

Answer: B—The option trade would lose less than the equivalent stock trade. The equivalent stock trade consisting of 1,000 shares would lose $20,000 because the delta of stock is always exactly 1.0. However, the call option delta would shrink as the price falls. In this case a $20 decrease in the stock price would result in the call option being only $5.00 in-the-money. For a $50 strike price call with 90 days left before expiration and implied volatility of 30%, the delta would fall to around 78%. The actual change in value for this trade would be $18,890.

Additional comments regarding the volatility smile:

It is important to distinguish between the volatility smile and the term *structure of volatility*, which measures the effect of time on implied volatility. Term structure can be visualized in a plot of implied volatility for at-the-money options versus expiration month. Its behavior tends to compress the shape of the smile curve as the maturity date increases. If we create a family of volatility smile curves, one curve per month, we will find that the shape of the curve becomes less pronounced as time advances. This behavior is illustrated in Figure 1.8, which displays March and April 2008 volatility smiles for Apple Computer. The chart was constructed using contract prices at the market close on March 14 (AAPL trading at $127). Volatility is measured on the y-axis and strike price on the x-axis.

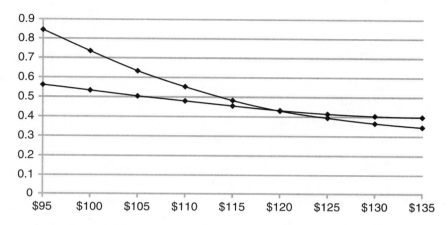

Figure 1.8   March and April 2008 volatility smile for Apple Computer. Data collected near the market close on March 14, 2008, with Apple trading at $127. Upper line = March; lower, flatter line = April. Volatility is displayed on the y-axis and strike price on the x-axis.

The volatility smile represents an important distortion of the Black-Scholes pricing model. As illustrated in Figure 1.8, option values decrease relative to a flat smile as the strike price increases. Near the right side of the chart, they are less expensive than predicted by a non-adjusted Black-Scholes model. This distortion causes out-of-the-money calls to be heavily discounted. From a trading perspective these pricing variations can be interpreted to mean that volatility will fall if the stock rises. Conversely, the high values placed on low strike prices are an indication that volatility will likely rise if the stock falls. This behavior is evident in most stocks, equity indexes, and the closely followed CBOE Volatility Index. The form of the smile is different for other financial instruments. Currency options, for example, are priced with a symmetrical volatility. Experienced traders sometimes use this information to create a table containing the correct implied volatility for each expiration date and strike price.

46. Equity and index options expire on Saturday following the third Friday of each month. As a result, option contracts still have 1 day remaining before expiration when the market closes on Friday. Although some stocks may continue to trade in the after-hours session, large price changes are unlikely. These dynamics have the potential to cause significant price distortions. For example, $120 strike price calls for a stock trading at $119 with 1 day left before expiration and implied volatility of 40% would theoretically be worth 60¢. However, the value of the option is limited because it cannot be traded by a public customer after the Friday close. Any money paid for such an option would probably be lost. As a result, such options typically trade for no more than 5¢ at the close despite the remaining time. How can the value be rationalized using traditional pricing methodologies such as Black-Scholes?

Answer: Because there is essentially no time left for the stock to trade, implied volatility shrinks rapidly as the market close approaches. It is not uncommon for options to open the day with 40% implied volatility and close with less than 1%. When the distortion disappears, at-the-money and out-of-the-money options lose all of their remaining value. Figure 1.9 displays the fair value for an out-of-the-money $120 strike price call on a stock trading at $119 with 1 day of time remaining. Despite being $1 out-of-the-money with only 1 day left, its initial trading price is 60¢. Collapsing implied volatility reduces the value to $0.00 by the end of the day. These dynamics make sense because the stock has essentially no volatility and the options cannot be traded after the close.

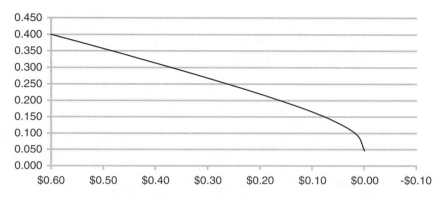

Figure 1.9   Fair trading price versus implied volatility for a $1 out-of-the-money call option on the final trading day of an expiration cycle. Call prices are displayed on the x-axis, volatility on the y-axis.

47. Suppose you were short $100 strike price calls and $90 strike price puts on a stock that traded at $95 at the close on expiration Friday—that is, both options were $5 out-of-the-money. Why might it be unwise to leave these options assuming they will expire worthless?

    Answer: The underlying stock could react to news that is released after the market closes and the options, which are likely to be in the hands of a broker, can be exercised on Saturday. Even if the stock does not trade in the Friday after-hours session, the anticipation of a large move on Monday can drive execution, forcing the trade to be covered at a substantial loss using Monday's stock prices.

48. Investors often use options to create "synthetic stock" positions. Which of the following positions is equivalent to 100 shares of a stock trading at $100?

   A.   1 long $100 call + 1 short $100 put

   B.   1 long $105 call + 1 short $95 put

   C.   1 long $95 call + 1 short $100 put

   Answer: A—1 long $100 call + 1 short $100 put is equivalent to 100 shares of stock.

49. With regard to question #48, can you explain why only the first choice is correct? Hint: The delta of an at-the-money call is roughly 0.50, and the corresponding put has a delta of –0.50.

   Answer: The long call is equivalent to 50 shares of stock (0.5 delta × 100 shares per contract). On the put side we are short a negative delta, which is equivalent to being long. Because the same math applies, the put position is also equivalent to 50 shares of long stock. Adding together the number of delta-equivalent shares for both sides gives us a value of 100 shares.

   Each of the other choices includes options with a net delta greater or less than 1.

50. Would the $100 strike price call/put combination of question #49 have still equaled 100 shares of stock if the underlying had been trading at $103?

> *Answer:* Yes. Both deltas would have been shifted by an equivalent amount. The following table presents an example. The first pair of entries displays the value of a position that is short 10 puts and long 10 calls using the $100 strike with the stock trading at $103. The second pair of entries reveals the new price after a $3 increase in the underlying stock price. Both positions are built around 35% volatility, 28 days remaining before expiration, and a risk-free interest rate of 3.5%.

Stock Price ($)	Call ($)	Put ($)	Delta	Value	10 Contr. Net ($)
103.00	5.77		0.65	5,770	
103.00		2.50	−0.35	−2,500	3,270
106.00	7.87		0.75	7,870	
106.00		1.61	−0.25	−1,610	6,260

Note that a $3 increase in the underlying stock price increased the value of the position $2,990, from $3,270 to $6,260. This change almost exactly equals that of 1,000 shares of stock.

51. How does time decay figure into the value of a synthetic long
    stock position like that of the preceding two problems?

Answer: As expiration approaches, the put delta becomes more
negative and the call delta becomes less positive. These
changes are revealed in the following table. The first pair of
entries contains prices, deltas, and position values for an at-the-
money short put/long call combination with 28 days remaining
before expiration. The second pair of entries displays the exact
same position at expiration with the underlying stock still trading at the $100 strike price.

Stock Price ($)	Days Remaining	Call ($)	Put ($)	Delta	Value	10 Contr. Net ($)
100	28	4.00		0.53	4,000	
100	28		3.73	−0.47	−3,730	270
100	0	0.00		0.50	0	
100	0		0.00	−0.50	0	0

Note that if the underlying stock remains at the strike price
until expiration, the position loses $270. Stated differently, the
10 contract synthetic stock position has an initial cost of $270,
which is ultimately lost to time decay if the stock remains at the
starting price.

52. Can you calculate the underlying stock price increase that would be necessary to offset the $270 loss in question #51?

    Answer: Because a 10 contract position is equivalent to 1,000 shares, we would need only a 27¢ increase in the underlying stock price (0.27 × 10 contracts × 100 shares per contract). This simple calculation works because on any given day—including expiration day—the position behaves as if it were stock. If the stock closed 27¢ in-the-money at expiration, the call would be worth 27¢ and the put would be worth $0.00. The final position would then be worth $270—exactly the time value of the original trade.

53. Does the synthetic stock position of the preceding five questions have a collateral requirement? (Assume stock trading at $100, 10 short $100 puts, 10 long $100 calls.)

    Answer: Yes. Because the puts are uncovered, the requirement is equal to 20% of the value of the underlying stock plus the revenue realized from the short sale. The base requirement would be 1,000 shares × 0.20 × $100 per share = $20,000. Adding the sale price of the options increases the value by $3.73 × 1,000 = $3,730. Total required collateral is, therefore, $23,730.

54. Based on the answer to question #53, can you estimate the
"opportunity" cost associated with this trade? (Opportunity
cost is related to interest that could be earned on money that
must be set aside to capitalize the trade in addition to any losses
incurred.)

Answer: The trade has an opportunity cost equal to the
following:

Interest on $23,730 collateral

Interest on $4,000 for the long call purchase

Loss of $270 from time decay

Assuming 3.5% interest, the trade would cost approximately
$351 for 1 month. One year of interest would be equal to .035
× ($23,730 + $4,000) = $970.55. Dividing by 12 and adding the
$270 time decay loss gives ($970.55 / 12) + $270 = $350.88.

55. Based on the answer to question #54, how does the cost of a
synthetic long stock position compare to actually owning the
stock?

Answer: 1,000 shares of a $100 stock would cost $100,000. The
1 month opportunity cost of this trade at 3.5% would be
$292—slightly less than the cost of the synthetic position. The
major cost of the synthetic position is the $270 of time decay
inherent to the structure.

56. If the synthetic position has a slightly higher cost of ownership, why would an investor not simply buy the stock?

    Answer: The synthetic 1,000 share position outlined in the previous questions can be purchased using less than $30,000. The stock position would cost more than three times as much. However, if the stock could be purchased on margin, it would cost only $50,000 in addition to interest charged by the broker. At 3.5%, the 1 month interest charge would be ($50,000 × 0.035) / 12 = $146. The ability to exploit margin borrowing dramatically reduces the acquisition cost.

57. Given the following information, can you estimate the price of the call option? (Hint: Time decay accelerates during the final week of an expiration cycle.)

Stock Price ($)	Call Strike ($)	Days Remaining	Risk-Free Interest	Volatility	Theta	Call Price ($)
100.00	100	7	0.015	0.75	−0.30	???

    Answer: Because of the steepening shape of the time decay curve, average theta approximately doubles during the final few days of an expiration cycle. That is, doubling the value given in the table will closely approximate the average time decay experienced by the options during the final week. Using this principle, we can assume an average time decay of 60¢ × 7 days, which yields a price of $4.20 for the call option.

Summary

This chapter was designed to provide a series of practical exercises that highlight important aspects of option pricing theory. It was meant to complement the many excellent texts that already exist on the subject, in addition to hundreds of academic research papers. Modern option pricing began with the publication of the Black-Scholes formula in 1973. Today, more than 35 years later, this elegant formula still forms the foundation of most option pricing activities. In this context we should distinguish between the price of an option and its value. Option pricing theory, including Black-Scholes and its extensions, can be used to determine the value of an option; the market determines its actual trading price. Sometimes the two differ considerably. For example, during early 2008 the implied volatility of options on financial stocks climbed steeply as a sub-prime lending crisis generated billions of dollars of losses among these institutions. In many cases actual prices were no longer based on historical volatility of the underlying stocks, but on the market's perception of risk. Plugging actual trading prices into the Black-Scholes formula sometimes gave implied volatilities of more than 500%. Furthermore, the volatility smile—an important extension to the Black-Scholes model—steepened considerably causing out-of-the-money put options to be priced with even higher implied volatilities. Such distortions are the source of pricing theory refinements that allow the market to accommodate unusual situations.

The calculations used throughout this book are based on the Black-Scholes formula. Many of the problems extend the model with implied volatilities that vary across different strike prices and expiration dates in addition to unique situations such as the dividend arbitrage scenario outlined at the end of Chapter 5, "Complex Trades— Part 2." Although the chapters can be reviewed in any order, they were designed as a progression that begins with long put and call positions and progresses to complex multipart trades spanning different strike prices and expiration dates. In all cases the goal was to create scenarios that can be addressed using basic principles.

2

Purchasing Puts and Calls

Simply stated, purchasing a call is a directional bet with higher leverage than an equivalent stock purchase. Purchasing puts is equivalent to shorting stock. Long puts and calls have many advantages over stock. Most notable is the flexibility to use different strike prices and expiration dates to accommodate a variety of expectations for the performance of the underlying stock. "Bullish" and "bearish" are broad terms, and the simple purchase or short sale of a stock does not adequately represent all bullish or bearish views. Suppose, for example, that you believe a stock might suddenly rise sharply as the result of an impending news event. That expectation is much different from a long-term somewhat positive view that can be summarized with the phrase "good long-term investment." Skillful call buying strategies can be tailored to accommodate either view.

Call and put buying also has the advantage of leverage, a dynamic that ultimately impacts the size of a portfolio that can be purchased. Consider the difficulties faced by an investor trying to purchase a portfolio of stocks with $10,000. A single trade consisting of 100 shares of a $100 stock would consume the entire budget. The same amount of money, however, could purchase a fairly broad portfolio of calls across many different securities. This approach allows an investor to use calls to gain exposure to expensive large cap stocks without bearing the prohibitive costs usually associated with owning those stocks. The same can obviously be said for buying puts versus shorting stocks. Short sales have margin requirements that are generally much larger than the cost of purchasing an equivalent portfolio of puts.

Skillfully choosing the right mix of long and short-dated expirations and strike prices allows an investor to distribute risk, maximize profit, and capitalize on different types of price change behavior. Even more important is the ability to respond with a corrective strategy when a stock moves the wrong way. For example, stock owners have only two choices for responding to a price decline: sell some or all of the stock, or buy more to "average down" the purchase price. Neither is a particularly good choice. Option traders have far better choices that involve shifting to different strike prices and/or selling calls to offset some of the loss. An option trader can recover from a loss, sometimes with a profit, even if the stock never returns to its previous price. Option traders can also take advantage of strategies that lock in profits after a sharp rise or fall. Stock investors are limited here as well because their only choice is to sell some or all of their stock or, in the case of a short position, to cover all or some of their trade. With luck the stock will reverse direction and provide a new trading opportunity.

In this section we will explore the dynamics associated with purchasing and owning puts and calls. Many of the questions will involve the kind of adjustments mentioned previously. Strictly speaking, these discussions reach beyond the basics of call and put buying into the realm of position management. Such extensions are appropriate because every option purchased must eventually be sold, and the jump to selling additional contracts as position adjustments is relatively small. These discussions are also intended as an introduction to more complex position management scenarios that will be explored in later sections.

Basic Dynamics (Problems #1–#7)

1. Suppose you buy $100 strike price calls for $2.50. Assuming that you hold the position until expiration, what price must the underlying stock achieve on expiration day for your trade to break even?

   Answer: $102.50.

2. Most option positions are not held until expiration because large upward or downward spikes usually intervene. Suppose you purchased 10 contacts of a call option for $1.50 and the stock spiked upward, driving the price to $3.75. An excellent strategy might be to sell enough of the contracts to pay for the original trade and hold the remainder in anticipation of further increases. How many contracts would you need to sell to pay for the original trade?

   Answer: 4 contracts. The original trade cost $1.50 × 10 contracts × 100 shares per contract = $1,500. Selling 4 contracts for $3.75 would recover the entire $1,500 ($3.75 × 4 contracts × 100 shares per contract).

3. Would you be more likely to hold the remaining 6 contracts if the spike occurred near or far from expiration?

Answer: As expiration approaches, time decay accelerates, and the chance of additional large upward spikes shrinks rapidly with each passing day. In the final few days it almost never makes sense to continue holding option contracts that have a large profit. Suppose, for example, that the large upward spike was 3 standard deviations and only 5 days remain before expiration. It is very unlikely that two spikes of this magnitude will occur within one week. Additionally, regression toward the mean often erodes some of the gain as other investors take profit and the stock sells off. If the large upward spike occurs in the after- or before-hours session, it would be wise to close the options as soon as the market opens. Finally, if the stock is far in-the-money close to expiration, the option will have a delta of 1.0 and the decision to continue holding the option is tantamount to holding an equivalent number of shares of the underlying stock. Most option positions are not designed to be synthetic stock and, therefore, should not be held when they display that characteristic.

4. The term "leverage" is often misused. Generally speaking, a call owner will realize greater percentage gains and losses than a stockholder for the same size movement of the underlying because the call provides greater leverage. Which of the following long call positions provides greater leverage?

   A. 100 contracts costing $0.24/$10 out-of-the-money

   B. 10 contracts costing $2.57/at-the-money

Answer: A—$0.24 option/$10 out-of-the-money provides much more leverage. The following table contains the sample trades used to structure this question. Implied volatility was set at 35%, 70 days remained before expiration, and the risk free interest rate was 3.5%.

Stock ($)	Strike ($)	Call ($)
40	50	0.24
40	40	2.57
45	50	1.14
45	40	6.03

In the second pair of entries, the stock has risen from $40 to $45. At-the-money options have more than doubled from $2.57 to $6.03, and out-of-the-money options have more than quadrupled from $0.24 to $1.14.

5. Would the results in question #4 have changed if the scenario played out with half as much time left (35 days) in the option contracts?

Answer: The exaggeration increases sharply as expiration approaches. In this particular case, an option pricing calculator can be used to show that the at-the-money $40 calls would increase in value from $1.79 to $5.44 (3 times), while the out-of-the-money $50 calls would increase a much larger percentage from 4¢ to 48¢ (12 times).

6. Why does the comparison break down when the time left is reduced to just a few days?

Answer: Except in situations where implied volatility is extraordinarily high, options that are 25% out-of-the-money are valueless with only a few days left. As expiration approaches, out-of-the-money leverage continues to increase until a point is reached where even a large move of the underlying fails to affect the nearest strike price. For example, with implied volatility of 35% and the stock trading at $40, a 1 standard deviation 3-day price change would be just $1.28. The position would, therefore, be 7.9 standard deviations out-of-the-money. The calculation is as follows:

Timeframes in 1 year	365/3 = 121.67
Annualization factor	Sqrt (121.67) =11.03
Volatility for 3 days	0.35 / 11.03 = 0.032
1 StdDev change	0.032 × $40 = $1.28

Because the chance of a 7.9 standard deviation change is vanishingly small, the $50 calls would have virtually no value with the stock trading at $40 and only 3 days left before expiration.

7. Leverage can be deceiving because it works in percentages rather than absolute amounts. In question #4 we compared the performance of out-of-the-money and at-the-money options for a stock whose price increased $5. With 70 days remaining before expiration, $10 out-of-the-money calls climbed from $0.24 to $1.14 while the value of at-the-money calls increased from $2.57 to $6.03. In percentage terms, the value of out-of-the-money options increased 375% while at-the-money options climbed a more modest 135%. In absolute terms, however, at-the-money options gained considerably more. If the at-the-money investment was 10 contracts, how many out-of-the-money contracts would you need to achieve the same absolute gain?

Answer: Approximately 38 contracts. The comparison is displayed in the following table (OTM = out-of-the-money, ATM = at-the-money).

OTM Call ($)	38 Contracts ($)	Gain ($)
0.24	912	
1.14	4,332	3,420

ATM Call ($)	10 Contracts ($)	Gain ($)
2.57	2,570	
6.03	6,030	3,460

At-the-money calls gained $3,460. Because the out-of-the-money calls grew in value by $0.90 ($90 per contract), we can divide to find the appropriate number of contracts:

$3,460 / $90 per contract = 38.4 contracts

Protecting Profit (Problems #8–#19)

There is no shortage of frustrated investors who, after making a wise and profitable investment, have experienced losses because they failed to protect their profit. The problem often occurs when a stock rallies early in an expiration cycle before falling back below the original price. Furthermore, because options experience time decay, a stock can rally during the early part of the cycle and the profit can be lost by expiration if the price does not continue climbing. The following problems were designed to address a variety of basic concepts surrounding profit protection for simple long call positions. (All calculations in this section are based on a 3.5% risk-free interest rate.)

8. Consider the trade parameters outlined in the following table. The first line of the table represents an initial position consisting of 10 calls that are $5.00 out-of-the-money with 70 days left before expiration. The second line represents the same trade 4 days later after the stock has climbed $7.00. Because the delta of these options is relatively high (42%), and a considerable amount of time remains before expiration (70 days), the option price increases by a substantial amount (78%).

Stock ($)	Call Strike ($)	Days Rem.	Call Price ($)	Delta	Volat.	10 Contr. ($)
100	105	70	4.33	0.42	0.35	4,330
107	105	66	7.69	0.60	0.35	7,690

A conservative investor would take action to protect profit. Following are some of the many choices that are available. Which of the following would not make sense? Which, if any, protect 100% of the profit?

A. Liquidate the entire position

B. Liquidate enough of the position to pay for the initial trade

C. Sell calls at a higher strike price with the same expiration

D. Sell calls at a lower strike price with the same expiration

E. Close the trade and simultaneously purchase calls at a higher strike (roll up)

F. Close the trade and simultaneously purchase calls at a lower strike (roll down)

G. Sell calls with an earlier expiration and same or higher strike

H. Sell calls with an earlier expiration and lower strike

I. Short an equivalent number of shares of stock based on the call delta

Answer: Liquidating the entire position (choice A) is the only choice that protects 100% of the profit under all circumstances. Choices D, F, and H do not make sense. D and H each involve creating a bearish position by selling more valuable calls that have a higher delta and a lower strike price. Each of these trades would profit from a price decline of the underlying. Choice F increases exposure to downward moves of the underlying by creating a more expensive long position with a higher delta. In this scenario all the profit remains at risk in addition to the added cost of the new trade.

Rolling up to a higher strike (E) can lock in some of the profit by creating a new lower-cost position similar to the initial trade. The amount of profit that is protected depends on the amount of money put at risk in the new position.

Selling calls at a higher strike price (C) and selling calls with the same or higher strike price and an earlier expiration (G) are similar strategies in that each protects some of the profit. Unlike rolling up, these strategies cap the potential gain because they contain a short component.

Liquidating enough of the position to pay for the initial trade (B) prevents an overall loss but leaves all the profit at risk.

Shorting an equivalent amount of stock as measured by the delta (I) creates a position similar to a long straddle. Additional profit would be generated by either a sharp increase or sharp decline in the stock price. Alternatively, a reduced number of shares can be shorted as a hedge against a price reversal. The number of shares chosen should reflect the investor's level of bullishness. One solution is to short enough shares of stock to create a position with a net delta equal to that of the original trade.

9. Suppose that after the large price spike in question #8 you decided to keep the position unchanged—that is, long 10 calls at the $105 strike price with the stock trading at $107. How many stock-equivalent shares would you be long? How do the costs of the two positions compare?

   Answer: 10 contracts with a delta of 0.60 is equivalent to 600 shares of stock. Since the stock is trading at $107, the cost would be $107 × 600 = $64,200. From the table in question #8, we know that the options are worth $7,690.

10. Why, in question #9, would an investor be willing to pay $64,200 for stock that is fundamentally equivalent to a $7,690 option position? Can you compare the values of the two positions if the stock falls $2.00 and continues trading at the strike price until expiration? How would the positions compare if the stock remained at $107 until expiration?

    Answer: If the underlying falls $2.00 and remains at or below the strike price until expiration, the entire $7,690 would be lost. The same price decline would generate a loss of only $1,200 for an investor holding 600 shares of stock.

    If the stock remains $2.00 in-the-money until expiration, the option trade will lose $5.69 while the stock position will not lose anything.

11. If you kept the position until expiration, the stock remained at $107, and you didn't sell any offsetting calls, would you have a profit?

Answer: The trade would lose $2,330. Our original 10 contracts that cost $4,330 would be worth $2,000 if the stock remained $2 in-the-money until expiration. A full accounting would also include the opportunity cost of the money and any expenses associated with trading. The stock would need to trade $4.33 in-the-money at expiration for the uncovered trade to generate a profit ($109.33).

12. In question #8, how many shares of stock would we have needed to purchase to match the $3,360 gain realized by the option position in the first 4 days? How does the percentage gain compare with that of the option trade?

    Answer: 480 shares would be needed to generate a $3,360 gain from a $7 increase in the stock price (480 × $7 = $3,360). The initial purchase price would have been $48,000 and the gain would have been 7%—the percentage gain for the option trade was more than 10 times larger.

13. For the scenario outlined in question #8, we can lock in some of our gain by selling calls at a higher strike price. If the stock price declines, some of the loss will be offset by the premium collected in the sale of the higher strike price calls. Conversely, if the stock continues to rise, our gain will be capped as the short call moves into-the-money. Choices with the same expiration as our long position are displayed in the following table.

Stock ($)	Call Strike ($)	Days Remaining	Call Price ($)	Delta	Volatility	10 Contr. ($)
107	110	66	5.33	0.47	0.35	5,330
107	115	66	3.56	0.36	0.35	3,560
107	120	66	2.29	0.26	0.35	2,290

Recall that in question #8 the stock is trading $2 in-the-money at $107, and our long calls have risen in value from $4.33 to $7.69. Which option with the same expiration date as our original trade would offer the best protection if the stock remains at that price? What would the total profit for the combined trade be at expiration?

Answer: If the stock remains at $107 until expiration, the best choice among those with the same expiration date would be the $110 strike for $5.33. At expiration our long call at the $105 strike price would be worth $2.00 and we would keep $5.33 of premium from the short sale. Since our original trade cost $4.33 we would have a total profit of $3.00 ($2.00 + $5.33 − $4.33). The combined trade consisting of 10 long and 10 short contracts would generate a profit of $3,000. Without the short sale we would have lost $2.33 to time decay ($2,330 for 10 contracts).

14. In question #13 we could have hedged our trade with a closer-dated option instead of one with the same expiration date. The following table contains the relevant choices. (Note that options with the same strike price as the trade we are protecting [$105] are included because the expiration date is different.)

Stock ($)	Call Strike ($)	Days Remaining	Call Price ($)	Delta	Volatility	10 Contr. ($)
107	105	38	6.05	0.60	0.35	6,050
107	110	38	3.69	0.44	0.35	3,690
107	115	38	2.09	0.29	0.35	2,090
107	120	38	1.10	0.18	0.35	1,100

Which short call position generates the largest return if the stock trades at $110 on the final day of the closer-dated expiration shown in the table?

Answer: If we decided to sell the $110 call with the nearer expiration and the stock closed this timeframe at $110, we would keep the entire $3.69 premium. Short calls at the $105 strike price would need to be repurchased for $5 at expiration. Since they are initially worth $6.05, the profit from this sale would be only $1.05. Higher strike prices provide no advantage over the sale of the $110 call because they generate less income.

15. In questions #13 and #14, which of the two short call positions, far- or near-dated, delivers the largest profit at the time of the earlier expiration?

    Answer: The short $110 call with the nearer expiration delivers a profit of $3.69. This amount is equal to 69% of the total value of the longer-dated option that sold for $5.33 in problem #13. Since only 38 of the 66 days originally left in the longer-dated contracts have passed, we know that the options could not have lost more than 58% of their initial value (0.58 × $5.33 = $3.09). We can predict, therefore, that the nearer-dated short call position delivered at least 60¢ of additional time decay.

16A. Assume that the underlying stock continues to rise at the rate indicated in questions #13 and #14—that is, the stock trades at $107 with 66 days remaining, and $110 with 29 days remaining before expiration. Can you identify the next option to sell when the near-dated $110 calls expire? The following table contains relevant call prices for the remaining expiration date. (Note that when the near-dated option expires, there are actually 28 days remaining in the longer-dated contracts [66 days – 38 days]. However, because equity options expire on Saturday, we sell new options on the preceding Friday with 29 days remaining. The table was designed to reflect this one-day difference in pricing.)

Stock ($)	Call Strike ($)	Days Remaining	Call Price ($)	Delta	Volatility	10 Contr. ($)
110	110	29	3.05	0.42	0.35	3,050
110	115	29	1.55	0.26	0.35	1,550
110	120	29	0.72	0.14	0.35	720

Answer: We know that the stock traded at $107 with 66 days remaining and $110 on the final trading day of the near expiration when 29 days remained. If the stock continues to rise at this rate, we can expect it to trade at just over $112 at the time of the next expiration. We can derive this result simply by drawing a line through the two points. The chart is displayed in Figure 2.1.

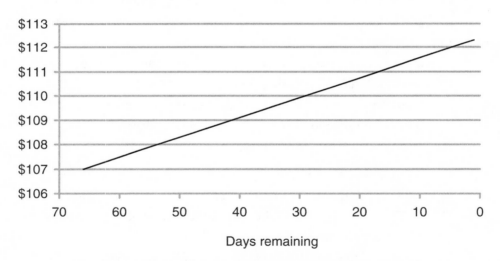

Figure 2.1   Expiration trading price projection for stock trading at $107 with 66 days remaining before expiration and $110 with 29 days remaining. Days remaining are displayed on the x-axis, projected price on the y-axis.

If we sell the $115 call and the stock ends the expiration cycle at $112, we will keep the entire $1.55. Conversely, if we sell the $110 strike price call for $3.05 and the stock closes at $112 on expiration Friday, our short trade will generate only $1.05 of profit after we repurchase the option for $2.00.

16B. Assuming that we follow the path implied by question #16A—
that is, we hedge our long $105 call position by first selling $110
calls with 38 days remaining and then $115 calls when the first
hedge expires—what will our total profit be if the stock closes
the final expiration cycle at $112?

Answer: $7.91 ($7,910 for 10 contracts). Our long position is
worth $7.00 at expiration with the underlying stock trading at
$112. Additionally, we sold 2 sets of options including $110 calls
for $3.69 and $115 calls for $1.55. Total revenue for the trade,
therefore, is $7.00 + $3.69 + $1.55 = $12.24. We must subtract
the cost of our original long position to obtain the final profit
($12.24 – $4.33 = $7.91). If each trade in the sequence involved
10 contracts, our total profit would be $7,910. Calculated as a
percentage of the initial trade, the profit would be 183%.

17. In questions #15 and #16 we used a line drawn through two
price points to predict that the stock would trade below $115 at
the end of the expiration cycle. Is this assumption reasonable
given the implied volatility listed in the accompanying table
(35%)?

Answer: The table lists implied volatility as 35%. With 29 days
remaining and the stock trading at $110, we can calculate the
size of a 1 standard deviation change as follows:

Timeframes in 1 year	365 / 29 = 12.59 timeframes
Annualization factor	Sqrt (12.58) = 3.55
Volatility for 29 days	0.35 / 3.55 = .099
1 StdDev change	.099 × $110 = $10.89

If the implied volatility is appropriate, then a $5 price increase to $115 during the remaining 29 days represents a change of only about half of a standard deviation. The normal distribution predicts that 62% of all price changes will be larger than 0.5 standard deviations. Statistically, however, half of these can be expected to be price increases and half will be decreases. Using the normal distribution, we can estimate that the probability of the stock trading above $115 at expiration is only 31%. This number can be arrived at using Excel's normal distribution function or a table in a statistics textbook.

In the case of Excel, the function NORMSDIST(0.5) = 0.691. This result represents the percentage of price changes for the 29-day timeframe that fall below +0.5 standard deviations. Because half the changes are negative, we can subtract these to determine the percentage that falls between 0.0 and +0.5 (0.691 – 0.50 = 0.191). The remaining 31% of the positive changes lie above +0.5 StdDev.

18. In question #8 after the rapid increase to $107, how many shares would we need to short to create a delta-neutral position that exactly offsets the long calls? How many shares would we need to short to create a long position that is delta-equivalent to the original trade?

Answer: 600 shares of stock would offset 10 calls with a delta of 0.60 (10 contracts × 100 shares per contract × 0.60). Alternatively, shorting 180 shares of stock would reduce the effective delta from 0.60 to 0.42, the value of the original trade.

19. If we created the delta-neutral position described in question #18 and the stock fell $10, would the complete set of trades be profitable at expiration? If so, what would the percent gain be on an annual basis?

    Answer: Yes. If the price fell $10, the short stock trade would gain $6,000 and our original long call position, which cost $4,330, would expire worthless. The combination would yield a profit of $1,670. The gain would be 2.4% calculated as follows: $1,670 profit / ($66,000 short stock + $4,330 long calls). Since there were 66 days remaining before expiration, we can annualize the number by multiplying by 365 / 66. Without compounding, the result would be 13.3% per year.

Defensive Action (Problems #20--#38)

The previous set of problems focused on strategies for protecting profit. Although this problem is a good one to have, we must also be prepared to take defensive action to recover from losses. The following problems address basic issues surrounding such strategies. (All calculations in this section are based on a 3.5% risk-free interest rate.)

20. Consider the trade parameters outlined in the following table. The first line of the table represents an initial position consisting of 10 calls that are $5.00 out-of-the-money with 70 days left before expiration. The second line represents the same trade 4 days later after the stock has fallen $7.00. Because the delta of these options is relatively high (42%), and a considerable amount of time remains before expiration (70 days), the option price decreases by a substantial amount (57%).

Stock ($)	Call Strike ($)	Days Remaining	Call Price ($)	Delta	Volatility	10 Contr. ($)
100	105	70	4.33	0.42	0.35	4,330
93	105	66	1.85	0.24	0.35	1,850

With the stock moving in the wrong direction and our trade losing more than half its value, it would be wise to take corrective action. Following are some of the many choices available. Can you identify the most logical choices? Which would not make sense? Which is the most conservative?

A. Liquidate the entire position and absorb the loss

B. Close the current trade and then structure a new position that is short the current strike and long a lower strike (also called a bull spread)

C. As in choice B, close the current position and then structure a bull spread using lower strike prices for both sides of the new trade

D. Keep the long position and sell calls at a higher strike with the same expiration

E. Keep the long position and sell calls at a lower strike with the same expiration

F. Close the trade and simultaneously purchase calls at a higher strike (roll up)

G. Close the trade and simultaneously purchase calls at a lower strike (roll down)

H. Keep the current long position and sell calls with an earlier expiration and the same or higher strike

I. Keep the current long position and sell calls with an earlier expiration and a lower strike

J. Purchase another 10 contracts at the original strike to "average down" the price

K. Short an equivalent number of shares of stock based on the call delta

Answer: Liquidating the entire position (choice A) is the only choice that prevents any further losses. As such it is the most conservative choice. Choices E and I do not make sense because they create bearish positions by selling more valuable calls that have a higher delta and a lower strike price. Each of these trades would profit if the underlying stock declines. While such a strategy might make sense for a stock that has recently fallen sharply, there are more efficient ways to structure a bearish position. It is unlikely that we would keep our long $105 strike price calls as part of a bearish structure.

Choice G increases exposure to downward moves of the underlying by creating a more expensive long position with a higher delta. If the stock continues to decline, our losses would be magnified. Very aggressive investors sometimes take this approach because they count on mean reversion, a force that can sometimes reverse a sharp decline. Choice J is philosophically similar—a very bullish investor might consider the decline an opportunity to purchase additional contracts at a reduced price. This approach should be considered only by investors who limit their original purchase and can accept a larger loss on the combined trade.

Rolling up to a higher strike (F) limits further losses by reducing the cost of the position. However, it generally does not make sense to purchase farther out-of-the-money calls on a stock that is declining.

Choices B, C, D, and H are logical solutions for an investor who remains bullish. Each creates a new trade structure that lowers the break-even point while capping the potential gain. Some, but not all, reduce the maximum possible loss. With each structure it is possible to recover the full loss and realize a profit at expiration.

As before, shorting a delta-equivalent number of shares (K) creates a position that embodies many of the dynamics of a long straddle. Profit would be generated by either a sharp increase or sharp decline in the stock price. The number of shares can be calibrated to reflect the investor's level of bullishness or bearishness; a bullish investor might short a small number of shares as a hedge, whereas a more bearish investor would likely select enough shares to match the delta of the stock. A very bearish investor might short more shares than required to match the delta of the calls. In the new bearish position the existing calls would serve as a hedge to protect the short stock position in the event of a price increase.

21. How many stock-equivalent shares were represented in the original trade? How many are represented in the same position after the $7 price decline?

    Answer: The original position was equivalent to 420 shares of stock. After the decline, at a delta of 0.24, the position represents only 240 shares of stock.

22. Which would have suffered the greater loss, 420 shares of stock or the original long call position consisting of 10 contracts at the $105 strike price? Why is there a difference if the positions are delta-equivalent?

    Answer: The stock position would have lost $2,940 ($7 × 420 shares) while the long calls would have lost only $2,480. The stock position suffers a greater loss because its delta is always 1.0, whereas the call delta continually declines as the underlying moves away from the strike price.

23. For the scenario outlined in question #20, we can offset some of the loss by creating a new position consisting of long and short calls. Since the stock is trading at $93, the relevant strikes are $95, $100, $105, and $110. What are the possible trade structures composed of 10 long and 10 short calls using these strikes and expiration? Do any of the new scenarios preserve the original 10 long $105 calls?

Answer: Only one scenario preserves the original long position. The choices are:

$5 gap between strikes

10 long $105 calls/10 short $110 calls

10 long $100 calls/10 short $105 calls

10 long $95 calls/10 short $100 calls

$10 gap between strikes

10 long $100 calls/10 short $110 calls

10 long $95 calls/10 short $105 calls

$15 gap between strikes

10 long $95 calls/10 short $110 calls

24. The following table contains pricing information that can be used to structure the new trade.

Stock ($)	Call Strike ($)	Days Remaining	Call Price ($)	Delta	Volatility	10 Contr. ($)
93	110	66	1.06	0.16	0.35	1,060
93	105	66	1.85	0.24	0.35	1,850
93	100	66	3.08	0.36	0.35	3,080
93	95	66	4.89	0.49	0.35	4,890

Can you create a table that compares the maximum gain and loss for each of the six new positions? The table should also reflect the maximum gain and loss for each position after subtracting the initial loss that resulted from the $7 stock price decline.

Answer: The following table describes the maximum gain that can be achieved for each trade if the stock closes at or above the short strike price at expiration. The original long position is included at the top of the table for comparison.

Long Call Strike ($)	Short Call Strike ($)	Initial Value ($)	Expiration Value ($)	Max Profit ($)	Net Profit ($)	10 Contr. Gain ($)
105	—	1.85	no limit	no limit	no limit	no limit
105	110	0.79	5.00	4.21	1.73	1,730
100	105	1.23	5.00	3.77	1.29	1,290
95	100	1.81	5.00	3.19	0.71	710
100	110	2.02	10.00	7.98	5.50	5,500
95	105	3.04	10.00	6.96	4.48	4,480
95	110	3.83	15.00	11.17	8.69	8,690

For example, to calculate the values for the $95/$105 strike price combination, we would first subtract the value obtained from selling the short side from the cost of the long side ($4.89 − $1.85 = $3.04). If the stock moves far into-the-money, the long side will be worth $10.00 more than the short side. Subtracting the cost of the trade from this value yields the maximum profit of $6.96. By subtracting the $2.48 loss associated with the initial $7 stock decline, we can determine the maximum overall profit of the trade ($6.96 − $2.48 = $4.48). In dollar terms, a 10-contract position structured using the $95/$105 strikes would return $4,480 when the initial trade loss is included in the calculation.

The next table describes the maximum loss that will be realized if the stock falls dramatically and both sides end the expiration cycle out-of-the-money. The original long position is, once again, included at the top of the table for comparison.

Long Call Strike ($)	Short Call Strike ($)	Initial Value ($)	Expiration Value ($)	Max Loss ($)	Net Loss ($)	10 Contr. Loss ($)
105	—	1.85	0.00	−1.85	−4.33	−4,330
105	110	0.79	0.00	−0.79	−3.27	−3,270
100	105	1.23	0.00	−1.23	−3.71	−3,710
95	100	1.81	0.00	−1.81	−4.29	−4,290
100	110	2.02	0.00	−2.02	−4.50	−4,500
95	105	3.04	0.00	−3.04	−5.52	−5,520
95	110	3.83	0.00	−3.83	−6.31	−6,310

For example, the maximum loss for the same strike price combination used previously ($95/$105) would be equal to the cost of the new position plus the initial loss that resulted from the $7 stock decline ($3.04 + $2.48 = $5.52). Restated in dollar terms, the combined loss would be $5,520 if the stock traded below $95 at expiration.

25. Which combination offers the largest risk-adjusted maximum return? Can you calculate the magnitude of the price change in standard deviations that would be necessary to achieve this return?

Answer: The $95/$110 strike price combination offers the best risk-adjusted return. The following table compares each choice by subtracting the maximum loss from the maximum gain for each position.

Long Call Strike ($)	Short Call Strike ($)	Max Gain ($)	Max Loss ($)	Risk Adjusted Max Return ($)
105	—	unlimited	–4,330	—
105	110	1,730	–3,270	–1,540
100	105	1,290	–3,710	–2,420
95	100	710	–4,290	–3,580
100	110	5,500	–4,500	1,000
95	105	4,480	–5,520	–1,040
95	110	8,690	–6,310	2,380

We can calculate the value of a 1 standard deviation price change over 66 days for a $93 stock with implied volatility of 35%.

Timeframes in 1 year	365 / 66 = 5.53 timeframes
Annualization factor	Sqrt (5.53) = 2.35
Volatility for 66 days	0.35 / 2.35 = 0.149
1 StdDev change	0.149 × $93 = $13.86

Maximum profit will be realized if the stock trades at or above $110 at expiration—a $17 price increase in 66 days. This increase is equal to 1.2 standard deviations ($17.00 / $13.86). In statistical terms, the stock has a 12% chance of trading above this level at expiration. This value can be obtained using Excel's NORMSDIST function.

The maximum return threshold for each adjusted trade is displayed in standard deviations in the following table.

Long Call Strike ($)	Short Call Strike ($)	Max Gain ($)	Distance to Max Gain in StdDev
105	—	unlimited	—
105	110	1,730	1.23
100	105	1,290	0.87
95	100	710	0.51
100	110	5,500	1.23
95	105	4,480	0.87
95	110	8,690	1.23

26. Risk-adjusted profiles can be deceiving because the maximum loss for most trades is larger than the maximum gain. For example, a short call position worth $10,000 has unlimited potential loss but a maximum return of only $10,000. Probabilities need to be applied to complete the analysis. If the naked calls are 2 standard deviations out-of-the-money for the timeframe involved, the chance of the stock expiring below the strike price is around 98%.

Why is the situation described in the preceding problems different? Is the risk-adjusted return a fair assessment?

Answer: The situation is different because each adjusted trade will suffer the maximum loss if the stock continues to fall or remains at $93. Moreover, each trade loses money if the stock fails to rise enough to pay back the initial cost. Stated differently, the original loss of $2.48 will be magnified if the stock does not rise enough to pay back the cost of the adjusted position. Considering that the stock has just experienced a sharp decline, it may be foolish to bet on such a reversal. In the case of a short call position that is 2 standard deviations out-of-the-money, the stock can rise substantially and the calls can still expire worthless.

27. How do the risk-adjusted alternatives from the table in question #25 compare with simply holding the original long $105 calls? You may find it helpful to think about price changes in standard deviations.

   Answer: If we keep the original position, our upside is unlimited and our downside is $4,330—the cost of the original trade. The adjusted trades vary considerably. For example, the $95/$100 strike price combination is severely limited with regard to upside potential and loses virtually the same amount of money as the original trade if the stock fails to rally. Conversely, the $95/$110 combination has the potential to ultimately lose $1,980 more than the original trade but caps the maximum gain at $8,690. The following table compares the returns that would be realized in each scenario with the stock trading at $105 and $110 on expiration day. Each of these price changes is reasonable; $105 would represent a 0.87 standard deviation change and $110 would correspond to 1.2 standard deviations. As before, the original long position is displayed in the first row of the table.

Long Call Strike ($)	Short Call Strike ($)	Initial Value ($)	Original Loss ($)	Net Profit at $105	Net Profit at $110
105	—	1.85	2.48	−4,330	670
105	110	0.79	2.48	−3,270	1,730
100	105	1.23	2.48	1,290	1,290
95	100	1.81	2.48	710	710
100	110	2.02	2.48	500	5,500
95	105	3.04	2.48	4,480	4,480
95	110	3.83	2.48	3,690	8,690

Profit for each row is calculated by subtracting the original loss plus the cost of the new trade from the value of the position at expiration. For example, the $95/$105 combination had an initial cost of $3.04. Adding the previous loss of $2.48 provides us with the total cost that must be recovered for the trade to be profitable ($5.52). At expiration with the stock trading at $105, the long $95 calls would be worth $10 and the short $105 calls would expire worthless—the position would be worth $10. Subtracting the cost that must be recovered including the original loss yields a profit of $4.48, or $4,480 for 10 contracts. Because the long and short sides of the trade are both in-the-money, further increases in the price of the underlying stock have no effect.

Despite having unlimited potential upside, the original long position yields the lowest return of the group for modest increases in the underlying stock price. At $105, the original trade suffers the greatest loss—$4,330—and at $110 it barely generates any profit. Conversely, the most profitable trade at $105 is the $95/$105 combination because the long side is worth $10 and the short side expires worthless. The same dynamics cause the $95/$110 combination to deliver the largest profit if the stock closes at $110 on expiration day.

28. At what expiration price does the original trade become the best alternative? How many standard deviations must the stock move to reach this price?

Answer: The largest maximum gain for any of the adjusted positions is $11.17 for the $95/$110 combination with the stock trading at, or above, $110 on expiration day. The original trade will not generate this much profit unless the underlying stock rises to $120.50 by expiration. This value is obtained by adding the required profit ($11.17) to the initial cost ($4.33 including the original loss) to determine the distance above the strike price that the stock must reach. Adding these values together and subtracting the $105 strike yields a value of $120.50. Only if the underlying stock trades above this price at expiration will the original trade provide the largest profit of the group.

We can determine the magnitude of this change by subtracting the starting price ($93) from the endpoint ($120.50) and dividing by the value of a 1 standard deviation change ($13.85).

$120.50 – $93.00 = $27.50

$27.50 / $13.85 = 2 standard deviations

29. In question #28 we determined that the original trade would be the best alternative only if the stock climbed more than 2 standard deviations by expiration. These dynamics provide a rationale for the adjustment. Stated differently, the adjusted trades have lower break-even points than the original. This strategy makes perfect sense for an investor who remains bullish and wants to remain long despite a recent price decline.

Can you create a table that displays the break-even point for each of the adjusted trades? Be sure to include the original $4.33 loss that triggered the adjustment.

Answer: The following table displays break-even points for each adjusted trade. As before, the original long position appears in the first row for comparison.

Long Call Strike ($)	Short Call Strike ($)	Starting Position ($)	Initial Loss ($)	Total Deficit ($)	Break Even ($)
105	—	1.85	2.48	4.33	109.33
105	110	0.79	2.48	3.27	108.27
100	105	1.23	2.48	3.71	103.71
95	100	1.81	2.48	4.29	99.29
100	110	2.02	2.48	4.50	104.50
95	105	3.04	2.48	5.52	100.52
95	110	3.83	2.48	6.31	101.31

Each break-even point is determined by adding the total cost to the long strike price. For example, the initial cost of the $95/$100 combination is $1.81. Adding the original $2.48 loss yields a deficit of $4.29 that must be recovered. To meet this condition the stock must close more than $4.29 above the long strike. Note that we are attempting to make up a $4.29 deficit with strike prices that are spaced by only $5. This combination, therefore, can never generate more than 71¢ of profit. The severely limited profit potential for the $95/$100 combination is offset by the lowest break-even point of the group.

Surprisingly, the combination with the greatest profit potential ($95/$110) does not have the highest break-even point. The relatively low break-even point for this trade is directly related to the relatively low strike price of the long side ($95). Conversely, the high break-even point for the $105/$110 combination is a function of the high strike price of the long side.

30. Assuming a larger initial loss, do any of the previous strike price combinations have the potential to generate a positive return if the combination of original loss and new initial trade price is greater than $5?

    Answer: Combinations with $10 or $15 spacing can generate more than $5 of profit to overcome a larger initial loss. Choices from our list include the following:

    $10 gap between strikes

    10 long $100 calls/10 short $110 calls

    10 long $95 calls/10 short $105 calls

    $15 gap between strikes

    10 long $95 calls/10 short $110 calls

    Much larger initial losses would necessitate restructuring the list of choices to include strikes lower than $95.

31. How many shares of stock would be delta-equivalent to the $95/$110 strike price combination?

    Answer: We know from the table displayed in question #24 that the $95 strike price delta is 0.49 and the $110 strike price delta is 0.16. Subtracting short from long yields a net delta of 0.33. Multiplying for 10 contracts gives a stock equivalency of 330 shares (10 contracts × 100 shares per contract × 0.33).

32. In the previous scenarios we accommodated a $7 price decline by structuring trades with a variety of strike price combinations and the same expiration date. We could also have chosen to sell calls with a nearer expiration.

The following table displays two possible choices that expire approximately one month earlier (38 days remain before expiration). The first row contains the original long position that still has 66 days left.

Stock ($)	Call Strike ($)	Days Remaining	Call Price ($)	Delta	Volatility	10 Contr.($)
93	105	66	1.85	0.24	0.35	1,850
93	105	38	0.86	0.16	0.35	860
93	100	38	1.80	0.29	0.35	1,800

However, in order to calculate maximum potential gains and losses, we need additional information about the value of the far-dated long position at the time of expiration of the short side. The following table displays prices for the long $105 call at the two relevant short strikes, $100 and $105, coincident with expiration of the short side (28 days remain on the long side).

Stock ($)	Call Strike ($)	Days Remaining	Call Price ($)	Delta	Volatility	10 Contr.($)
105	105	28	4.20	0.53	0.35	4,200
100	105	28	2.04	0.33	0.35	2,040

How do these two choices compare for maximum potential profit?

Answer: The expiration price and maximum gain with 28 days remaining in the long $105 calls are listed in the following table.

Long Call Strike ($)	Short Call Strike ($)	Initial Value ($)	Expiration Value ($)	Max Profit ($)	Net Profit ($)	10 Contr. Gain ($)
105	—	1.85	no limit	no limit	no limit	no limit
105	105	0.99	4.20	3.21	0.73	730
105	100	0.05	2.04	1.99	−0.49	−490

Total profit is calculated by subtracting the cost of each trade from the maximum value when the short side expires. Reducing this amount by the original loss ($2.48) yields the net profit. For example, selling $105 calls after the initial price decline reduces the cost of the long side by 86¢ to $0.99. With the short side expiring at-the-money, the long $105 calls are worth $4.20. Subtracting the net cost of the original trade (99¢) yields a profit of $3.21. Further reducing this gain by the amount of the initial loss ($2.48) yields a net profit of only 73¢ or $730 for 10 contracts. Note that if the stock only rises to $100 by the time of the near expiration, the long side will not appreciate enough to pay back the original $2.48 loss. This result might seem surprising because the short $100 call, which has decayed to zero, initially sold for $1.80—nearly the same price as the long call.

33. Does the $100/$105 combination make any sense if it cannot generate a profit? Why would an investor make this adjustment?

    Answer: It is important to remember that the initial trade lost $2.48 when the stock declined $7. Both trades have the potential to significantly reduce that loss. The $105/$105 combination can fully reverse the loss and generate a profit of $730; the $100/$105 combination can reduce the loss from $2,480 to $490. In return for diminished upside potential, the less favorable combination offers greater protection if the stock remains at $93 or falls further.

34. Can the stock rise far enough at any point in the expiration cycle to raise the price of the near-dated $105 call above its far-dated equivalent? Can the two sides achieve the same value?

Answer: The price of the near-dated call cannot exceed the price of its far-dated equivalent if implied volatility is the same on both sides. However, pending events such as earnings releases can distort the term structure so that implied volatility for the near-dated option is much higher than for its far-dated counterpart. However, this distortion disappears at expiration because the option can never be worth more than the amount that the stock is in-the-money. At expiration the near-dated $105 call can never be worth more than its far-dated counterpart.

35. Figure 2.2 displays the net value of the $105/$105 short/long combination at expiration for stock prices above and below the strike price. (The original $2.48 loss is not included.) Stock prices are measured on the x-axis, net value of the option position on the y-axis. Can you explain the sharp drop that occurs as the stock crosses the strike price?

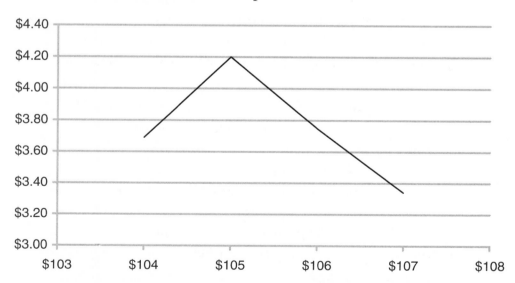

Figure 2.2   Value of a one-month calendar spread (short $105 call/long $105 call) for stock prices just above and below the strike. Prices are calculated at expiration of the near-dated short side using 35% volatility.

Answer: The value drops off steeply because the delta of the short side rises to 1.0 when the underlying stock crosses the strike price, and the long side, with one month remaining before expiration, has a delta of only about half as much (0.53). If the stock trades at or below the strike price, the short side has no value. The sharp transition from no value and a delta of 0.0 to in-the-money value and a delta of 1.0 creates the profile seen in the figure. If the stock climbs far enough, both deltas will rise to 1.0 and both options will have essentially the same value.

36. What is the maximum potential loss for each combination? In each case, what conditions cause the maximum loss?

Answer: For the $105/$105 short/long combination, the maximum loss occurs with the stock far below the strike price at expiration. In this scenario, both sides are worthless and the net cost of the initial trade ($0.99) is lost. The initial value of 99¢ is also lost if the stock moves very far above the strike price where both sides have the same value. In either case, the maximum loss is equal to the original net cost of the position—99¢.

The $100/$105 short/long combination is different because the short side will be worth $5.00 more than the long side if the stock trades far above the strike price at expiration. In this scenario, we would be forced to close the trade and buy back the short side for a $5.00 loss. Because both sides were initially worth approximately the same amount, the $5.00 difference would be equal to the entire loss. Conversely, if the stock trades far below the strike price at expiration, both sides collapse to zero and nothing is lost because the initial trade cost only 5¢.

In summary, both positions experience their maximum loss if the stock trades far above the strike price at expiration—$5.00 for the $100/$105 combination and 99¢ for the position built solely around the $105 strike. The single strike position also experiences its maximum loss if the stock trades far below the strike price.

37. Based on the previous discussion and analysis, which of the two near-dated adjustments would be more appropriate for a strongly bullish investor—10 short calls at the $105 strike or 10 short calls at the $100 strike?

    Answer: Shorting the $105 strike is more appropriate for a bullish investor because it yields limited losses for very large increases of the underlying stock and larger losses in the event of additional declines. Conversely, the $100 strike is fully hedged against additional stock declines but provides a much smaller return if the stock rises. Worse still, a steep rise in the stock generates a significant loss if the lower strike is shorted. It is, therefore, difficult to imagine that a bullish investor would structure this position.

38. Assume that we sell the $105 call as our original correction and the stock climbs to $105 at the time of the near expiration—that is, we keep the premium from the $105 short call and realize a $3.21 profit on the new trade. How much money is at risk if we keep the position without selling another hedge in the remaining month?

    Answer: $4.20 is at risk because that is the value of the far-dated long $105 call.

Term Structure, Volatility Skews, and Theta (Problems #39–#46)

39. As previously mentioned, volatility has a term structure that causes it to vary between expiration dates. Anticipated events such as earnings can further distort the term structure so that implied volatility is significantly higher for one expiration than another. These distortions disappear after the event has passed.

    Consider the following table of option prices for a $150 stock that reports quarterly earnings just a few days after the near expiration. The first set of calls expires in 15 days, and the second set in 43 days. Because of the pending earnings announcement, implied volatility is inflated 25% (50% versus 40%) for the second set. (Calculations are based on 1.5% risk-free interest rate.)

Stock Price ($)	Call Strike	Days Remaining	Volatility	Call Price ($)	Theta
150	150	15	0.4	4.90	−0.16
150	155	15	0.4	2.87	−0.15
150	160	15	0.4	1.55	−0.12
150	165	15	0.4	0.77	−0.09
150	150	43	0.5	10.39	−0.12
150	155	43	0.5	8.23	−0.12
150	160	43	0.5	6.43	−0.12
150	165	43	0.5	4.97	−0.11

    In percentage terms, what would you expect the minimum price distortion to be for the far-dated options listed in the table? Which strike price has the most inflated value and which has the least?

Answer: The price of at-the-money options will be inflated in approximate proportion to the increase in implied volatility (25%). In-the-money options experience smaller price distortions while out-of-the-money options experience larger percentage increases. Assuming 25% inflation for the $150 call yields a noninflated price of approximately $8.30 ($10.39 / 1.25 = $8.31).

Figure 2.3 charts the price distortion in percentage terms on the y-axis against strike price on the x-axis for options in the preceding table.

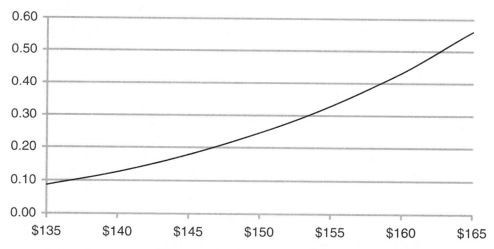

Figure 2.3   Price distortion in percentage terms for different strikes with volatility inflated 25% and the underlying stock trading at $150. The increase in call prices is measured on the y-axis in percent, and strike prices are displayed on the x-axis.

40. Based on the information presented in question #39, which of the following positions is the most statistically sound?

    Long far-dated $150 call/short near-dated $150 call

    Long near-dated $150 call/short far-dated $150 call

    Long far-dated $165 call/short near-dated $165 call

    Long near-dated $165 call/short far-dated $165 call

Answer: Long near-dated $165 call/short far-dated $165 call leverages the greatest distortion because the far-dated call is overpriced by more than 50%. The position is long 40% volatility and short 50%. Another way to think about the trade is that it is long a $0.77 option and short a $4.97 option that is really worth only $3.18. Because of its inflated price, the short far-dated option returns more time decay than its near-dated, correctly priced counterpart. (The short side returns 37% more time decay than the correctly priced option.)

It is important to realize that the trade dynamics change once the near-dated side expires, because rolling forward requires purchasing expensive current month calls. Additionally, keeping the trade open until the distortion-causing event implies a certain level of risk related to the complexities of trading against an earnings announcement.

Many complex positions can be created to exploit the kinds of volatility distortions generated by earnings, expiration, and other special events. It is impossible to fully take advantage of all the possibilities without considering structures that are both long and short, puts and calls across different timeframes. For example, in the current scenario we would be much better off selling overpriced far-dated puts and calls against similar current-month long positions. We could, for example, sell far-dated $165 calls and $145 puts against a long position consisting of near-dated options at the same or closer strikes. The dynamics are complex, and we will return to such structures throughout this book in various contexts.

Many investors mistakenly believe that puts are simply the opposite of calls. That view is flawed for two specific reasons that are each related to distortions in implied volatility. First, implied volatility tends to rise steeply in response to sudden declines in the price of the underlying security. This effect tends to magnify the value of a long put position as the stock moves toward the strike price. Second, out-of-the-money put prices are normally inflated to accommodate the risk of a large downward spike. This implied volatility skew, also referred to as the "volatility smile," has been an important factor in put pricing since the 1987 stock market crash when billions of dollars were lost in short out-of-the-money put positions.

41. The volatility skew for a particular stock can become severe when the market perceives that there is a significant risk of negative news. Consider the following table, which reveals implied volatility and put prices for a stock with a steep volatility skew. The table contains information for two different expirations and four strike prices. (Calculations are based on a 1.5% risk-free rate of return.)

Stock Price ($)	Put Strike ($)	Days Remaining	Volatility	Put Price ($)	Delta
44	45	15	0.70	3.04	−0.53
44	40	15	0.84	1.28	−0.26
44	35	15	1.04	0.58	−0.12
44	30	15	1.27	0.28	−0.05
44	45	43	0.64	4.37	−0.49
44	40	43	0.73	2.46	−0.30
44	35	43	0.87	1.47	−0.18
44	30	43	1.02	0.87	−0.10

Assume that over the next 7 days the stock price declines to $34. Can you predict the new implied volatilities for the $35 and $30 strikes for both expirations?

Answer: After the decline, the stock trades $1 below the $35 strike. Assuming that the volatility smile remains approximately the same, both the $35 strike and the $30 strike should be priced as the $45 and $40 strikes were before the price decline. The values would be 70% for the $35 strike and 84% for the $30 strike in the near expiration. The far expiration implied volatilities would be 64% and 73%, respectively.

42. Which of the two $45 strikes would yield the larger profit after
the price decline—near- or far-dated? What would the approximate prices be?

Answer: Because they are far in-the-money ($11 for a $34
stock), both puts can be expected to trade for approximately
$11. The near-dated option that traded for $3.04 would have a
profit of $7.96, and the far-dated option would gain $6.63. In
percentage terms, the near option would gain 262% and the far
option 152%.

43. Using basic principles, can you predict which strike price would
be the best investment and which would be the worst for both
expirations? Why?

Answer: The $40 put was consistently the best investment, and
the $30 put was the worst. If the stock trades for $34 at the time of
the first expiration, the near-dated $45 put will be worth $11
(262% profit), and the near-dated $40 put will be worth $6 (369%
profit). The exceptionally large profit of the $40 strike is caused by
its transition from $4 out-of-the-money to $6 in-the-money. This
large swing causes the delta to fall from –0.26 to –1.0. The delta
swing would be nearly as large with 8 days remaining after the initial downward spike. The $45 option experiences a smaller change
in delta because it was initially in-the-money with a delta of –0.53.
For the $35 put trading $1 in-the-money, we can estimate that the
new delta will fall between –0.55 and –0.60. This estimate is supported by the delta of the $45 put before the decline (initial delta
of the $35 put was –0.12).

The $30 put loses all its value if it remains out-of-the-money. It
also suffers the largest decrease in implied volatility from 127%
to 84%, and the smallest increase in delta (we can estimate the
maximum delta from the $40 strike price option before the
decline).

These dynamics also apply to the far-dated options. The $40 put that initially traded for $2.46 is now $6 in-the-money with more than one month left before expiration. The $30 put experiences a large decline in implied volatility from 102% to 73% while remaining $4 out-of-the-money.

The following table summarizes these observations and predictions. It parallels the original version displayed in question #41 but reflects the $10 underlying price decline along with 7 days of time decay. The original volatility skew is preserved.

Stock Price ($)	Put Strike ($)	Days Remaining	Volatility	Put Price ($)	Delta
34	45	8	0.64	10.99	−1.00
34	40	8	0.67	6.07	−0.94
34	35	8	0.70	1.98	−0.59
34	30	8	0.84	0.33	−0.14
34	45	36	0.56	11.10	−0.93
34	40	36	0.58	6.63	−0.79
34	35	36	0.64	3.26	−0.51
34	30	36	0.73	1.33	−0.25

44. Implied volatility often falls and the skew flattens after an anticipated event passes. Suppose that, in the previous question, the $10 price decline was met with a return to historical implied volatility and the smile disappeared.

    Which, if any, of the original positions lose money? Do any still return a profit? Can you explain the results using basic option trading concepts? (Assume that each of the near-dated options experiences an implied volatility collapse to 40%, and the far-dated options return to 35%.)

Answer: Because the $45 puts are $11 (24%) in-the-money, we can safely assume that each trades for very close to $11—a substantial profit for either expiration date. The same dynamic exists for the $40 strike price, which, as previously discussed, generates more profit than the other members of the group.

Because the stock is trading $1 below the $35 strike, we can assume that the $35 put is worth at least $1.00 plus a certain amount of time premium. Original prices for the $35 put with the stock trading at $44 were $0.58 in the near month and $1.47 in the far-dated expiration. All of this value was time premium because the options were $11 out-of-the-money. Even slashing each value by half still leaves 29¢ of time decay in the near option and 70¢ in the far option. Although these are unrealistically low estimates, the near put would still be worth at least $1.29 and its far-dated counterpart at least $1.70. (Actual values for these options are $1.40 and $2.03.)

We can, therefore, assume that each of the first three strikes—$45, $40, $35—generates a positive return in both expiration timeframes.

The $30 strike is different from the other three because it remains $4 out-of-the-money after the price decline. Because it originally had the largest implied volatility, it is also the most affected by the newly flattened skew. For comparison purposes, it is helpful to restate distance to the strike in terms of standard deviations. For the near expiration, the original value is given by the following:

Timeframes in 1 year	365 / 15 = 24.3 timeframes
Annualization factor	Sqrt (24.3) = 4.93
Volatility for 15 days	1.27 / 4.93 = 0.26
1 StdDev change	0.26 × $44 = $11.33
Distance to $30 strike	$14/$11.33 = **1.24 StdDev**

Although the original price was $14 from the strike, it was only 1.24 standard deviations away because of the high volatility (127%). Repeating this calculation with the stock at $34, 8 days remaining before expiration, and implied volatility of only 40% yields the following:

Timeframes in 1 year	365 / 8 = 45.6 timeframes
Annualization factor	Sqrt (45.6) = 6.75
Volatility for 8 days	0.40 / 6.75 = 0.059
1 StdDev change	0.059 × $34 = $2.01
Distance to $30 strike	$4/$2.01 = **1.99 StdDev**

Surprisingly, in terms of standard deviations the stock is further from the strike after the price decline than before. Similar dynamics hold true for the far-dated option, which begins and ends the scenario approximately 1.1 standard deviations out-of-the-money.

These very rough calculations reveal that the stock has not moved closer to the strike in option pricing terms. (Actual pricing calculations give post-decline values of $0.01 for the near-dated option and $0.22 for the far-dated option.)

45. Unanticipated negative news often causes both a rapid decline in the stock price and a rise in implied volatility. The following table depicts such an event in terms of underlying price, volatility, and days remaining before expiration. Four different strikes are shown before and after the drawdown. Predrawdown prices are given in the table and theta is included for all entries. (Calculations are based on a 1.5% risk-free rate of return.)

Stock Price ($)	Put Strike ($)	Days Remaining	Volatility	Theta	Put Price ($)
120.00	120	15	0.44	–0.14	4.24
120.00	115	15	0.47	–0.13	2.38
120.00	110	15	0.51	–0.11	1.32
120.00	105	15	0.56	–0.08	0.74
105.00	120	8	0.88	–0.21	
105.00	115	8	0.94	–0.30	
105.00	110	8	1.02	–0.38	
105.00	105	8	1.12	–0.43	

Without knowing the final option prices, can you determine which strike delivers the largest return measured in percent? Which delivers the largest return in absolute dollars?

Answer: The $105 put experiences the largest percent gain while the $120 option increases the most in absolute terms.

We can predict that the $120 put experiences the largest absolute gain because it has the largest negative delta throughout the entire scenario and, therefore, gains the most for each incremental downward movement of the stock. Because the stock falls to $105, we can also assume that the price of the $120 put rises above $15. The table also reveals that the $120 put continues to experience 21¢ per day of time decay after the drawdown. Because this option is deep in-the-money, the rate of time decay will slow in the final few days and finally reach $0.00 on the last day, leaving the option value at $15. Knowing that theta shrinks from $0.21 to $0.00 allows us to reduce this number by half to approximate the average decay of the final week ($0.21 / 2 × 8 days = $0.84). Adding together the minimum values ($15 in-the-money + 84¢ of additional time decay) sets a floor of $15.84 on the final price of the $120 put, and suggests a profit of at least $11.60 for the trade.

The $105 put gains the most in percentage terms as it transitions from a far out-of-the-money, relatively inexpensive option with a very low delta, to an at-the-money option with a delta approaching –0.50. This option also benefits from the steepened volatility skew which has increased its implied volatility from 56% to 112%. We can estimate the final value of this option because the table lists its theta as 43¢ per day and there are only 8 days remaining before expiration. Multiplying 43¢ × 8 days sets a minimum floor of $3.44 on the value. However, time decay accelerates in the final week for at-the-money options, and we can roughly double this value to estimate the price of the put with 8 days remaining ($0.43 × 8 days × 2). This estimate yields a value of $6.88—an increase of more than 800% over the initial price of 74¢.

(Note that theta values are negative in the table, and that adding theta to an option price reduces its value by 1 day's worth of time decay.)

46. The following table compares $110 put prices for two different expirations. Initially, the near-dated option has 15 days left, and its far-dated counterpart has 43 days. The first pair of entries contains beginning and ending prices for the near-dated trade, and the second pair displays corresponding values for the far-dated trade recorded on the same days. (Calculations are based on a 1.5% risk-free rate of return.)

Stock Price ($)	Put Strike ($)	Days Remaining	Volatility	Theta	Put Price ($)
120.00	110	15	0.51	–0.11	1.32
105.00	110	0	0.00	0.00	
120.00	110	43	0.50	–0.08	3.79
105.00	110	28	0.75	–0.15	

Which trade generates the most profit at the time of the near expiration? Which generates the greatest return measured in percent? (Note: The far-dated option has 28 days left on expiration day of the near option.)

Answer: Because the near option expires $5 below the strike price, it is worth $5. Total profit is $3.68 (279%).

The far-dated option would provide a larger return if the position were closed on this date. As before, we can set a floor for its value using theta, which the table lists as 15¢ per day with 28 days remaining. Multiplying gives a value of $4.20. Adding this value to the distance that the option is in-the-money yields a minimum price of $9.20. Since the initial trade was priced at $3.79, we can conclude that the minimum profit is $5.41. Additionally, this number is conservative because time decay will accelerate over the remaining 28 days and the average will be larger than 15¢ per day. However, no reasonable increase can generate a value large enough to exceed the 279% return of the near-dated option. For example, assuming that 30¢ per day of time remains in the far-dated option yields a price of $13.40 and a profit of $9.61 (254%).

Additional notes for problems #45–#46:

In problems #45 and #46 we used theta to estimate the prices of several options. The following tables provide the precise values.

Problem #45

Stock Price ($)	Put Strike ($)	Days Remaining	Volatility	Theta	Put Price ($)
120.00	120	15	0.44	−0.14	4.24
120.00	115	15	0.47	−0.13	2.38
120.00	110	15	0.51	−0.11	1.32
120.00	105	15	0.56	−0.08	0.74
105.00	120	8	0.88	−0.21	16.13
105.00	115	8	0.94	−0.30	12.34
105.00	110	8	1.02	−0.38	9.27
105.00	105	8	1.12	−0.43	6.94

Problem #46

Stock Price ($)	Put Strike ($)	Days Remaining	Volatility	Theta	Put Price ($)
120.00	110	15	0.51	−0.11	1.32
105.00	110	0	0.00	0.00	5.00
120.00	110	43	0.50	−0.08	3.79
105.00	110	28	0.75	−0.15	11.53

Summary

Many investors mistakenly believe that puts and calls can be used as simple proxies for short or long stock positions. This chapter was designed to dispel that belief. Option positions differ from stock positions in many ways—they suffer time decay and eventually expire; they have a threshold or strike price that must be crossed for the contracts to have any value at expiration; they provide varying levels of leverage that can be mathematically described (delta); their value depends, in part, on the volatility of the underlying security. These complex dynamics often lead to the scenario where an investor correctly predicts the direction of a stock but still loses money on what seems to be a well-planned option trade. Even the simplest trades can be dynamic and complex to manage.

The discussions in this chapter strayed beyond simple put and call buying to include hedging and other positional adjustments designed to protect profit. These extensions are intended as a springboard to the chapters that follow.

3

Covered Puts and Calls

Covered positions are used by conservative investors who are willing to accept a cap on their maximum gain in return for a hedge that can offset potential losses. Covered calls—long stock combined with short calls—are the most popular and best understood. Many investors find that covered calls are more profitable than simple long stock positions when the tendency is to hold the stock for a long period.

Bearish investors often take the same approach by shorting a stock and selling puts. As we will see, covered put positions display trading dynamics that are very different from their covered call counterparts. Most of the difference is related to spikes in implied volatility that often occur when a stock suddenly falls. Implied volatility spikes increase the price of the put side of a trade and, therefore, affect the way the trade must be managed.

It is also important to note that covered calls and covered puts are logically different with regard to the mechanism by which they are exercised. The two sides of a covered call are directly linked; the option is exercised by calling away the covering stock from the investor who sold the call. Conversely, when a put is exercised, the owner sells (puts) the stock to the investor who originally sold the option. If the original sale was covered with short stock, the investor who is assigned would simply offset his or her loss by purchasing the stock that was originally borrowed to create the trade. Both trades are covered in the sense that no additional collateral is required to protect the short put position.

In the option trading world it is more common to structure covered positions without any stock at all. Long calls substitute for long stock, and long puts replace short stock. A short option position is considered covered if the account is long a corresponding number of option contracts having more favorable terms—that is, the same or farther expiration date, and the same or closer strike price. These rules add additional complexity because the two sides of the trade can have different expiration dates. Various structures are possible and an appropriate set of names has evolved to describe them. Vertical spreads include long and short options with the same expiration date; calendar spreads span different expirations with the same strike price; diagonals have different strikes and expirations. Generally speaking, it is much more important to understand the trading dynamics of each structure than to memorize the names.

Finally, the term "covered" should not be misinterpreted as an indication that uncovered positions are always more dangerous. A single uncovered short put presents no more risk than 100 shares of long stock. Many investors miss this subtlety and lose the opportunity to create a large portfolio that benefits both from price movement and time decay.

In this section we will explore various covered positions, including pure option trades that span multiple expirations. We previously touched on covered trades in our discussion of simple long call positions. In that context we were either protecting profit after a rally or taking defensive action in response to a price decline. This section builds on those discussions with trades that are structured as covered positions from the outset. (All calculations for this chapter are based on a 1.5% risk-free interest rate.)

Traditional Covered Positions Involving Stock and Options (Problems #1–#23)

1. Which of the following positions are considered covered? (Assume a stock price of $47.)

   A. long 1,000 shares
      short 10 contracts—current month $50 call

   B. long 1,000 shares
      short 15 contracts—current month $50 call

   C. long 1,000 shares
      short 10 contracts—distant month $40 call

   D. short 1,000 shares
      short 10 contracts—current month $40 put

   E. short 1,000 shares
      short 10 contracts—distant month $60 put

   F. long 10 contracts—current month $50 put
      short 10 contracts—distant month $50 put

   G. long 10 contracts—current month $50 put
      short 10 contracts—distant month $40 put

   H. long 10 contracts—distant month $70 call
      short 10 contracts—current month $60 call

   I. long 10 contracts—distant month $60 call
      short 10 contracts—current month $60 call

   J. long 10 contracts—distant month $50 call
      short 10 contracts—current month $55 call

   Answer: A, C, D, E, I, and J are covered. B is short 5 extra contracts. F and G are short the far-dated option. H is short the closer strike price. A short position can be covered by an equivalent number of shares of stock or the same number of option contracts with more favorable terms. The phrase "more favorable" refers to contracts that have the same or farther expiration date, and a strike price that is the same or closer to the underlying security. Stated differently, the covering options must have at least as many days left before expiration and a strike price that is at least as valuable as the short side of the trade.

2. Which trade is more bullish for a stock trading at $47?

    A. long 1,000 shares
        short 10 contracts—current month $50 call

    B. long 1,000 shares
        short 10 contracts—current month $55 call

Answer: B—the $55 call has less value and offers less downside protection in return for greater potential upside.

3. What is the maximum profit for the long stock/short call position shown in the following table? What stock price yields the maximum profit at expiration of the short call?

Stock Price	Long Shares	Short Call Price	Short Call Strike	Short Call Contracts
$47.00	1,000	$3.50	$50	10

Answer: $6,500 with the stock trading at $50. The stock will have a $3 profit, and the short call will expire worthless, returning $3.50 × 10 contracts = $3,500.

4. What would the break-even point be for question #3 at expiration of the short option.

   Answer: $43.50. This amount is equal to the initial purchase price of the stock minus the amount of premium taken in by selling 10 calls.

5. Suppose in question #3 we had chosen to sell deep in-the-money $30 calls for $17.50 instead of the $50 calls mentioned in the problem. Which short option position will provide the best return if the stock climbs to $50? Which provides the most protection if the stock falls to $45.

   Answer: With the stock at $50, we would be forced to buy back the $30 call for $20 (a $2.50 loss), and our stock would have a $3 profit. Our overall gain would, therefore, be only 50¢ as opposed to the $6.50 profit of the trade described in question #3.

   Conversely, if the stock declines to $45, the long stock position will lose $2 and the short $30 calls will be worth $15 ($2.50 profit). The overall position will, therefore, gain 50¢. Under the same circumstances, the short $50 calls will expire worthless and the entire $3.50 of premium will remain in the account, providing an overall profit of $1.50 ($2 loss on the long stock position + $3.50 gain from the short call position). Once again the short $50 calls provide the larger return.

6. At what expiration price are the two trades of the previous question equal? Which trade performs better if the stock falls further?

    Answer: A $3 decline in the stock price from $47 to $44 yields the same profit (50¢) for both trades because each of the short choices returns $3.50 at that price. The short $50 call that originally sold for $3.50 expires worthless, and the short deep in-the-money $30 call that originally sold for $17.50 would be worth $14 (its original price included 50¢ of time premium).

    The short $30 call offers extended protection if the stock declines below $44. Because DITM options have a delta near 1.0, the call price will decline in direct proportion to the stock price until the price falls below $30.

    Unfortunately, most options trading books and courses over-simplify the dynamics of complex positions. The most serious oversimplifications are those that evaluate positions at expiration and ignore the real time-management issues. Calculating the value of a position at expiration is far easier than deciding how to react to sharp price spikes that occur while the trade is open. Most of the remainder of this section is devoted to problems that address these issues.

7. The following table displays pricing data for the $50 call of problem #3 at four different stock prices with 54 days left before expiration. Suppose, as before, we purchased 1,000 shares of stock at $47 and sold 10 calls. What would the loss be if the stock fell to $44 after only 5 days and we closed the trade? What portion of the $3.50 downside protection were we able to take advantage of? Why?

Stock Price ($)	Call Strike ($)	Call Price ($)	Volatility	Days Remaining	Theta
47	50	3.50	0.65	54	−0.04
46	50	3.06	0.65	54	−0.04
45	50	2.66	0.65	54	−0.04
44	50	2.29	0.65	54	−0.04

Answer: Because the option has an initial value of $2.29 with the stock trading at $44, and theta is 4¢ per day, we can assume that it would be worth $2.09 after 5 days of time have passed ($2.29 − $0.04 × 5 days). Subtracting from the original value ($3.50) that we obtained by selling the option with the stock trading at $47 yields a gain of only $1.41. This gain offsets $1,410 of the $3,000 loss in the stock position. The difference ($1,590) is the final loss after we sell our 1,000 shares of stock and buy back the short calls for $2.09.

We were only able to utilize 40% of the original downside protection of the short $50 calls; the remaining 60% is locked up in time decay that can only be realized by keeping the trade open until expiration.

Note: When the underlying stock is trading out-of-the-money, theta can be used to accurately predict the price of an option over a relatively short timeframe. In this example, 5 days represents less than 10% of the remaining time, and all the option value is derived from time premium. Theta, therefore, is a very accurate measure of time decay and it can be used to predict the option price.

8. Consider the following scenario: You have a bearish view of a stock that is trading at $47, so you establish a covered put position by shorting 1,000 shares and selling $40 puts × 10 contracts. Two days later, the stock reacts to very negative financial rumors by plunging nearly 15%. With the stock now trading at $40, implied volatility soars to 180%. This scenario, depicted in the following table, was fairly common among financial stocks during the first quarter of 2008, when implied volatilities occasionally exceeded 400%.

Stock Price ($)	Strike ($)	Days Remaining	Put Price ($)	Volatility	Delta
47.00	40	54	1.66	0.65	–0.22
40.00	40	52	10.58	1.80	–0.37

Does this trade lose money? If so, would closing the trade be a good strategy for preventing further loss? What are the relevant numbers?

Answer: The trade will lose a substantial amount of money if it is closed after the large downward price spike. While the short stock position has gained $7,000 ($7 × 1,000 shares), the short put position has lost $8,920 (10 contracts × $8.92). Immediately closing the trade will cost $1,920. This unrealized loss is caused by the implied volatility spike that adds a substantial amount of time premium to the short option position. Closing the trade would be equivalent to throwing away the value of this premium.

9. If we keep the trade described in question #8, which of the following would be better?

    A. Stock falls another $5 to $35.

    B. Stock rises $5 to $45.

Answer: A. Our position would benefit if the stock continues falling because we are more likely to lock in the maximum gain at expiration when all remaining time premium has run out. If the stock closes at $45 on expiration day, we will keep $1.66 from the short put and gain $2 on our short stock position—the final gain will be $3.66 or $3,660. Conversely, if the stock falls another $5 before expiration, we will realize the maximum gain—$7 for the short stock plus $1.66 of time premium from the short put. Specifically, we will buy back 1,000 shares of short stock at $35 for a $12,000 profit, and the short put position, now $5 in-the-money, will lose $3.34 ($3,340). Total profit for the trade will, therefore, be $8,660.

10. Assume a scenario similar to that of the previous problem with one difference—we sell 10 puts at the $45 strike instead of $40. As before, we are short 1,000 shares of stock, the stock plunges to $40, and implied volatility climbs to 180%. These events are outlined in the following table.

Stock Price ($)	Strike ($)	Days Remaining	Put Price ($)	Volatility	Delta
47.00	45	54	3.59	0.65	−0.38
40.00	45	52	13.90	1.80	−0.43

We would likely establish this position because we are less bearish and would prefer the greater protection of the $45 put. Suppose that after the sharp decline we decide to buy back the $45 puts and sell the next lower strike—$40, as described in the following table.

Stock Price ($)	Strike ($)	Days Remaining	Put Price ($)	Volatility	Delta
40.00	40	52	11.71	2.00	−0.35

If the stock remains at this price until expiration, which short put provides the greater return? Why? Is the new trade more or less bearish than the original?

Answer: At expiration the $45 put will be worth $5 and the $40 put will be worth $0. Subtracting these values from their post-decline prices reveals that the $45 put has $8.90 of residual time premium whereas the $40 put has $11.71. Therefore, if the stock remains at this price and we hold the position until expiration, the $40 put will generate more profit. However, the transaction is complex because buying back the $45 put for $13.90 locks in a loss of $10.31 which is ultimately recovered in the sale of the $40 put. We can calculate the returns for each scenario as shown in the next two tables.

Scenario #1—Keep $45 short put until expiration (profit = $5,590)

Trade	Open	Close	Profit/Loss ($)
Short stock	Short 1,000 shares at $47	Buy to cover 1,000 shares at $40	7,000
$45 put	Sell 10 contracts at $3.59	Buy back 10 contracts at $5.00	−1,410

Scenario #2—Close $45 put and sell $40 put (profit = $8,400)

Trade	Open	Close	Profit/Loss ($)
Short stock	Short 1,000 shares at $47	Buy to cover 1,000 shares at $40	7,000
Short $45 put	Sell 10 contracts at $3.59	Buy back 10 contracts at $13.90	−10,310
Short $40 put	Sell 10 contracts at $11.71	Expires worthless	11,710

The new trade is less bearish than the first. It replaces a short put with a delta of −0.43 with a new option having a delta of

–0.35. Since short stock has a delta of –1.0, the original trade has a net delta of –0.57 and the replacement trade has a net delta of –0.65. In more practical terms, the short $40 puts provide less protection against a recovery in the stock price and allows greater profit if the stock continues falling.

11. How would the two scenarios outlined in the previous trade compare if the stock rallied back to $45 by expiration? (The scenarios are listed next.)

Scenario #1
short 1,000 shares at $47 and sell $45 puts (10 contracts)
stock falls to $40
keep trade as is
stock rallies back to $45

Scenario #2
short 1,000 shares at $47 and sell $45 puts (10 contracts)
stock falls to $40
buy back $45 puts and sell $40 puts
stock rallies back to $45

Answer: Scenario #1 generates more profit because short $45 in-the-money puts provide greater protection against a rally than short $40 out-of-the-money puts. The two scenarios are outlined in the tables that follow.

Scenario #1—Keep $45 short put until expiration (profit = $5,900)

Trade	Open	Close	Profit/Loss ($)
Short stock	Short 1,000 shares at $47	Buy to cover 1,000 shares at $45	2,000
$45 put	Sell 10 contracts at $3.59	Expires worthless	3,590

Scenario #2—Close $45 short put and sell $40 put (profit = $3,400)

Trade	Open	Close	Profit/Loss ($)
Short stock	Short 1,000 shares at $47	Buy to cover 1,000 shares at $45	2,000
$45 put	Sell 10 contracts at $3.59	Buy back 10 contracts at $13.90	−10,310
$40 put	Sell 10 contracts at $11.71	Expires worthless	11,710

12. What is the maximum profit at expiration for the position outlined in the following table?

Position	Stock Price	Strike ($)	Option Price ($)	Days Rem.	Volatility
Long call	100	105	5.76	33	0.65
Short call	100	115	2.93	33	0.65

Answer: $7.17—the difference between the two strikes minus the cost of the original trade.

$5.76 long call – $2.93 short call = $2.83 original cost

$115 – $105 = $10.00 maximum value at expiration

$10.00 maximum value – $2.83 original cost = $7.17 maximum profit

13. In problem #12, are there any conditions that would cause the trade to gain more than $7.17 before expiration?

Answer: No, the maximum profit can only be obtained at expiration with the long call $10 in-the-money and the short call expiring worthless. No underlying price change at any point in the expiration cycle can yield a value for the long call that is $10 more than the value of the short call. The only exceptions are related to large differential volatility swings. The maximum profit can increase if implied volatility of the long call rises sharply relative to that of the short call. Distortions of this magnitude are extremely rare.

This section explores scenarios that involve a series of covered calls spanning four months. The sequence begins at December expiration with the stock trading at $104, and ends at April expiration with the stock at $108. Many different strike price and expiration date combinations are possible. We might, for example, respond to changes in the underlying stock price by selling a new batch of calls at a different strike each month. Alternatively, we could simplify the process by selling April calls once at the beginning of the process. Selecting the latter option, however, does not rule out the possibility of reacting to changes by adjusting the short call position.

The following table contains relevant pricing information for each of the four expirations. Because options expire on Saturday, each row contains a Friday start date and a Saturday expiration. For example, the first group expires on Saturday 1/19/2008 and the next group begins on the previous Friday 1/18/2008. The goal is to settle the current position and sell new options before the market close on the final trading day of the expiration cycle. Extending this logic to the final group in the table, we see that all trades are closed on Friday 4/18/2008 for options that expire the next day.

Stock Price ($)	Start Date	Expiration Date	Days Remaining	Strike($)	Call Price ($)	Volatility	Delta
104	12/21/2007	1/19/2008	29	105	4.86	0.45	0.50
104	12/21/2007	1/19/2008	29	110	2.97	0.45	0.36
104	12/21/2007	1/19/2008	29	115	1.72	0.45	0.24
104	12/21/2007	1/19/2008	29	120	0.94	0.45	0.15
112	1/18/2008	2/16/2008	29	115	4.42	0.45	0.45
112	1/18/2008	2/16/2008	29	120	2.75	0.45	0.32
112	1/18/2008	2/16/2008	29	125	1.63	0.45	0.21
112	1/18/2008	2/16/2008	29	130	0.92	0.45	0.14
97	2/15/2008	3/22/2008	36	100	4.23	0.45	0.45
97	2/15/2008	3/22/2008	36	105	2.60	0.45	0.32
97	2/15/2008	3/22/2008	36	110	1.52	0.45	0.21
97	2/15/2008	3/22/2008	36	115	0.85	0.45	0.13
94	3/21/2008	4/19/2008	29	95	4.35	0.45	0.50
94	3/21/2008	4/19/2008	29	100	2.51	0.45	0.34
94	3/21/2008	4/19/2008	29	105	1.35	0.45	0.21
94	3/21/2008	4/19/2008	29	110	0.68	0.45	0.12
108	4/18/2008	4/19/2008	1	95	13.00	0.01	1.00
108	4/18/2008	4/19/2008	1	100	8.00	0.01	1.00
108	4/18/2008	4/19/2008	1	105	3.00	0.01	1.00
108	4/18/2008	4/19/2008	1	110	0.00	0.01	0.00

14. For the timeframe beginning on 12/21 and ending on 4/19, which trade sequence generates the larger return? In percentage terms, what is the overall profit for this trade?

Purchase 1,000 shares of stock on 12/21 and sell on 4/18.

or

Purchase 1,000 shares of stock and, for each expiration, sell 10 contracts at the first strike that is at least $5 out-of-the-money. As mentioned earlier, each option trade should be settled, and the next batch of calls sold, on an expiration Friday (12/21, 1/18, 2/15, 3/21). All trades are finally settled at the market close on 4/18.

Answer: The stock position alone returns $4,000 while the covered call sequence returns $4,830. The following table outlines the gain or loss of the short call position at each expiration.

Expiration Date	Initial Stock Price ($)	Expiration Stock Price ($)	Strike ($)	Initial Call ($)	Final Call ($)	Gain/ Loss ($)
1/19/2008	104	112	110	2.97	2.00	0.97
2/16/2008	112	97	120	2.75	0.00	2.75
3/22/2008	97	94	105	2.60	0.00	2.60
4/19/2008	94	108	100	2.51	8.00	−5.49
					Total	0.83

The first three expirations return a profit of $6.32 but the final expiration loses $5.49, for a total short call return of only $0.83 ($830). Adding together the stock and short call profits yields a net return of $4,830. Since the total cost of the trade was 1,000 shares of long stock at $104, the percent gain is $4,830 / $104,000 = 4.64%.

15. In problem #14, what was the return for the short call portion of the trade? Was it necessary to set aside funds to collateralize the short calls?

Answer: In each case the short calls were covered with long stock so additional collateral was not required. Initial trade prices were $2,970, $2,750, $2,600, and $2,510—an average of $2,710. Dividing the return by this amount ($830 / $2,710) reveals that the short calls generated a profit equal to 31% of their value. Because there was no additional expense associated with the short calls, the revenue from their sale flows directly to the bottom line as profit that is measured against the cost of the long stock position (see problem #14).

16. In problem #14, would we have generated more profit by selling the nearest out-of-the-money strike for each month and taking in more premium, or selling the next further strike and taking in less premium?

Answer: Moving out to the next strike yields significantly more profit. Selling the closest out-of-the-money strike for each expiration results in a loss of $2.14 ($2,140) for the combined short option trades. Moving one strike beyond those of question #14 has the opposite effect—it generates a positive return of $3.22 ($3,220). The following tables provide detail for both cases.

Close Strikes

Expiration Date	Initial Stock Price ($)	Expiration Stock Price ($)	Strike ($)	Initial Call ($)	Final Call ($)	Gain/ Loss ($)
1/19/2008	104	112	105	4.86	7.00	−2.14
2/16/2008	112	97	115	4.42	0.00	4.42
3/22/2008	97	94	100	4.23	0.00	4.23
4/19/2008	94	108	95	4.35	13.00	−8.65
					Total	−2.14

Far Strikes

Expiration Date	Initial Stock Price ($)	Expiration Stock Price ($)	Strike ($)	Initial Call ($)	Final Call ($)	Gain/ Loss ($)
1/19/2008	104	112	115	1.72	0.00	1.72
2/16/2008	112	97	125	1.63	0.00	1.63
3/22/2008	97	94	110	1.52	0.00	1.52
4/19/2008	94	108	105	1.35	3.00	−1.65
					Total	3.22

In summary, the closest OTM strike results in a loss of $2,140; the next strike generates $830; the far strike yields $3,220.

17. How do the short call trades of the preceding three questions compare in percentage terms?

Answer: See the following table.

	Average Call Price ($)	Return ($)	Return
Nearest OTM Strike	4.47	−2.14	−48%
Nearest strike > $5 OTM	2.71	0.83	31%
Nearest strike > $10 OTM	1.55	3.22	207%

18. Why is the return so much larger for calls sold at the far strike price? (Hint: Measuring distances to strikes and price changes in standard deviations is helpful.)

   Answer: Assuming a stock price near $100, we can calculate the approximate value of a 1 standard deviation price change for each 1-month timeframe as shown here:

Timeframes in 1 year	12
Annualization factor	Sqrt (12) = 3.46
Volatility for 1 month	0.45 / 3.46 = 0.13
1 StdDev change	0.13 × $100 = $13

   The greatest loss (4/19 expiration) was caused by a price change of just over 1 standard deviation ($94 – $108) that was protected by an option sale of $4.35 for a strike just $1.00 out-of-the-money. Total protection for this sale was, therefore, only $5.35, or less than 0.5 StdDev. Selling calls that protect against small price changes is a bearish strategy that assumes mispriced volatility. The 1/19 expiration displayed similar dynamics: The short $105 call lost 44% on a price increase of approximately 0.6 StdDev.

19. In problem #17 we discovered that the largest return was generated by selling new options each month that were close to 1 standard deviation OTM. Suppose we decided, instead, to sell one batch of calls for the entire timeframe (120 days) that were approximately the same distance (1 StdDev) from the $104 starting price. Which row in the following table would be most relevant? How would the results compare to the monthly option sales of the previous problems?

Stock Price($)	Start Date	Exp. Date	Days Rem.	Strike ($)	Call Price ($)	Volat.	Delta
104	12/21/07	4/19/08	120	125	4.22	0.45	0.29
104	12/21/07	4/19/08	120	130	3.30	0.45	0.24
104	12/21/07	4/19/08	120	135	2.57	0.45	0.19
104	12/21/07	4/19/08	120	140	1.99	0.45	0.16

Answer: We can calculate the value of 1 StdDev for the 120 day timeframe as shown here:

Timeframes in 1 year[1]	65 / 120 = 3.04
Annualization factor	Sqrt (3.04) = 1.74
Volatility for 120 days	0.45 / 1.74 = 0.26
1 StdDev change	0.26 × $104 = $27.04

[1] We use calendar days for this calculation to precisely measure the fraction of a year that is represented by the entire timeframe. If we were calculating a daily price change, number of trading days (252) would provide a more appropriate metric.

Using these values, we can assume that we would sell the $130 strike price for $3.30 ($26 OTM). Since the stock closed at $108 on expiration day, the full amount would be realized as profit. In this case, the simple trade would generate approximately the same return as the more complex monthly sequence of option sales.

20. With regard to risk, how does the long-dated trade of problem #19 compare with that of the monthly trades? Do the results validate or conflict with option pricing theory?

Answer: Delta closely approximates the chance of an option expiring in-the-money. The monthly short trades had deltas of 0.24, 0.21, 0.21, and 0.21; the long-dated trade had a delta equal to 0.24. We can, therefore, conclude that the risk of expiring in-the-money was approximately equal for monthly and long-dated short calls. These dynamics make sense because monthly and long-dated strike choices were both based on a 1 standard deviation price change.

The results are a strong validation of option pricing theory because equal risks yielded comparable profits regardless of the timeframe. Selling more expensive closer strikes was not a good strategy because potentially larger profits were offset by greater risks that occasionally materialized into substantial losses.

Option traders frequently make the mistake of selling seemingly expensive near-dated options that exhibit high levels of time decay. This approach is flawed because correctly priced options have balanced risk:reward profiles regardless of the timeframe. However, monthly short sales can provide an advantage in rising volatility environments—bear markets being the most notable case. The following problems are designed with this concept in mind.

In this section we will explore scenarios that involve a series of covered puts spanning four months. The following table contains relevant pricing information. As before, each section's start date corresponds to expiration Friday of the previous section. The sequence begins at December expiration with the stock trading at $106, and ends at April expiration with the stock at $66.

Stock Price ($)	Start Date	Expiration Date	Days Remaining	Strike ($)	Call Price ($)	Volatility	Delta
106.00	12/21/2007	1/19/2008	29	105	4.79	0.45	-0.44
106.00	12/21/2007	1/19/2008	29	100	2.71	0.45	-0.30
106.00	12/21/2007	1/19/2008	29	95	1.34	0.45	-0.17
106.00	12/21/2007	1/19/2008	29	90	0.57	0.45	-0.09
98.00	1/18/2008	2/16/2008	29	95	3.48	0.45	-0.38
98.00	1/18/2008	2/16/2008	29	90	1.76	0.45	-0.23
98.00	1/18/2008	2/16/2008	29	85	0.75	0.45	-0.12
98.00	1/18/2008	2/16/2008	29	80	0.26	0.45	-0.05
103.00	2/15/2008	3/22/2008	36	100	3.78	0.41	-0.38
103.00	2/15/2008	3/22/2008	36	95	2.01	0.41	-0.24
103.00	2/15/2008	3/22/2008	36	90	0.92	0.41	-0.13
103.00	2/15/2008	3/22/2008	36	85	0.35	0.41	-0.06
78.00	3/21/2008	4/19/2008	29	75	3.75	0.60	-0.37
78.00	3/21/2008	4/19/2008	29	70	1.95	0.60	-0.23
78.00	3/21/2008	4/19/2008	29	65	0.85	0.60	-0.12
78.00	3/21/2008	4/19/2008	29	60	0.30	0.60	-0.05
66.00	4/18/2008	4/19/2008	1	75	9.00	0.01	-1.00
66.00	4/18/2008	4/19/2008	1	70	4.00	0.01	-1.00
66.00	4/18/2008	4/19/2008	1	65	0.00	0.01	0.00
66.00	4/18/2008	4/19/2008	1	60	0.00	0.01	0.00

21. For the timeframe beginning on 12/21 and ending on 4/19, which trade sequence generates the larger return?

   Short 1,000 shares of stock on 12/21 and close the trade on 4/18.

   or

   Short 1,000 shares of stock and, for each expiration, sell 10 puts at the first strike that is at least $5 out-of-the-money. As mentioned earlier, each option trade should be settled, and the next batch of puts sold, on an expiration Friday (12/21, 1/18, 2/15, 3/21). All trades are finally settled at the market close on 4/18.

   Answer: The stock position returns $40,000 while the covered put sequence subtracts $14,570. The net result is a profit of $25,430. The following table outlines the gain or loss of the short put position at each expiration.

Expiration Date	Initial Stock Price ($)	Expiration Stock Price ($)	Strike ($)	Initial Put ($)	Final Put ($)	Gain/ Loss ($)
1/19/2008	106	98	100	2.71	2.00	0.71
2/16/2008	98	103	90	1.76	0.00	1.76
3/22/2008	103	78	95	2.01	17.00	−14.99
4/19/2008	78	66	70	1.95	4.00	−2.05
					Total	−14.57

22. When a company reports very negative financial news that shocks the market, the resulting stock drawdown is normally accompanied by a sharp increase in implied volatility. Spikes of 300%, 400%, and even 500% are not uncommon in these situations.

Consider a covered put position that is short 1,000 shares of stock at $107 and 10 puts at the $105 strike as outlined in the following table. Line 1 of the table displays the starting put position, and line 2 reveals the results after a severe downward price spike accompanied by a large increase in implied volatility from 30% to 170%.

Stock Price ($)	Days Rem.	Strike($)	Put Price ($)	Volat.	Delta	Theta
107	29	105	2.61	0.30	−0.39	−0.06
80	25	105	31.61	1.70	−0.65	−0.26

How much money has the trade lost? Assuming that both implied volatility and stock price remain constant, how many days must elapse before the trade reaches a break-even point? How much will the trade recover if the stock closes at $80 on expiration day? What will the final profit be?

Answer: With 25 days remaining before expiration, the trade has lost $2 ($27 gain on short stock offset by $29 loss on short puts).

With a theta of −$0.26, approximately 8 days must elapse to recover the $2 loss ($0.26 × 8 = 2.08).

If the stock closes the expiration timeframe at $80, the trade will be worth $6.37 calculated as shown here:

Profit from short stock	$27.00
Sale of short put	$2.61
Cost to repurchase short put	−$25.00
Trade profit	$4.61

The final profit realized at expiration is a $2.61 improvement over the $2.00 loss experienced after the large downward spike displayed in the table. Overall, the combined stock and option trades generated a profit of $4,610.

23. Suppose that in problem #22 we responded to the sharp price decline by buying back our original short put position for $31.61 and selling new puts at a lower strike. Which of the choices shown in the following table generates the largest profit if the stock falls another $10? Which generates the most profit if the stock rises? Which choices generate at least as much return as the original $105 put if the stock remains at $80 until expiration?

Stock Price ($)	Days Rem.	Strike($)	Put Price ($)	Volat.	Delta	Theta
80	25	75	11.28	1.70	−0.36	−0.26
80	25	70	8.78	1.70	−0.30	−0.25
80	25	65	6.60	1.70	−0.24	−0.22

Answer:

Decline to $70: If the stock falls another $10, the short $70 strike that sells for $8.78 will generate the largest profit—the short stock will generate an additional $10 and $8.78 of premium will be realized when the options expire out-of-the-money. The more valuable $75 puts will generate $6.28 ($11.28 initial sale − $5.00 cost to repurchase), and the $65 puts will return the sale price ($6.60).

Protection against a rally: Of the three choices, the highest strike ($75) provides the most protection against a stock rally—it has the most negative delta and the most value. However, the original $105 short puts would provide superior protection. Keeping this trade open is the best choice if a price reversal seems likely.

Stock remains at $80: At the time of the downward spike, the original $105 puts were $25 in-the-money but traded for $31.61. Subtracting intrinsic from actual value ($31.61 – $25.00) reveals that the contracts had $6.61 of remaining time premium that must decay away before expiration. We can use this number for comparison against the three new choices, which each return their full sale price at expiration as they expire out-of-the-money. The first two choices yield higher returns than the original trade ($11.28 and $8.78). The third choice provides approximately the same return ($6.60).

Pure Option Covered Positions (Problems #24–#28)

The following section focuses on covered positions composed of equal numbers of long and short options in which the long side has more favorable terms (same or later expiration and same or closer strike). Many investors who trade covered positions favor this approach because it requires less capital, limits downside exposure, and benefits from leverage.

The following two tables display relevant pricing information for the problems that follow. The first table is organized by month and strike price. As before, each section's start date corresponds to expiration Friday of the previous group. The sequence begins at December expiration with the stock trading at $104, and ends at April expiration with the stock at $133.

The second table is composed of a single set of entries that span the entire timeframe. It provides long-dated option prices that complement those of the previous table.

Monthly Expirations

Stock Price ($)	Start Date	Expiration Date	Days Remaining	Strike ($)	Call Price ($)	Volatility	Delta
104	12/21/2007	1/19/2008	29	105	4.86	0.45	0.50
104	12/21/2007	1/19/2008	29	110	2.97	0.45	0.36
104	12/21/2007	1/19/2008	29	115	1.72	0.45	0.24
104	12/21/2007	1/19/2008	29	120	0.94	0.45	0.15
112	1/18/2008	2/16/2008	29	115	4.42	0.45	0.45
112	1/18/2008	2/16/2008	29	120	2.75	0.45	0.32
112	1/18/2008	2/16/2008	29	125	1.63	0.45	0.21
112	1/18/2008	2/16/2008	29	130	0.92	0.45	0.14
117	2/15/2008	3/22/2008	36	120	5.35	0.45	0.46
117	2/15/2008	3/22/2008	36	125	3.60	0.45	0.35
117	2/15/2008	3/22/2008	36	130	2.34	0.45	0.25
117	2/15/2008	3/22/2008	36	135	1.47	0.45	0.18
103	3/21/2008	4/19/2008	29	105	4.37	0.45	0.47
103	3/21/2008	4/19/2008	29	110	2.63	0.45	0.33
103	3/21/2008	4/19/2008	29	115	1.49	0.45	0.21
103	3/21/2008	4/19/2008	29	120	0.80	0.45	0.13
133	4/18/2008	4/19/2008	1	105	28.00	0.01	1.00
133	4/18/2008	4/19/2008	1	110	23.00	0.01	1.00
133	4/18/2008	4/19/2008	1	115	18.00	0.01	1.00
133	4/18/2008	4/19/2008	1	120	13.01	0.01	1.00

Long-Dated Expirations

Stock Price ($)	Start Date	Expiration Date	Days Remaining	Strike ($)	Call Price ($)	Volatility	Delta
104	12/21/2007	4/19/2008	120	100	13.53	0.48	0.62
104	12/21/2007	4/19/2008	120	105	11.17	0.48	0.55
104	12/21/2007	4/19/2008	120	110	9.15	0.48	0.48
104	12/21/2007	4/19/2008	120	115	7.45	0.48	0.42
104	12/21/2007	4/19/2008	120	120	6.02	0.48	0.36
104	12/21/2007	4/19/2008	120	125	4.84	0.48	0.30
104	12/21/2007	4/19/2008	120	130	3.87	0.48	0.26
104	12/21/2007	4/19/2008	120	135	3.07	0.48	0.21
104	12/21/2007	4/19/2008	120	140	2.44	0.48	0.18

24. Assume we purchase $105 calls with 120 days remaining and sell near-dated calls each month to offset time decay. Which sequence of strike prices would be most appropriate if our view is completely neutral as opposed to bearish or bullish? What would be the profit engine for such a trade?

Answer: Consistently selling the most expensive option (closest strike) creates positions that are essentially neutral because both sides have similar deltas. The trade would be designed to profit from time decay. The sequence is listed in the following table. (Note that we sold the $110 strike for the final month because we were already long the $105 strike.)

Expiration Date	Strike ($)	Call Price ($)
1/19/2008	105	4.86
2/16/2008	115	4.42
3/22/2008	120	5.35
4/19/2008	110	2.63

25. What would the profit or loss be in problem #24 for a trade consisting of 10 short and 10 long calls?

Answer: The collective trade gains $2.09 ($2,090 for 10 contracts), as shown in the next table.

Position	Expir. Date	Initial Stock Price ($)	Expir. Stock Price ($)	Strike ($)	Initial Call ($)	Final Call ($)	Gain/ Loss ($)
Short	1/19/2008	104	112	105	4.86	7.00	−2.14
Short	2/16/2008	112	117	115	4.42	2.00	2.42
Short	3/22/2008	117	103	120	5.35	0.00	5.35
Short	4/19/2008	103	133	110	2.63	23.00	−20.37
Long	4/19/2008	104	133	105	11.17	28.00	16.83
						Total	2.09

26. Would purchasing the far-dated $100 call create a more bullish or bearish position? Why? (Note: Assume that we would also adjust the short April position by shifting from the $110 call to the $105 call.)

Answer: Initially it would appear that the higher delta of the $100 call represents a more bullish view. (The $105 strike of problem #25 had a delta of 0.55 and the new delta is 0.62.) However, the new trade is more bearish because it shifts the optimal return point from $110 to $105.

The largest price increase occurred in April, and we are adjusting both the short and long positions for this month. On the long side we pay an additional $2.36 for the $100 strike, whereas the new short call only generates an additional $1.74. (Strike price spacing remains the same.) This difference represents an increased cost of $0.62 that is lost if the underlying stock closes above or below both strikes at expiration. However, if the stock closes April expiration nearly unchanged at $105, lowering both strikes provides a $5.00 improvement because the long side of the trade moves $5.00 in-the-money while the short side remains worthless. Since the initial position cost is increased by $0.62, the net improvement at expiration is $4.38. This improvement is reduced as the stock moves away from the $105 strike in either direction.

We can verify these numbers by calculating the return for each position with the stock trading at $105 at expiration. The original trade—long $105 calls / short $110 calls—would lose $8.54 if the stock closed April expiration at $105 ($11.17 loss on the long side offset by $2.63 gain on the short side). Shifting the strikes down $5.00 adjusts these values so that the long side loses only $8.53 ($13.53 initial cost – $5.00 value at expiration) which is partially offset by a gain of $4.37 on the short side for a net loss of $4.16. The improvement from an $8.54 loss to $4.16 loss is exactly equal to $4.38.

27. How would a trade structured using the far-dated $100 call for the long side and each month's nearest OTM strike for the short side compare with the position of problem #25?

Answer: Based on the answer to problem #26, we can predict that the new trade will generate a return that is $620 smaller—$1,470 as opposed to $2,090 for the original trade. The details are outlined in the following table.

Position	Expir. Date	Initial Stock Price ($)	Expir. Stock Price ($)	Strike ($)	Initial Call ($)	Final Call ($)	Gain/ Loss ($)
Short	1/19/08	104	112	105	4.86	7.00	–2.14
Short	2/16/08	112	117	115	4.42	2.00	2.42
Short	3/22/08	117	103	120	5.35	0.00	5.35
Short	4/19/08	103	133	105	4.37	28.00	–23.63
Long	4/19/08	104	133	100	13.53	33.00	19.47
						Total	1.47

28. Would the preceding trade yield a larger return if we sell monthly calls that are approximately 1 standard deviation out-of-the-money? How would we structure both sides of the trade so that it is still considered covered—that is, the long side has more favorable terms?

Answer: First we must calculate the value of a 1 StdDev price change for each timeframe.

Near-Dated Options

Timeframes in 1 year	12
Annualization factor	Sqrt (12) = 3.46
Volatility for 1 month	0.45 / 3.46 = 0.13
1 StdDev change	0.13 × $104 = $13.52
1 StdDev change	0.13 × $112 = $14.56
1 StdDev change	0.13 × $117 = $15.21
1 StdDev change	0.13 × $103 = $13.39
Average 1 StdDev change	$14.17

Far-Dated Options

Timeframes in 1 year	365 / 120 = 3.04
Annualization factor	Sqrt (3.04) = 1.74
Volatility for 120 days	0.48 / 1.74 = 0.276
1 StdDev change	0.28 × $104 = $28.70

Using these numbers as a guide, we can select appropriate strikes and construct a table that includes prices and other relevant information.

Expiration Date	Initial Stock Price ($)	Strike ($)	Initial Call ($)	Delta
1/19/2008	104	115	1.72	0.24
2/16/2008	112	125	1.63	0.21
3/22/2008	117	130	2.34	0.25
4/19/2008	103	115	1.49	0.21

However, the requirement to select long-dated options with more favorable terms caps our strike price at $115. Additionally, because we have chosen this strike for the short April call, we must move closer and purchase the far-dated $110. This option is only $6.00 (0.21 StdDev) out-of-the-money for the 120-day timeframe. We can now complete a table that outlines the entire trade.

Position	Expir. Date	Initial Stock Price ($)	Expir. Stock Price ($)	Strike($)	Initial Call ($)	Final Call ($)	Gain/ Loss ($)
Short	1/19/08	104	112	115	1.72	0.00	1.72
Short	2/16/08	112	117	125	1.63	0.00	1.63
Short	3/22/08	117	103	130	2.34	0.00	2.34
Short	4/19/08	103	133	115	1.49	18.00	−16.51
Long	4/19/08	104	133	110	9.15	23.00	13.85
						Total	3.03

Reducing the risk of each short trade by selecting more distant strikes increased the return by 45% to $3,030. Additionally, with regard to the initial trade outlined in problem #25, the cost of the long April call was reduced by $2.02 while the short April call price only changed $1.14. Strike price spacing remained the same at $5. This dynamic locked in an additional 88¢ of profit because the stock closed above both strikes at April expiration.

Additional notes for problems #24–#28:

In the previous five problems the April price increase was the predominant force affecting profit. However, we have calculated that a 1 StdDev price change for the 120-day timeframe is approximately $29 and, therefore, the rise from $104 to $133 should not be considered a surprise. Unfortunately, it is difficult to structure covered calls against the April $130 or $135 strike on a monthly basis because some of the short sale candidates have virtually no value. More specifically, both the January and the April $135 calls would be worth only 10¢ at the time of sale. Generally speaking, it is more reasonable to allow short-term risk parameters for each short option sale to drive strike price selection.

Summary

Our discussion began with traditional covered calls that are structured with long stock and an equivalent number of short calls. As we have seen, the dynamics of position management change dramatically when long calls are substituted for long stock or long puts replace short stock, because stock always has a delta of 1.00 and options obviously do not.

The present discussion focused on covered trades in which the short side has less favorable terms and potential losses are somewhat limited. The next section will expand this discussion to include trade structures in which the time decay of a far-dated long position is offset by near-dated options with a more favorable strike price. Such trades, because they are uncovered, require a more sophisticated approach to risk management.

Finally, we will build on these dynamics with more complex structures that involve ratios where the two sides—long and short—contain different numbers of contracts. These trades can take many different forms, including some that are quite complex. All variations include uncovered short components. Risk management will play an increasingly important role as the complexity increases. Generally speaking, not losing money is the most efficient way for an option trader to generate a profit.

4

Complex Trades—Part 1

The preceding chapter focused on covered trades that limit the potential loss of a short option position. Covered trades also provide downside protection for the complementary long position. However, this downside protection is limited to the value of the short option, and that value is realized only at expiration. These dynamics can be problematic for stock investors seeking more balanced positions in an unstable market.

Option traders generally solve this problem by structuring pure option positions that do not involve stock. Rather than purchasing 1,000 shares of stock and selling a call that is worth $2.50, an option trader might choose to purchase a $5.00 call and sell a $2.50 call at a more distant strike price. In this case, the total risk is limited to $2.50 regardless of how far the stock falls. As we saw in the preceding chapter, this simple vertical spread has a risk:return profile that is much different from a stock-based covered call.

A bearish investor might choose to take the other side of this trade by selling the lower strike and purchasing the higher one. The trade would have a $2.50 credit and the potential loss, in the event that the stock rises, would be capped by the long option. Despite the cap, this trade is not considered covered because the short option has a more favorable strike price. Collateral is required, but the cost is also capped by the difference between the strikes. We will explore the dynamics of this trade, also known as a bear spread, in the opening sections of this chapter.

The bear spread, like its bullish counterpart, is a relatively simple trade. Unlike the bull spread, which is long the more favorable strike, it can only generate profit from time decay. The full credit of the original trade is realized at expiration if the stock remains at or below the lower strike price.

These two trades, along with their stock-based counterparts, are excellent springboards for discussing more complex structures. The goal in placing more complex trades is to take advantage of the leverage offered by options while managing risk. With those goals in mind, we will explore a variety of trade structures and their financial implications. (All calculations for this chapter are based on a 1.5% risk-free interest rate.)

Vertical Spreads (Problems #1–#15)

This section compares different vertical structures that can be created using puts or calls. The following table contains relevant pricing information for two different trades. Each is represented by a pair of entries containing both long and short components. The first pair outlines a position that is short $100 calls and long $105 calls. The second is long $100 puts and short $95 puts. This information is used in problems #1–#11.

Position	Stock Price ($)	Strike ($)	Volatility	Days Remaining	Contract Price ($)
Short call	100	100	0.40	29	4.55
Long call	100	105	0.40	29	2.57
Long put	100	100	0.40	29	4.43
Short put	100	95	0.40	29	2.29

1. Is the first trade (calls) bearish or bullish? Is the second trade (puts) bearish or bullish?

   Answer: Both trades are bearish because they generate profit if the stock price falls.

2. What is the maximum profit for each trade described in problem #1? What conditions generate the maximum profit for each trade?

   Answer: The first trade, structured using calls, is established for a credit because the short side is more expensive than the long side ($4.55 – $2.57 = $1.98). The maximum profit is generated if the stock closes at or below $100 on expiration day because the premium of the short side is fully realized.

   The second trade, established for a debit, is capped by the lower strike price. It potentially generates $5 (the difference between the strikes) minus the initial debit of $2.14 ($4.43 – $2.29). The maximum gain ($2.86) is realized if the stock closes at or below $95 on expiration day.

   These parameters are summarized in the following table.

Trade	Max Profit ($)	Calculation	Condition
Call	1.98	4.55 – 2.57	Stock at or below $100 on expiration day
Put	2.86	5.00 – (4.43 – 2.29)	Stock at or below $95 on expiration day

3. What is the maximum loss for each trade? What conditions cause the maximum loss for each trade?

Answer: Both trades lose money if the stock rallies. The first trade will be short the difference between the strikes ($5.00) if the stock closes at or above $105 at expiration. Because it was initially established for a credit ($1.98), it will lose the difference ($5.00 – $1.98). Losses are capped by the strike price difference.

The second trade was established for a $2.14 debit. This money will be lost if the stock closes at or above the higher of the two strikes on expiration day. These parameters are summarized in the table that follows.

Trade	Max Profit ($)	Calculation	Condition
Call	3.02	5.00 – (4.55 – 2.57)	Stock at or above $105 on expiration day
Put	2.14	4.43 – 2.29	Stock at or above $100 on expiration day

4. How does each trade perform if the stock remains at $100 until expiration?

Answer: The first trade was established for a $1.98 credit. The full credit will be realized if the stock closes at $100 on expiration day. The second trade, however, was a debit spread costing $2.14. The full cost of the trade is lost at expiration if the stock closes at $100.

5. What is the break-even point for each trade?

Answer: The first trade breaks even when the cost to close the position exactly equals the original credit of $1.98. That point will be reached when the stock is $1.98 in-the-money with respect to the short strike price at expiration ($101.98).

The second trade breaks even if the stock is far enough in-the-money with respect to the long side to repay the initial debit. That point is reached if the stock trades $2.14 in-the-money with respect to the long strike ($97.86).

6. Which trade is more bearish?

Answer: The second trade is designed around a more bearish view because it anticipates a lower stock price at expiration. As we saw in the preceding problem, the first trade, composed of long and short calls, breaks even if the stock rises slightly to $101.98. The second trade, composed of long and short puts, will lose money if the stock does not fall below $97.86.

7. How would the two trades previously described compare with shorting an equivalent number of shares of stock at $100?

Answer: Unlike the pure option trades, the stock short sale has no limits with regard to potential gain or loss. However, short stock outperforms both of the other trades if the stock price declines. The following table presents results for three expiration prices: $95, $100, $105.

Expiration Stock Price ($)	Long $105 Call Short $100 Call	Long $100 Put Short $95 Put	Short Stock ($)
95	1.98	2.86	5.00
100	1.98	−2.14	0.00
105	−3.02	−2.14	−5.00

8. Which of the following structures would most closely mirror the performance of the previous problem's short stock if the underlying declines 1 standard deviation?

Position	Stock Price ($)	Strike ($)	Volatility	Days Remaining	Contract Price ($)	Delta
Short call	100	90	0.40	29	11.09	0.84
Long call	100	105	0.40	29	2.57	0.36
Long put	100	100	0.40	29	4.43	−0.47
Short call	100	100	0.40	29	4.55	0.53
Long put	100	110	0.40	29	11.20	−0.78

Answer: First we must calculate the value of a 1 StdDev price change.

Timeframes in 1 year	365 / 29 = 12.59
Annualization factor	Sqrt (12.59) = 3.55
Volatility for 29 days	0.4 / 3.55 = 0.11
1 StdDev change	0.11 × $100 = $11
New stock price	$100 − $11 = $89

The first trade will realize the full value of the short sale and lose the cost of the long purchase—total gain will be $8.52 ($11.09 − $2.57).

The second position is a synthetic short sale that almost exactly duplicates the performance of short stock in both directions. The long put will be worth $11, which is an $11.12 gain over the original trade in which both sides were almost exactly the same price ($11.00 – $4.43 + $4.55).

The third trade, composed of a long DITM put, has an initial delta of only –0.78. Although the delta will quickly rise to 1.00, the overall trade will not generate the full $11 profit of the synthetic short position. At expiration with the stock trading at $89, the $110 put will be worth $21. Subtracting the original cost yields a profit of $9.80 ($21.00 – $11.20).

9. The original put trade outlined in problem #1 (long $100 puts/short $95 puts) had a maximum potential profit of $2.86. Would shifting to higher strikes (long $110 put/short $105 put) increase or decrease the maximum potential profit? What would the effect be of structuring the same trade using strike prices that are very deep in-the-money?

Answer: The maximum potential profit shrinks as the strike prices are increased. In extreme cases, in which both options are very deep in-the-money, the long put will cost $5.00 more than the short put because it is $5.00 further in-the-money and there is no time premium in either contract. As the stock falls, the long put will continue being worth $5.00 more than the short put and no profit will be generated. The following table lists option prices and maximum potential profits for this example at various strikes.

Strikes

Long/Short	Long Put ($)	Short Put ($)	Max Profit ($)
115/110	15.50	11.20	0.70
110/105	11.20	7.45	1.25
105/100	7.45	4.43	1.98
100/95	4.43	2.29	2.86
95/90	2.29	0.99	3.70
90/85	0.99	0.34	4.35

10. In problem #9 how does increasing the strike prices affect the deltas of the two puts? How does the relative difference change?

Answer: As the strike prices are raised, the deltas of both sides will decrease, with the short delta decreasing faster than the long delta. The values will continue to converge until they reach −1.00 and both sides are deep in-the-money. After this point is reached, the prices will differ by an amount equal to the space between the strikes.

11. Suppose, as before, that we establish a trade that is long $100 puts and short $95 puts. How will the maximum potential profit of our trade be affected if a sharp downward spike skews prices so that options are priced with a relatively steep volatility smile—that is, implied volatility can be visualized on a constantly steepening curve that rises with lower strikes.

Answer: A steep volatility smile will disproportionately raise the value of the lower strike, the overall position will become shorter, and interim profit will shrink. However, the maximum potential profit at expiration, with both options deep in-the-money, will remain the same because the higher strike will still be worth $5.00 more than the lower strike.

12. Problems #1–#10 assumed that implied volatility when the trades were launched was 0.40 for all strikes. Suppose, however,

that options for these problems were originally priced with a more common volatility smile as outlined in the following table.

Strike	Implied Volatility
105	0.40
100	0.45
95	0.53
90	0.64

In general terms, how would these changes affect maximum profit and loss for the original put and call trades? (The next table summarizes the differences; as before, each pair of entries outlines the long and short sides of a single trade.)

Position	Stock Price ($)	Strike ($)	Original Volatility	Skewed Volatility
Short call	100	100	0.40	0.45
Long call	100	105	0.40	0.40
Long put	100	100	0.40	0.45
Short put	100	95	0.40	0.53

Answer: The potential gain is increased and the potential loss is decreased for both trades because in each case the short side has a lower strike price than the long side, and lower strikes are relatively more expensive.

For the call trade, if the stock declines and both sides expire worthless, the more expensive short sale will yield more profit. Conversely, if the stock rises sharply, the increased value of the short sale will buffer the loss.

The put trade has similar dynamics—more profit is realized if the stock falls because the cost to repurchase the short $95 put is closer to its initial sale price. Similarly, the loss that is experienced if the stock rises is buffered by the increased revenue from the short sale.

13. Which trade, put or call, gains the most from the volatility skew described in problem #12? Why?

    Answer: The put trade gains more because the curve that describes the volatility skew steepens as the strike price falls. The call trade has an implied volatility gap of 5% between the strikes while the put trade exhibits an 8% difference.

14. The following table displays two trades that are each based on the volatility skew of problems #12 and #13. The first is long $95 calls and short $100 calls; the second is shifted up one strike (long $100 calls/short $105 calls). Without knowing the exact prices, can you predict which trade generates the most profit if the stock closes the expiration cycle at $100?

Position	Stock Price ($)	Strike ($)	Volatility	Days Remaining
Long call	95	95	0.53	29
Short call	95	100	0.45	29
Long call	95	100	0.45	29
Short call	95	105	0.40	29

    Answer: The first trade (long $95 call/short $100 call) generates a profit and the second trade loses money. More specifically, the profit of the first trade is equal to $5 minus the original cost; the second trade loses an amount equal to its original cost.

    These dynamics remain intact for all pricing structures because every possible combination of initial prices will yield some profit for the $95/$100 trade and at least a small loss for the $100/$105 trade.

15. Is it mathematically possible to structure a volatility smile that would reverse the results of problem #14 causing the second trade to be more profitable than the first? Is there a practical reason that such a structure cannot exist?

    Answer: It is mathematically possible to structure a volatility smile that generates a substantial loss for the $95/$100 combination and a smaller loss for the $100/$105 trade. In this structure the initial cost of the $95/$100 trade must be more than $5 so that the trade ultimately loses money at expiration when the gap collapses to $5. The skew must also cause the $100/$105 combination to have an initial price that is lower than the amount lost in the $95/$100 trade. An example based on an extremely steep volatility smile is provided in the table that follows.

Position	Stock Price ($)	Strike ($)	Volatility	Days Remaining	Contract Price ($)
Long call	95	95	0.84	29	9.00
Short call	95	100	0.36	29	2.00
Long call	95	100	0.36	29	2.00
Short call	95	105	0.30	29	0.50

At expiration the $95/$100 combination collapses from $7 to $5 and the second trade loses its initial value of $1.50. These dynamics reverse the original situation presented in problem #14.

However, despite the mathematics, the initial pricing structure of the $95/$100 trade is impossible because it creates a riskless arbitrage that would immediately vanish. Option traders would sell the $95 call and purchase the $100 call to lock in a $2 profit at expiration. The gain would be realized regardless of the final underlying stock price. Market forces make it impossible for a position to cost more than the strike price spacing. These dynamics set limits on the steepness and overall shape of the volatility smile.

Calendar Spreads (Problems #16–#30)

16. The following table outlines a calendar spread that is long May calls and short April calls. The trade is initiated on Friday 3/21/2008, the day before March expiration. As revealed in the table, the short side expires on 4/19 and the long side on 5/17.

Position	Expiration Saturday	Stock Price ($)	Strike ($)	Volat.	Days Rem.	Contract Price ($)
Short call	4/19/2008	100	100	0.40	29	4.55
Long call	5/17/2008	100	100	0.40	57	6.41

What is the maximum potential gain for the trade at April expiration?

Answer: The maximum gain ($2.69) occurs at the strike price, which yields the largest possible return for the long side with the short side still expiring worthless. To calculate the long side gain, we must determine the price of the long call on expiration Friday 4/18. In this particular example we know that the price is exactly $4.55—the same as the initial value of the short call, priced with 40% volatility and 29 days remaining before expiration. The short side, because it expires at-the-money, becomes worthless.

Therefore, the initial trade that was long $1.86 ($6.41 – $4.55) is long $4.55 at April expiration for a total profit of $2.69 or $2,690 for every 10 contracts purchased.

17. What is the maximum potential loss for the trade described in problem #16? Based on the answers to this and the preceding problem, can you sketch the shape of the profit-loss curve for this trade?

Answer: The maximum loss ($1.86) occurs with the stock far below or far above the strike price at April expiration. In both cases the initial value of the trade is lost. If the stock closes April expiration far below the strike, both near-dated and far-dated options will lose all their value. Conversely, if the stock rises dramatically, placing both trades deep in-the-money, all time premium will vanish from the price calculations and the calls will trade for an amount that is equal to their distance above the strike. Stated differently, prices collapse to $0.00 for deep out-of-the-money options and converge on the same high price when the stock is deep in-the-money. These dynamics will be true regardless of expiration date if the stock rises or falls far enough. The expiration profile of this trade is displayed in Figure 4.1 for various underlying stock prices at April expiration.

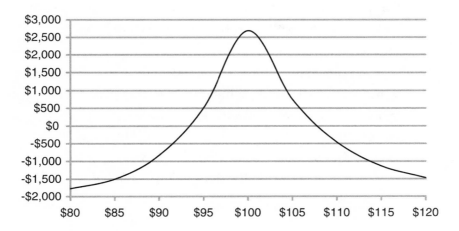

Figure 4.1   Calendar spread expiration profile for problems #16 and #17. Underlying stock prices at April expiration are displayed on the x-axis, profit of a 10-contract position on the y-axis.

18. Can you explain the slight asymmetry of the chart in problem #17 in terms of option pricing theory?

   Answer: The chart reveals a subtle asymmetry that is apparent when positions that are deep in-the-money (far right) are compared with those that are deep out-of-the-money (far left). These differences arise from the statistical parameters that underlie all approaches to option pricing. One simple explanation is that $100 strike price options are 25% out-of-the-money with the underlying stock trading at $80, but only 17% out-of-the-money with the underlying trading at $120. This difference causes option prices to collapse to zero more rapidly on the left side of the graph than the convergence to a high price on the right. In this example, with the stock trading at $120, the position is worth $390 ($1,470 loss). The symmetrically opposite position (stock at $80) is worth only $90 ($1,770 loss).

   This asymmetry, which is present across the entire chart, causes the right side to trail off more slowly than the left. For example, if the stock closes April expiration $10 in-the-money, the position will be worth $1,400 ($460 loss). The symmetrically opposite situation (stock at $90) is worth only $1,030 ($830 loss). These differences are quite significant. Our original $1,860 long position loses 45% if the stock falls $10, but only 25% if the stock rises $10.

19. Which of the graphs shown in Figure 4.2 correctly describes the relationship between implied volatility and the value of a calendar spread such as that of problem #16 (long far-dated $100 call, short near-dated $100 call with stock trading at $100)? Does rising implied volatility favor a calendar spread? If so, is there a downside?

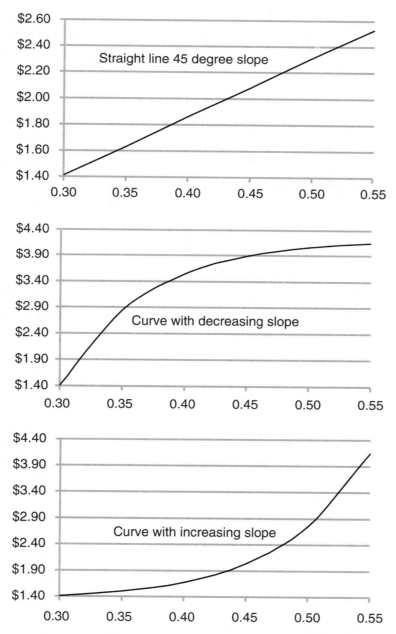

Figure 4.2   One of these three curves correctly describes the relation-ship between implied volatility and the value of a calendar spread. In each case, implied volatility is measured on the x-axis, the value of the position on the y-axis.

Answer: The first graph, straight line with a slope of approximately 45 degrees, is correct. As implied volatility increases, the gap between the short and long sides also increases. Generally speaking, rising implied volatility is beneficial to a traditional calendar spread in which the near-dated side is short and the far-dated side is long. However, rising implied volatility is normally accompanied by proportionally larger price changes of the underlying stock; large price changes adversely affect the value of a calendar spread. Therefore, volatility changes are beneficial only if implied volatility is mispriced to the upside.

20. How would the graph in problem #17 (Figure 4.1—calendar spread expiration profile) be affected if the options were priced with substantially higher implied volatility? Can you roughly sketch the differences? How are the maximum possible gain and loss affected?

Answer: The graph would be broader with a wider profit zone and a higher peak. Figure 4.3 displays the expiration profile of problems #16 and #17 (Figure 4.1) with implied volatility doubled from 40% to 80%. As before, the near-expiration underlying stock price appears on the x-axis, and the value of the calendar spread on the y-axis.

The following table provides break-even points for the calendar spread we have been discussing using implied volatilities of 40% and 80%.

Implied Volatility	Upper Break-Even ($)	Lower Break-Even ($)	Break-Even Spacing ($)
40%	107.77	93.45	14.32
80%	116.74	87.54	29.20

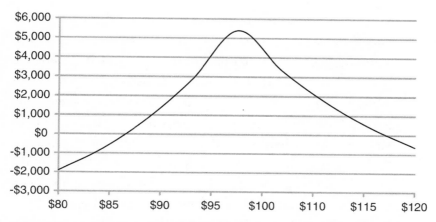

Figure 4.3   Calendar spread expiration profile for problems #16 and #17 with implied volatility doubled to 80%. Underlying stock prices at April expiration are displayed on the x-axis, profit of a 10-contract position on the y-axis.

The wider profit zone of the 80% implied volatility trade yields break-even points that are twice as far apart as those of the 40% trade. This profile is consistent with the answer to problem #19, which revealed a linear relationship between implied volatility and the overall position value.

The maximum possible gain and loss are similarly affected. For the trades we have been discussing, the maximum potential gain approximately doubles from $2,690 to $5,400. These values are visible in Figures 4.1 and 4.3. The maximum potential loss also doubles from $1,800 to $3,630. In Figure 4.1 these values fall just outside the range of the graph; they are farther from the edges in Figure 4.3 because the profit zone is wider.

21. How would the maximum possible loss and gain values of the preceding trade be affected if implied volatility climbed steeply after the trade was established?

Answer: If the stock remained at the strike price until expiration of the short side, the maximum gain would increase dramatically because the far-dated long side would experience price appreciation while the near-dated short side would still expire worthless. The maximum loss cannot increase after the trade is established because it equals the initial position cost. However, as we have seen, the break-even points are pushed farther apart and so are the maximum loss points. Stated differently, the trade can withstand larger price changes after implied volatility increases. These dynamics make sense because higher levels of implied volatility should offset the increased risk of a large price change when a stock becomes more volatile. Impending earnings releases are an excellent example. Holding a calendar spread through an earnings release is risky for stocks that have a history of surprising the market. This increased risk is offset by higher levels of implied volatility that widen the profit zone and buffer potential losses.

22. In general terms, how are the break-even points for the calendar spread described in problems #16–#19 affected by time? Can the trade still generate profit if the underlying stock crosses a break-even point early in the expiration cycle and remains at this price? Do these dynamics suggest a particular strategy for entry timing? (The trade we are discussing is long the far-dated $100 call and short the near-dated $100 call with the stock initially trading at $100.)

Answer: The trade has only a single break-even point at initiation—the stock price—and any underlying price change will lose money if very little time has elapsed. As expiration of the short side approaches, the break-even points move farther apart. However, the trade can never lose more than the initial investment—in this case, $1,860 for 10 contracts.

A trade that has crossed a break-even point and is losing money early in the expiration cycle can still become profitable as long as the underlying price stays within the profit zone calculated for expiration.

These dynamics suggest that a calendar spread placed near the end of an expiration cycle will benefit from accelerated time decay. This distortion increases as expiration approaches and the amount of profit generated per day from time decay rises.

23. Which of the two charts shown in Figure 4.4 accurately depicts the relationship between date of initiation and maximum potential profit of a traditional calendar spread (short near-dated option/long far-dated option)? In each case the x-axis shows the number of days remaining when the trade is initiated, and the y-axis displays maximum potential profit for a 10-contract position. Can you relate option pricing mathematics to the shape of the graph?

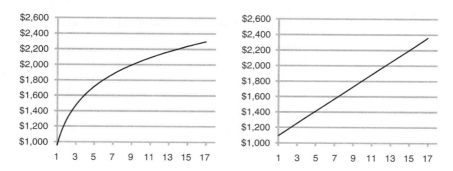

Figure 4.4   One of the two charts correctly describes the relationship between the number of days that remain before expiration when a calendar spread is initiated and the maximum potential value of the trade. In each case, days remaining before expiration are depicted on the x-axis, and maximum profit for a 10-contract position is shown on the y-axis.

Answer: The first graph (curve with decreasing slope) depicts the relationship between date of initiation and maximum potential profit of a calendar spread that is short a near-dated option and long a far-dated option. Time decay tends to accelerate as expiration approaches near the left side of the chart. The effect becomes very pronounced when fewer than 2 weeks remain before expiration. The second chart could be correct only if time decay were a constant process that did not accelerate. In this model, an at-the-money option with 30 days remaining would be worth precisely 10 times as much as the same option with 3 days; sellers of short-term options would be overly compensated for risk.

24. Without knowing the exact option prices, can you predict which of the two trades shown in the following table would generate the largest profit if the stock remains at the strike price until April expiration? Which delivers the most profit per day?

Position	Stock Price ($)	Strike ($)	Volatility	Days Remaining
Short call	100	100	0.40	30
Long call	100	100	0.40	58
Short call	100	100	0.40	4
Long call	100	100	0.40	32

Answer: Based on the previous discussion, we can predict that the maximum profit is larger for the longer-dated trade (first pair in the table). However, despite the brief timeframe, the second trade delivers much more profit per day because of accelerated time decay near the end of the expiration cycle.

The next problem will explore risk-based calculations that will further test these assumptions.

25. The following table extends the preceding problem with option prices, break-even points, and maximum potential profit for each position. Pricing data at April expiration with the stock trading at $100 is included for reference (pair of entries below the gray line). Note that 1 day remains in the contracts because they are priced at the close on expiration Friday. As before, both positions are $100 calendar spreads, the stock is trading at $100 when each position is initiated, and implied volatility is 40%. Using this data, can you compare the risk-adjusted returns for the two trades?

Position	Days Rem.	Contr. Price ($)	Contr.	Position Total ($)	Max Profit ($)	Low Break-Even	High Break-Even
Short call	30	4.63	10				
Long call	58	6.47	10	1840	2690	93.38	107.85
Short call	4	1.68	10				
Long call	32	4.79	10	3110	1420	96.94	103.48
Short call	1	0.02	10				
Long call	29	4.55	10	4530			

Answer: Because the timeframes differ, we need to transform the distance from $100 to each break-even point into standard deviations before comparing the trades. Following are the calculations for both high and low break-evens.

30 Days Remaining

Timeframes in 1 year	365 / 30 = 12.17
Annualization factor	Sqrt (12.17) = 3.49
Volatility for 1 month	0.4 / 3.49 = 0.115
1 StdDev change	0.115 × $100 = $11.50
Distance to high break-even	$107.85 − $100 = $7.85
High break-even StdDev	$7.85 / $11.50 = 0.68 StdDev

| Distance to low break-even | $100 – $93.38 = $6.62 |
| Low break-even StdDev | $6.62 / $11.50 = 0.58 StdDev |

4 Days Remaining

Timeframes in 1 year	365 / 4 = 91.25
Annualization factor	Sqrt (91.25) = 9.55
Volatility for 4 days	0.4 / 9.55 = 0.042
1 StdDev change	0.042 × $100 = $4.20

| Distance to high break-even | $103.48 – $100 = $3.48 |
| High break-even StdDev | $3.48 / $4.20 = 0.83 StdDev |

| Distance to low break-even | $100 – $96.94 = $3.06 |
| Low break-even StdDev | $3.06 / $4.20 = 0.73 StdDev |

These calculations reveal that the distance to each high or low break-even point is relatively small—less than 1 StdDev. The 30-day trade averages 0.63 StdDev and the 4-day trade averages 0.78 StdDev. The differences are minor. In the 4-day case approximately 42% of all price changes can be expected to fall outside the break-even point; the figure rises to 52% for the 30-day case. We will explore the use of the cumulative normal distribution function to calculate the percent chance of a price change falling within the profit zone in problem #28.

On a risk-adjusted basis, therefore, the return is much smaller for the 4-day trade because the maximum potential gain is roughly half ($1,440 versus $2,710) and the maximum possible loss is 69% larger ($3,110 versus $1,840). These dynamics make sense because the timeframe is much shorter and it should not be possible to consistently generate the same return in 4 days as in 30 days. Moreover, it is not uncommon for implied volatility to shrink as expiration approaches. This additional adjustment further reduces the profit potential of very short-term trades at the end of an expiration cycle.

26. How would the maximum potential gain and loss for the 4-day trade of problem #25 be affected if the initial implied volatility for the near-term option were reduced from 40% to 20%? Can you fill in the missing blanks in the following table?

Position	Days Remaining	Volatility	Contract Price	Contracts	Position Total ($)	Max Profit ($)
Short call	4	0.40	1.68	10		
Long call	32	0.40	4.79	10	3110	1440
Short call	4	0.20	Blank_1	10		
Long call	32	0.40	4.79	10	Blank_2	Blank_3
Short call	1	0.01	0.02	10		
Long call	29	0.40	4.55	10	4530	

Answer: Halving the volatility of the near-dated at-the-money option causes the value to fall by half. The initial value $1.68 will be reduced to $0.84. The change increases the initial cost of the trade by $0.84 and reduces the maximum profit by the same amount. For a 10-contract position the initial cost will rise by $840 to $3,950 and the maximum profit will be reduced to $580.

Blank_1 $0.84
Blank_2 $3,950
Blank_3 $580

27. Which of the following three trades is most bullish? Which is most bearish? Can you quantify the bullish or bearish nature of each position?

Position	Stock Price ($)	Strike ($)	Volat.	Days Rem.	Contr. Price ($)	Delta	10 Contr. Position ($)
Short call	100	90	0.40	29	11.09	0.84	
Long call	100	90	0.40	57	12.42	0.78	1330
Short call	100	100	0.40	29	4.55	0.53	
Long call	100	100	0.40	57	6.41	0.54	1860
Short call	100	110	0.40	29	1.33	0.22	
Long call	100	110	0.40	57	2.84	0.31	1510

Answer: The first position on the list ($90 calendar spread) is the most bearish, and the third ($110 calendar spread) is the most bullish. Positions structured around the $90 strike achieve their maximum profit if the stock falls $10; the $110 calendar spread achieves its maximum profit if the stock rises $10 to close the expiration timeframe at the strike. An investor would structure a position around the $90 strike if he or she anticipated a drawdown in the underlying stock. The $110 strike would be chosen by a bullish investor who expected a price increase.

We can use overall position delta to quantify the results of initial price changes. Subtracting the short delta from its long counterpart for each trade yields the results shown in the following table.

Position	Net Delta
$90 calendar spread	−0.06
$100 calendar spread	0.01
$110 calendar spread	0.09

Because the $110 calendar spread has an initial delta equal to 0.09, the trade will gain 9¢ if the underlying stock immediately rises $1. Conversely, the same increase will cause the $90 calendar spread to lose 6¢. These changes are extremely small, but they validate the directional character of each trade. The bearish structure will lose value if the stock does not fall toward the strike, and the bullish trade will lose value if the stock fails to rally.

28. When you're structuring a calendar spread, it is important to manage risk by considering both the direction and distance to the maximum profit point, and the magnitude of the price change that will cause a loss in each direction. These dynamics are especially important for asymmetric trades like the $90 and $110 calendar spreads described previously, in which the maximum profit point is below or above the starting point.

    The following table lists break-even points for the three trades outlined in the preceding problem.

Position	Lower Break-Even ($)	Upper Break-Even ($)
$90 calendar spread	82.85	98.62
$100 calendar spread	93.45	107.77
$110 calendar spread	100.78	121.17

Can you create a new table that measures the distance to each break-even point and maximum profit point in standard deviations? Based on this information, which trade represents the most favorable risk:reward profile? Can you estimate the probability of losing money for each trade? (Assume the parameters of the previous problem—29 days remaining before expiration of the short side with implied volatility set at 40%.)

Answer: First we must calculate the value of a 1 standard deviation change for a $100 stock with 40% implied volatility across a timeframe of 29 days.

Timeframes in 1 year[1]	$365 / 29 = 12.59$
Annualization factor	$\text{Sqrt} (12.59) = 3.55$
Volatility for 29 days	$0.40 / 3.55 = 0.113$
1 StdDev change	$0.113 \times \$100 = \$11.30$

[1] We use calendar days for this calculation to precisely measure the fraction of a year that is represented by the entire timeframe. If we were calculating a daily price change, number of trading days (252) would provide a more appropriate metric.

Using these numbers, we can assemble a table that reveals the distance to each break-even point in standard deviations. In each case we must subtract the initial price ($100) from the break-even price, and divide by the size of a 1 standard deviation price change ($11.30).

Position	Lower Break-Even (StdDev)	Upper Break-Even (StdDev)
$90 calendar spread	−1.52	−0.12
$100 calendar spread	−0.58	0.69
$110 calendar spread	0.07	1.87

Reading from the table, we can predict that the $110 calendar spread is profitable only if the stock rises more than 0.07 Std-Dev but less than 1.87 StdDev. Applying the cumulative normal distribution function, we can predict that 3.07% of all price changes will fall beyond the upper limit of 1.87 StdDev. The same calculations place 52.79% of the price changes below 0.07 StdDev. Summing both sides together gives the total percentage of price changes that can be expected to fall outside the profit zone (55.86%). These values are readily calculated using Excel's NORMSDIST function or a hand-held calculator with statistical capabilities. Figure 4.5 provides a visual representation of the individual components. The areas below the lower break-even point and above the upper break-even point are marked A and B respectively—calculations are displayed on the chart.

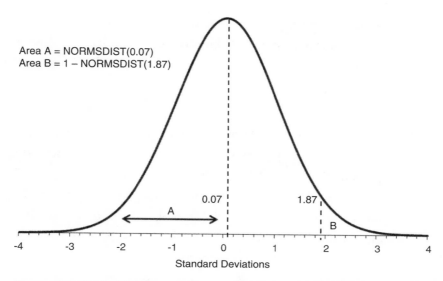

Figure 4.5   Probability calculations for a $110 calendar spread using the cumulative normal distribution function. Area A holds all price changes that fall below the lower break-even point (0.07 StdDev); area B contains price changes larger than 1.87 standard deviations. Summing the results together yields the percentage of price changes that can be expected to fall outside the profit zone.

Calculations for the three calendar spreads are listed in the following table. The "1-Sum" column displays the percentage chance of a 29-day price change landing within the profit zone for each trade.

Position	Calculation	Results	Sum	1-Sum
$110 calendar spread	NORMSDIST(.07)	0.528		
	1-NORMSDIST(1.87)	0.031	0.559	0.441
$100 calendar spread	NORMSDIST(−.58)	0.281		
	1-NORMSDIST(.69)	0.245	0.526	0.474
$90 calendar spread	NORMSDIST(−1.52)	0.064		
	1-NORMSDIST(−.12)	0.548	0.612	0.388

Subtle differences between the positions are apparent. Most significant is the elevated probability of obtaining a profit by structuring an at-the-money $100 calendar spread (47.4%).

Overall, however, the differences are relatively small, and an investor considering one of these trades would likely choose a strike price based on a bearish or bullish view of the underlying stock.

29. The following table contains two calendar spreads spanning different timeframes. In both cases the near-dated short side expires in 29 days. The long side of the first trade expires in 57 days; the long side of the second trade has a longer time-frame—183 days. Can you fill in the blanks and determine the maximum profit for the second trade? How would you rationalize these results with regard to time decay?

Position	Stock Price ($)	Strike ($)	Days Rem.	Contr. Price ($)	Pos. Total ($)	Theta	Max Profit ($)
Short call	100	100	29	4.55		−0.079	
Long call	100	100	57	6.41	1.86	−0.057	2.67
Short call	100	100	1	0.02		−0.020	
Long call	100	100	29	4.55	4.53	−0.079	
Long call	100	100	183	11.60	7.05	−0.032	Blank_3
Short call	100	100	1	0.02		−0.020	
Long call	100	100	155	Blank_1	Blank_2	−0.035	

Answer: Far-dated at-the-money options exhibit relatively flat time decay. This effect is visible in the table because theta for the second trade barely increases from −0.032 to −0.035 during the first month. Multiplying the average value (−0.0335) by the number of days that elapse (28) provides an exact value for the amount of time premium lost in the long side of the trade (−0.0335 × 28 = $0.94). Subtracting 94¢ from the original value ($11.60) yields a new value for the long $100 call with 155 days remaining ($10.66). Subtracting the tiny amount of premium (2¢) left in the short side gives a position total of $10.64. Finally, we can determine the maximum profit by subtracting the original position cost ($10.64 − $7.05 = $3.59). The answers are summarized here.

Blank_1 $10.66
Blank_2 $10.64
Blank_3 $3.59

30. The results of problem #29 seem to suggest that the profit of a calendar spread increases with the time gap between the two sides. Is there a downside to this trade structure? Would taking the other side of the trade—short the far-dated option/long the near-dated option—be a better choice from a risk:reward perspective?

Answer: Unfortunately, the profit of the second trade is much smaller than that of the first when measured as a percentage of the original investment. The first trade (28-day spacing) has a maximum profit potential of $2.67 or 144% of the original purchase price; the second trade (154-day spacing) generates more absolute profit ($3.59), but on a much larger initial investment ($7.05). In percentage terms, the second trade has a maximum potential return of only 51%.

Statistically speaking, it would make more sense to structure the second trade as a reverse calendar spread—short the far-dated side and long the near-dated side. Reversing our previous calculations yields a maximum potential gain of $7.05 against a $3.59 downside risk.

Diagonal Calendar Spreads Spanning Multiple Expirations and Strike Prices (Problems #31–#34)

31. The following table contains relevant pricing information for three different trades. Each is represented by a pair of entries composed of a short side and a long side. The trades are each initiated on Friday 3/21/2008, the day before March expiration. All three short sides expire on Saturday 4/19, the long sides expire on Saturday 5/17. Which of the three is most bullish and which is most bearish? How do the three trades compare with the stock trading at $105 at April expiration? Do the position deltas provide useful evidence?

Position	Stock Price ($)	Strike($)	Implied Volat.	Delta	Theta	Days Rem.	Exp. Sat.	Contr. Price ($)
Short call	100	105	0.40	0.36	–0.07	29	4/19	2.57
Long call	100	110	0.40	0.31	–0.05	57	5/17	2.84
Short call	100	105	0.40	0.36	–0.07	29	4/19	2.57
Long call	100	100	0.40	0.54	–0.06	57	5/17	6.41
Short call	100	110	0.40	0.22	–0.06	29	4/19	1.33
Long call	100	105	0.40	0.41	–0.06	57	5/17	4.35

Answer: The first trade (short $105/long $110) is the most bearish and the third (short $110/long $105) is the most bullish.

Trade #1

The first trade is initially long just 27¢. Maximum profit is realized at near-term expiration with the stock trading at $105. In this situation $2.57 of profit is realized from the short sale, and the long side will be worth approximately the same as its initial cost. We can estimate this value from the short side, which is initially $5.00 out-of-the-money with 29 days remaining. When the short side closes on 4/18, the long side will also have 29 days remaining. We can add a small premium (20¢) to account for the $5.00 increase in the underlying stock price. Using these dynamics, we can predict that the trade will yield a maximum profit of around $2.50.

If the stock rises sharply, the short side will be worth $5.00 more than the long side—that is, the position will transition from long $0.27 to short approximately $5.00 ($5.27 loss). Conversely, the maximum loss that can be realized in a price decline is the initial 27¢ paid for the trade.

Trade #2

The second trade achieves its largest gain if the stock closes at $105 on Friday 4/18 and the cost of the short side is realized as $2.57 of profit. To estimate the value of the long side, which is now $5.00 in-the-money, we must add a factor to account for the remaining 29 days of time decay. Early in the expiration cycle with 57 days remaining, theta was equal to 6¢ per day. It is reasonable to add 50% to this number to account for accelerated time decay that will occur as the end of the expiration cycle approaches. We can, therefore, estimate that time decay will add $2.61 to the option price ($0.09 × 29 days). Adding this value to the amount that the options are in-the-money ($5.00) yields a value of $7.61—a $1.20 profit for the long side. This value can be confirmed with a Black-Scholes calculator. Surprisingly, the estimate is exactly correct. By combining the profits of both sides, we can accurately estimate that the trade returns $3.77 ($2.57 from the short side and $1.20 from the long side).

If the stock rises sharply, placing both sides of the trade far in-the-money, the value will be equal to the difference between the strikes ($5.00). Subtracting the cost of the initial trade ($3.84) yields a total profit of $1.16. Conversely, the maximum loss that can be realized if the price declines sharply is equal to the initial purchase price ($3.84).

Trade #3

The third trade also achieves its largest gain if the stock closes at the strike of the short side ($110) on Friday 4/18. The dynamics are very similar to trade #2. The long side, now $5.00 in-the-money, is worth $5.00 plus remaining time decay. Using our previous calculation provides a conservative estimate of $7.61. This value is slightly low because it is based on the time decay for a much less expensive option that was priced before the stock climbed $10.00. However, despite the conservative nature of the estimate, the profit is still larger than that of trade #2. The short side generates a $1.33 return; the long side yields $3.26 ($7.61 – $4.35). Adding these values together gives a total profit of $4.59.

As before, as the stock rises sharply, the net value converges on $5.00. Subtracting the initial cost yields a profit of $1.98. The maximum loss in this case is $3.02—the initial cost of the trade.

We must also be able to compare the values of trades #2 and #3 at April expiration with the stock trading at $105. In this context we must assume that the options are fairly priced. Because the stock has traveled half the distance to the $110 strike with half the time remaining, the value of the $110 call should remain fairly constant near $4.35, and virtually all value in the trade will be generated by collapse of the short side to $0.00. The actual value of the long $110 call given by a Black-Scholes calculator is fairly close ($4.78) to this estimate; the $0.43 discrepancy in the price can be thought of as compensation for accelerating time decay. (Actual value of theta increases to 44¢ on the final trading day of the May expiration cycle with the stock at $105.)

These results are summarized in the next table.

	Max Gain ($)	Max Gain Price ($)	Deep OTM Gain/Loss ($)	Deep ITM Gain/Loss ($)
Trade #1	2.50	105	−0.27	−5.27
Trade #2	3.77	105	−3.84	1.16
Trade #3	4.59	110	−3.02	1.98

The bearish nature of the first trade is evident in the substantial ($5.27) loss that occurs when the underlying stock price rises sharply. The trade is also hedged against very large price declines because the prices and deltas of both sides are nearly equal. While clearly the most bearish of the group, it is not designed to profit from a large price decline.

Both trade #2 and trade #3 are bullish because they are designed to profit from large price increases. Trade #3 is more bullish because it anticipates a larger price increase. Its maximum gain is 22% larger, occurs $5.00 farther in-the-money, and is capped at a higher price ($1.98 versus $1.16). Furthermore, the trade will generate a substantially smaller gain than trade #2 if the stock rises only $5.00 by April expiration. As discussed previously, the long side just keeps pace with time decay, and virtually all profit is generated by collapse of the short side from $1.33 to $0.00. In summary, trade #2 generates nearly three times as much profit as trade #3 if the stock closes April expiration at $105—further evidence that trade #3 is built around a more bullish view.

Differences between long and short deltas are virtually identical for both trades. However, because the deltas are uniformly lower for trade #3, it can be concluded that both sides are farther out-of-the-money when the trade is initiated. Increased distance to the strikes provides additional verification that the trade is structured around larger underlying price changes.

32. The three graphs shown in Figure 4.6 are profit profiles for the trades outlined in problem #31. In each case the stock price at April expiration is represented on the x-axis, and position value is measured on the y-axis (unlabeled). Can you match each trade to its corresponding profile?

Answer:

A = first trade—short near-dated $105 call/long far-dated $110 call.

B = second trade—short near-dated $105 call/long far-dated $100 call.

C = third trade—short near-dated $110 call/long far-dated $105 call.

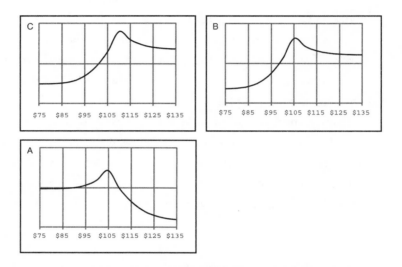

Figure 4.6   Profit profiles for trades described in problem #31. Stock price at April expiration appears on the x-axis, and position value is represented on the y-axis (unlabeled).

33. Which description best characterizes trade #3 of the previous two problems?

    A. Generates at least 65% profit if the underlying stock rises above the short side strike at expiration. Partially hedged against downside loss.

    B. Generates at least 30% profit if the underlying stock rises above the short side strike at expiration. Fully hedged against downside loss.

C. Generates at least 30% profit if the underlying stock rises above the short strike at expiration. Not hedged against downside loss.

D. Generates at least 65% profit if the underlying stock rises above the short side strike at expiration. Not hedged against downside loss.

E. Generates more than 100% profit if the underlying stock rises above the short side strike at expiration. Value of the position declines steadily beyond the strike. Partially hedged against downside loss.

Answer: D. The description can be supplemented with information about the maximum gain of 150% that occurs if the stock expires at the short side strike ($110).

34. As we have seen, bearish positions can be established using calls. The following table contains two bearish positions; the first is structured with calls, the second with puts.

Position	Stock Price ($)	Strike($)	Implied Volat.	Delta	Theta	Days Rem.	Exp. Sat.	Contr. Price ($)
Short call	100	100	0.40	0.53	−0.08	29	4/19	4.55
Long call	100	120	0.40	0.14	−0.03	57	5/17	1.10
Long put	100	100	0.40	−0.47	−0.08	29	4/19	4.43
Short put	100	90	0.40	−0.22	−0.04	57	5/17	2.20

Which trade would you consider to be the most bearish? What is the maximum potential gain and loss for each trade? Which generates the largest return if the stock declines a modest amount to $95 by April expiration? How do the position deltas relate to the bullish or bearish nature of each trade?

Answer: The put trade is more bearish because its maximum potential downside profit is larger and dependent on a large drawdown of the underlying stock. Stated differently, its structure anticipates a larger price decline. Additionally, the call trade generates a profit if the stock remains at $100, whereas the put trade loses money at this price.

Maximum Potential Gain

With the stock deep-in-the-money at April expiration, the put trade has a maximum value equal to the difference between the long and short strikes ($10.00). Subtracting the initial cost of the trade ($2.23) yields a maximum theoretical profit of $7.77.

Maximum profit for the call trade occurs at April expiration with the underlying stock trading at the short side strike ($100). The short side will have a value of $0.00 and the far-dated long side will have a very small value that can be closely estimated using theta of the initial trade to calculate the value lost over 28 days ($0.03 × 28 days = $0.84). Subtracting this amount from the starting price ($1.10) yields a remaining value of just 26¢. Adding together the initial short sale $3.45 and the final long value $0.26 reveals a maximum theoretical profit of $3.71.

This comparison reveals that the put trade has more than twice the profit potential of the call trade. Furthermore, the limited downside potential of the call trade becomes apparent if the stock falls sharply because no additional profit can be generated below $100.

Maximum Potential Loss

Maximum loss for the put trade occurs at April expiration with the underlying stock trading at the long side strike ($100). The long side collapses to $0.00, and the far-dated short side retains approximately half its initial value. As before, we can use initial theta to estimate the remaining value after 28 days of time decay ($0.04 × 28 days = $1.12). Subtracting from the original sale price ($2.20) yields a final value of $1.08. (This estimate is actually 8¢ higher than the value that is obtained with a Black-Scholes calculator.) Since the trade has transitioned from long $2.23 to short $1.00, the loss is equal to $3.23.

Maximum loss for the call trade occurs if the stock rises sharply placing both sides deep in-the-money. In this circumstance, the trade will be worth the difference between the strikes ($20.00). Subtracting the initial short value ($3.45) yields a maximum theoretical loss of $16.55.

These results are summarized in the following table.

Position	Max Gain ($)	Max Gain Comments	Max Loss ($)	Max Loss Comments
Short $100 call/long $120 call	3.71	At short strike ($100)	16.55	Deep in-the-money
Long $100 put/short $90 put	7.77	Deep in-the-money	3.23	At long strike ($100)

$5.00 Decline

If the stock closes April expiration $5.00 in-the-money, the long side of the trade will be worth $5.00. We can predict that the short side remains very close to its original value of $2.20 because the stock has moved half the distance to the $90 strike in half the time of the original trade (28 of 57 days). The original trade was net long $2.23 and our estimate yields a final value of $2.80 ($5.00 – $2.20) at expiration. (The short side value obtained using a Black-Scholes calculator is actually $2.09—just 11¢ less than our rough estimate). In broad terms, the put trade generates very little profit ($0.68) for a modest $5.00 price decline.

The call trade generates a much larger return ($3.45) at this price because both sides collapse to $0.00 and all premium from the original sale is realized as profit. One way to rationalize the value of the short side is to calculate the distance to the strike in standard deviations for the 29 days that remain in the trade.

29 Days Remaining

Timeframes in 1 year	365 / 29 = 12.59
Annualization factor	Sqrt (12.59) = 3.55
Volatility for 1 month	0.4 / 3.55 = 0.113
1 StdDev change	0.113 × $100 = $11.30

At $95 with 1 month remaining before expiration, the stock is $25 out-of-the-money (2.2 standard deviations by the calculation shown previously). Options that are 2 StdDev OTM have virtually no value (actual calculated price is 9¢). Therefore, the call trade generates a return approximately equal to $3.45, or five times the profit of the put trade if the stock declines only 0.5 StdDev.

Summary

The most important results of our discussion are summarized in the following table.

Position	Max Gain ($)	Max Loss ($)	Profit at $5 Decline ($)
Short $100 call/long $120 call	3.71 (at $100 strike)	16.55 (DITM)	3.45
Long $100 put/short $90 put	7.77 (DITM)	3.23 (at $100 strike)	0.68

Although both trades are bearish, the call trade generates approximately half the return of the put trade ($3.45 versus $7.77) if the stock declines dramatically. Conversely, the call trade is much more profitable for a modest decline of $5.00—approximately 0.5 standard deviations.

These dynamics are virtually impossible to predict by comparing the net deltas for the two starting positions (call = –0.39 / put = –0.25). However, the net deltas are important predictors of the initial response to a small rise or fall of the underlying stock. If, for example, the stock fell $1.00 immediately after the position was launched, the call trade could be expected to gain 39¢ while the put trade would gain 25¢.

Ratio Trades (Problems #35–#41)

35. The following table depicts a ratio trade composed of 10 long $80 calls and 20 short $85 calls. The trade is initiated with 36 days remaining before expiration and the underlying stock trading at $77.

Stock Price ($)	Strike ($)	Days Rem.	Delta	Contr. Price ($)	Contr.	Position Total ($)
77	80	36	0.41	2.65	10	
77	85	36	0.24	1.27	−20	110

What is the maximum potential loss for the trade? What is the maximum potential gain? What are the position values at expiration with the stock trading at $80, $85, $90, and $95?

Answer: The maximum gain at expiration occurs if the stock closes at the short strike and the long call is $5.00 in-the-money. Subtracting the initial trade value ($110) gives a total profit of $4,890 for 10 contracts.

The potential loss is unlimited because the trade continues to lose larger amounts of money as the expiration stock price rises above the short strike.

At $80 both sides expire worthless and the initial small trade value of $110 is lost. The maximum gain of $4,890 occurs at $85 (the short strike). At $90 the long side is $10 in-the-money and the short side is $5 in-the-money. Since the short side contains twice as many contracts as the long side, the values of both sides are equal at $10,000 and the total trade value is $0.00—the initial $110 is lost. Finally, at $95 the short side is worth $10 × 20 contracts or $20,000, the long side is worth $15 × 10 contracts or $15,000, and the net value is −$5,000. Adding the original trade value yields a final loss of $5,110 (we add the values because the trade transitions from long $110 to short $5,000). These results are summarized in the next table.

Expiration Stock Price ($)	Long Side	Short Side	Total ($)	Net ($)
80	$0 × 10	$0 × 20	0	−110
85	$5 × 10	$0 × 20	5,000	4,890
90	$10 × 10	$5 × 20	0	−110
95	$15 × 10	$10 × 20	−5,000	−5,110

36. In problem #35 we saw that the initial trade value was preserved at expiration if the stock climbed from $77 to just over
$90. However, the rate of climb is important because it affects
each day's mark to market value for the trade. One of the three
charts shown in Figure 4.7 depicts a rate-of-change profile that
holds the value of the trade constant. In each case the underlying stock price is represented on the x-axis and the number of
days remaining before expiration on the y-axis. Can you spot
the correct profile?

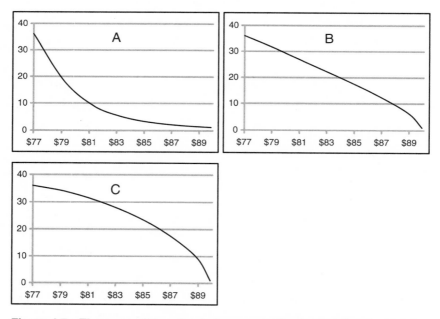

Figure 4.7   Three possible rate-of-change profiles for holding the value
of a ratio call spread constant. Underlying stock price is displayed on the
x-axis, days remaining before expiration on the y-axis.

Answer: B—The relationship between the stock price and time must be linear for the trade value to remain constant. Accelerated time decay in the final 24 hours causes a very subtle price distortion that is visible at the extreme right side of the graph.

37. Using the line defined in problem #36, can you predict—in general terms—the impact of a stock price increase to $83 with 28 days remaining? Where would this point appear on the graph?

    Answer: If the stock rises to $83 with 28 days remaining, the trade will yield a mark to market loss because the stock has risen too rapidly. This point appears above the line depicted in problem #36.

38. The following table displays relevant pricing information for four different trades. Each is designed to generate profit from a decline in the stock price. How do the trades compare with regard to bearishness—that is, how well does each perform when the underlying price declines by a certain amount?

Position	Stock ($)	Days Rem.	Strike($)	Contr.	Volat.	Delta	Contr.	Position Total ($)
Long put	102	100	37	4.12	0.400	−0.41	10	
Short put	102	90	37	1.02	0.400	−0.14	−30	1,060
Short put	102	100	65	5.71	0.400	−0.41	−10	
Long put	102	90	65	2.09	0.400	−0.20	20	−1,530
Short put	102	95	128	5.99	0.400	−0.33	−10	
Long put	102	85	128	2.67	0.400	−0.18	20	−650
Long call	102	105	128	8.56	0.400	0.51	10	
Short call	102	110	128	6.69	0.400	0.43	−20	−4,820

Answer: As we have seen before, the most efficient way to compare price changes spanning different timeframes is to convert all changes into standard deviations. This problem is structured around three different timeframes: 37 days, 65 days, and 128 days.

37 Days

Timeframes in 1 year	365/37 = 9.86
Annualization factor	Sqrt (9.86) = 3.14
Volatility for 37 days	0.40 / 3.14 = 0.127
1 StdDev change	0.127 × $102 = $12.95

65 Days

Timeframes in 1 year	365 / 65 = 5.62
Annualization factor	Sqrt (5.62) = 2.37
Volatility for 65 days	0.40 / 2.37 = 0.169
1 StdDev change	0.169 × $102 = $17.24

128 Days

Timeframes in 1 year	365 / 128 = 2.85
Annualization factor	Sqrt (2.85) = 1.69
Volatility for 128 days	0.40 / 1.69 = 0.237
1 StdDev change	0.237 × $102 = $24.17

Using these values, we can readily calculate the new stock price after a 1 or 2 standard deviation price decline. The following values are rounded to the nearest dollar.

37 Days

1 StdDev decline (approx)	$102 – $13 = $89
2 StdDev decline (approx)	$102 – $26 = $76

65 Days

1 StdDev decline (approx)	$102 – $17 = $85
2 StdDev decline (approx)	$102 – $34 = $68

128 Days

1 StdDev decline (approx)	$102 – $24 = $78
2 StdDev decline (approx)	$102 – $48 = $54

With these expiration closing prices we can calculate both the final value and the overall profit for each trade. Results of these calculations are displayed in the following tables for 1 and 2 standard deviation price declines.

Expiration Data for 1 Standard Deviation Decline

Position	Stock ($)	Strike ($)	Contracts Price ($)	Contracts	Position Total ($)	Profit/ Loss ($)
Long put	89.00	100	11.00	10		
Short put	89.00	90	1.00	–30	8,000	6,940
Short put	85.00	100	15.00	–10		
Long put	85.00	90	5.00	20	–5,000	–3,470
Short put	78.00	95	17.00	–10		
Long put	78.00	85	7.00	20	–3,000	–2,350
Long call	78.00	105	0.00	10		
Short call	78.00	110	0.00	–20	0	4,820

Expiration Data for 2 Standard Deviation Decline

Position	Stock ($)	Strike ($)	Contracts Price ($)	Contracts	Position Total ($)	Profit/ Loss ($)
Long put	76.00	100	24.00	10		
Short put	76.00	90	14.00	−30	−18,000	−19,060
Short put	68.00	100	32.00	−10		
Long put	68.00	90	22.00	20	12,000	13,530
Short put	54.00	95	41.00	−10		
Long put	54.00	85	31.00	20	21,000	21,650
Long call	54.00	105	0.00	10		
Short call	54.00	110	0.00	−20	0	4,820

Summary

The most bearish trades are structured to generate profit from a large price decline. Trades #2 and #3 fit this description because their profit is directly proportional to the size of the decline. (These trades are normally referred to as ratio put backspreads because they are long more contracts at the lower, less favorable strike.) As the underlying price declines, all deltas converge on 1.0 and the long side continues to grow at twice the rate of the short side.

Although both trades were similarly priced, nearly delta neutral, and structured with $10 strike price spacing at initiation, the longer-dated trade has a distinct advantage. A 2 standard deviation downward price change places the stock 36% in-the-money versus only 24% for the near-dated trade (calculated against the long side). Despite the timeframe difference, these moves are identical from a statistical perspective. The extremely bearish nature of these trades is evident when their performance is measured against a more modest 1 standard deviation change—both trades suffer a significant loss.

Trade #4 (ratio call spread) is the next most bearish. Anything less than a $3 price increase leaves both sides of this trade below the lowest strike, causing the value to collapse to $0.00. Close spacing ($5.00) of the strikes combined with the long timeframe (128 days) causes this trade to be net delta short (−0.35).

Trade #1, because of its 3:1 ratio, is the least bearish of the group. Although it generates the largest profit with the stock expiring near the short strike, it is also the most sensitive to additional price declines. Generally speaking, ratios larger than 2:1 must be managed carefully and are best initiated when the perceived chance of a large price spike is small. Such trades can be dangerous during earnings season or when news is anticipated.

39. Although three of the four trades outlined in problem #38 were initially very close to delta-neutral, their performance varied dramatically. Why is it difficult to use net delta to predict the outcome of each scenario?

    Answer: Delta is an excellent indicator for short-term, relatively small price changes. However, large price changes that span long periods are difficult to analyze using initial position delta.

40. Which trade from problem #38 would generate the most profit if the stock experienced a 2 standard deviation downward price spike immediately after the trade was initiated?

    Answer: Using the same method as before, we can calculate that the value of a 1-day, 1 standard deviation price change for a $102 stock with 40% volatility is approximately $2.14 ($2.57 using a 252-day trading year). This calculation sets the value for a 2 StdDev decline at $97 ($5.00). Such a decline early in the expiration cycle will have the largest effect on the trade with the largest delta imbalance—trade #4. The first trade, owing to its 3:1 ratio, will also be sensitive to a move of this magnitude, especially since the long side moves from out-of-the-money to in-the-money. As a result, its delta begins to rise significantly more slowly than the short side. This effect is exaggerated by the 3:1 ratio.

Although it is not necessary to have a Black-Scholes calculator to make this prediction, the actual results are interesting; trade #4 (call ratio) generates a $1,590 profit and trade #1 (3:1 put ratio) yields a $490 loss. The two put backspreads remain relatively unchanged because they are low ratios (2:1), are delta-neutral, and have significant time remaining before expiration.

41. Can you calculate the exact break-even price at expiration for the trade shown in the following table? What would the general formula be for calculating the break-even point for any ratio trade?

Position	Stock ($)	Strike ($)	Days Rem.	Contr. Price ($)	Contr.	Position Total ($)	Net
Long call	128	130	33	6.85	15	10,275	
Short call	128	145	33	2.37	–50	–11,850	–1,575

Answer: The expiration value of the short side is given by

$$5,000 \times (exp - \$145)$$

where *exp* is the stock price. Similarly, the value of the long side is given by

$$1,500 \times (exp - \$130)$$

For the trade to break even, it must remain short $1,575—that is, the short side must be $1,575 larger than the long side. Using these relationships, we can write an equation that solves for the expiration price.

$$5,000 \times (exp - 145) = 1,500 \times (exp - 130) + 1,575$$

Solving for *exp*, we obtain the following:

$$5,000\,exp - 725,000\,exp = 1,500\,exp - 195,000 + 1,575$$
$$5,000\,exp = 1,500\,exp - 531,575$$
$$3,500\,exp = 531,575$$
$$exp = \$151.879$$

Rounding to the nearest cent gives a break-even expiration price of $151.88. Using this value, we can extend the table with expiration prices.

Position	Stock ($)	Strike ($)	Days Rem.	Contr. Price ($)	Contr.	Position Total ($)	Net
Long call	128.00	130	33	6.85	15	10,275	
Short call	128.00	145	33	2.37	–50	–11,850	–1,575
Long call	151.88	130	0	21.88	15	32,820	
Short call	151.88	145	0	6.88	–50	–34,400	–1,580

We can use this calculation as a template for a general formula.

Short Shares × (*exp* – Short Strike) =

Long Shares × (*exp* – Long Strike) + Initial Credit

The formula for a position that is initially long (established for a debit) would be

Short Shares × (*exp* – Short Strike) =

Long Shares × (*exp* – Long Strike) – Initial Debit

In the second case, the long side must close expiration worth more than the short side by an amount equal to the cost of the original trade.

Summary

This chapter began with trades that span different strikes in the same month and progressed to relatively complex trades crossing multiple expiration dates and strike prices. We ended with a series of problems that compared different ratio structures with long and short components of different sizes.

Each of these structures will form an important springboard for the next chapter, which addresses complex multipart trades spanning various combinations of strike price and month. These trades require nimble and efficient execution and are generally found in the portfolios of private investors. Properly structured, they have the potential to deliver substantial profits against a backdrop of well-managed risk. Unlike large institutions that distribute risk across many investment vehicles and venues, private investors normally manage risk on a trade-by-trade basis. This dynamic significantly increases the value of complex multipart trades because a portfolio can be structured using a very small number of large positions.

5

Complex Trades—Part 2

Until this point our focus has been structures composed of puts or calls spanning different strike prices and/or expiration dates. This chapter extends those themes with more complex trades that contain three or more components. These structures, because of their complexity, offer additional advantages with regard to hedging and risk management. For example, using the ratios of the previous chapter as a springboard, we can structure a position containing three strikes that caps both the maximum gain and the maximum loss. These structures, commonly referred to as "butterfly trades," are quite popular among private investors.

This chapter also builds on previous discussions with trades that involve both puts and calls. Generally speaking, short put/call structures generate profit from time decay while the corresponding long positions bet on large underlying price changes. Stated differently, short put/call combinations succeed when implied volatility is overpriced, whereas the reverse structures, like all long positions, can be profitable only if volatility is understated. These structures, known as straddles and strangles, are the basis of more complex four-part trades that are both long and short, puts and calls. They can be built around a large number of strike-price and expiration-date combinations.

In some sense this chapter represents a fork in the road because these trades have specific characteristics that make them difficult for large institutions and perfect for private investors and small investment groups. Complex trades have many components and speed of execution is key to their success. Institutional investors placing very large trades containing thousands of contracts are unlikely to pursue such structures. Furthermore, bid-ask spreads represent a significant expense for a multisided trade, and the associated costs double if the position needs to be adjusted. The inefficiencies associated with unwinding and rebuilding complex positions amplifies the bid-ask spread problem, which is further aggravated by very large trades.

Large institutions also take a different approach to hedging than private investors because their portfolios are significantly larger and they can spread risk across many different investments. Conversely, most private investors are sensitive to the loss from a single failed trade, and it makes sense to build structures that are individually hedged. Trades that cap both the maximum gain and maximum loss tend to deliver more stable profit over time. This dynamic allows private investors with relatively few investments to realize the same stable return pattern as a large institution with an enormously diverse portfolio. In this regard, complex multipart trades can be thought of as being more conservative than the more familiar calendar, vertical, and diagonal spreads, ratios, or simple long or short option positions. However, as with any complex device containing many moving parts, management and fine-tuning are key success factors. The exercises in this chapter are designed to address this additional level of complexity. (All calculations for this chapter are based on a 1.5% risk-free interest rate.)

Butterfly Spreads (Problems #1–#8)

1. The following table depicts the three components of a typical long butterfly spread. What is the maximum potential profit at expiration? What is the maximum potential loss?

Position	Stock Price ($)	Strike ($)	Volat.	Days Remaining	Contract Price ($)	Contracts
Long call	90	95	0.45	29	2.63	10
Short call	90	100	0.45	29	1.39	−20
Long call	90	105	0.45	29	0.68	10

Answer: The maximum profit is achieved if the stock closes at the short strike on expiration Friday—the $100 and $105 strike calls will be worth $0.00, and the $95 strike calls will be worth $5.00 ($5,000 for 10 contracts). To determine the profit, we must subtract the cost of the initial position. Details for these calculations are displayed in the tables that follow.

Initial Position	Stock Price ($)	Strike ($)	Contr. Price ($)	Contr.	Position Total ($)	Grand Total ($)
Long call	90	95	2.63	10	2,630	
Short call	90	100	1.39	−20	−2,780	
Long call	90	105	0.68	10	680	530

Final Position	Stock Price ($)	Strike ($)	Contr. Price ($)	Contr.	Position Total ($)	Grand Total ($)
Long call	100	95	5.00	10	5,000	
Short call	100	100	0.00	−20	0	
Long call	100	105	0.00	10	0	5,000

Subtracting the initial cost from the final value yields a net profit of $4,470.

The maximum potential loss is equal to the cost of the initial long position, $530. We can demonstrate that this is the case by calculating the terminal position value with all three strikes deep in-the-money and subtracting the value of the starting position. The following table displays values for each strike with the stock trading deep in-the-money at expiration.

Final DITM Position	Stock Price ($)	Strike ($)	Contr. Price ($)	Contr.	Position Total ($)	Grand Total ($)
Long call	120	95	25.00	10	25,000	
Short call	120	100	20.00	−20	−40,000	
Long call	120	105	15.00	10	15,000	0

Subtracting the initial trade value yields a loss of $530 ($0 − $530). The exact same loss would be realized with the stock trading at or below $95 at expiration as all three positions would collapse to $0.

2. What would the maximum potential gain and loss be if we had taken the other side of the trade in problem #1 (10 short $95 calls, 20 long $100 calls, 10 short $105 calls)?

Answer: The maximum loss would occur at expiration with the stock trading at the center ($100) strike. The short $95 call would trade for $5.00, and the other two strikes would be worthless. We would, therefore, be short $5,000 at expiration. Reversing the trade outlined in problem #1 yields a starting credit of $530. Since the trade is initially short $530 and ultimately short $5,000 at expiration, the total loss is $4,470 (equal to the maximum gain of the long butterfly of problem #1).

The maximum gain for the short butterfly is realized with the stock trading above or below the three strikes at expiration. As before, the final position value will be $0. Because we have taken the opposite side of the trade, the initial $530 credit is retained as profit.

3. Using bid and ask prices from the following table, can you quantify the loss that would be realized if the trade were immediately unwound? Can the cost of the bid-ask spread be recovered through time decay?

Position	Stock Price($)	Strike($)	Bid($)	Ask($)	Delta	Vega	Theta	Contr.
Long call	90	95	2.60	2.70	0.36	0.095	–0.075	10
Short call	90	100	1.35	1.45	0.22	0.076	–0.060	–20
Long call	90	105	0.65	0.70	0.13	0.053	–0.041	10

Answer: Assuming that we buy at the ask and sell at the bid, our initial cost would be $700. On liquidation we would be able to recover only $350—a loss of 35¢ per contract (50%). Details of the calculation are presented in the next table.

Position	Strike ($)	Bid ($)	Ask ($)	Contracts	Open ($)	Close ($)
Long call	95	2.60	2.70	10	2700	2600
Short call	100	1.35	1.45	–20	–2700	–2900
Long call	105	0.65	0.70	10	700	650
				Totals	700	350

Time decay for the trade is very slow. The long side loses $0.116 per day (.075 + .041) and the short side returns $0.120 (0.06 × 2). Subtracting long from short yields a net time decay of only $0.004 per day ($4 per day for a 10-contract trade). Time decay, therefore, is not a feasible cost recovery mechanism.

4. Using the data from problem #3, can you explain why underlying price changes have only modest effects on the value of a butterfly spread? How would the trade be affected by a large change in implied volatility? How would the initial position value be affected if implied volatility were double that of problem #3 (90%)? (Hint: Think about overall trade delta and vega.)

Answer: Net delta for the starting position is nearly neutral. Furthermore, we can predict that the hedged structure of the position will preserve this neutrality. The initial value is equal to 0.36 – (0.22 × 2) + 0.13 = 0.05. We can also infer that delta will change very little if the underlying stock moves far in-the-money because all three deltas will converge on 1.00. For example, if the stock were to suddenly rise 100 points, placing all three strikes far in-the-money, the net delta would be given by $1.00 - (1.00 \times 2) + 1.00 = 0.00$. Likewise, if the underlying stock were to fall dramatically, all three deltas would collapse to 0.00; the net delta would fall from 0.05 to 0.00. Because the structure remains delta-neutral over a wide range of prices, the trade is relatively immune to price spikes in either direction.

Net vega of the initial position is also very close to neutral. The exact value is given by $0.095 - (0.076 \times 2) + 0.053 = -0.004$. Therefore, a 10% increase in implied volatility will reduce the value of the trade by only 4¢ (10×-0.004). Doubling the implied volatility of the starting position would correspond to a 45% increase. Multiplying by the net vega yields a decrease in the position value of 18¢ ($45 \times -0.004 = \$0.18$). Considering the magnitude of the implied volatility change, this value is very small.

5. The following table contains three different long butterfly trades. The first is initiated with 29 days remaining before expiration, the second has 92 days, and the third has 217 days. One of the trades is much more bullish than the other two. Can you compare the trades to determine which is the most bullish? (Hint: The comparison should take into account the distance to the point of maximum profit, timeframe of the trade, implied volatility, and underlying stock price.)

Position	Stock Price ($)	Strike ($)	Volatility	Delta	Days Remaining	Contracts Price ($)	Contracts	Net Cost ($)
Long call	90	95	0.45	0.36	29	2.63	10	
Short call	90	100	0.45	0.22	29	1.39	−20	
Long call	90	105	0.45	0.13	29	0.68	10	530
Long call	90	100	0.45	0.37	92	4.56	10	
Short call	90	110	0.45	0.22	92	2.36	−20	
Long call	90	120	0.45	0.13	92	1.16	10	1,000
Long call	90	130	0.45	0.19	217	2.89	10	
Short call	90	150	0.45	0.10	217	1.31	−20	
Long call	90	170	0.45	0.05	217	0.59	10	860

Answer: Since the trades are structured around different strike prices and expiration timeframes, we must restate the distance to each maximum profit point in standard deviations.

29 Days Remaining

Timeframes in 1 year	365 / 29 = 12.59
Annualization factor	Sqrt (12.59) = 3.55
Volatility for 29 days	0.45 / 3.49 = 0.127
1 StdDev change	0.127 × $90 = $11.43
Distance to maximum profit	$100 − $90 = $10
Distance in StdDev	$10 / 11.43 = 0.87 StdDev

92 Days Remaining

Timeframes in 1 year	365 / 92 = 3.97
Annualization factor	Sqrt (3.97) = 1.99
Volatility for 92 days	0.45 / 1.99 = 0.226
1 StdDev change	0.226 × $90 = $20.34
Distance to maximum profit	$110 - $90 = $20
Distance in StdDev	$20 / 20.34 = 0.98 StdDev

217 Days Remaining

Timeframes in 1 year	365 / 217 = 1.68
Annualization factor	Sqrt (1.68) = 1.30
Volatility for 217 days	0.45 / 1.30 = .346
1 StdDev change	0.346 × $90 = $31.14
Distance to maximum profit	$150 − $90 = $60
Distance in StdDev	$60 / 31.14 = 1.93 StdDev

The results reveal that the first two trades (29 and 92 days) are moderately bullish in that each is structured with a maximum profit point less than 1 standard deviation from the starting price. The third trade is more than twice as bullish because it relies on a nearly 2 standard deviation upward move of the stock to reach the maximum profit point of $150.

6. In problem #5 can the net delta of each trade be used to determine bullishness? Why?

Answer: No—the net deltas are essentially neutral for each trade (0.05, 0.06, and 0.04, respectively). The numbers do not reveal the bullish or bearish nature because time decay is a more important factor for a butterfly spread than starting delta. Small initial price changes will not materially affect the value of any of the three positions.

7. In the following table, the trade, structured with puts, is bearish because it profits from a decline in the underlying stock price. Can you design an equivalent trade using calls?

Position	Stock Price ($)	Strike($)	Volat.	Delta	Days Rem.	Contr. Price($)	Contr.	Net Cost ($)
Long put	105	105	0.45	−0.47	29	5.24	10	
Short put	105	100	0.45	−0.32	29	3.02	−20	
Long put	105	95	0.45	−0.19	29	1.52	10	720

Answer: We can structure a call position that will perform exactly the same way using the same strikes—10 long $105 calls, 20 short $100 calls, 10 long $95 calls. At expiration, with the stock trading at the maximum profit point (the middle strike), the position will be worth $5 because the long $95 call will be $5 in-the-money and the other options will be worthless.

These dynamics hold true for all expiration prices. For example, if the stock declines to $103, the call trade will be worth $2 ($8 for the long $95 call and $3 × 2 for the short $100 call). The put trade will also be worth $2 because the long $105 put will be $2 in-the-money and the other options will be worthless.

The call-based trade shown in the next table will perform identically to the put trade outlined previously.

Position	Stock Price ($)	Strike($)	Volat.	Delta	Days Rem.	Contr. Price($)	Contr.	Net Cost ($)
Long call	105	105	0.45	0.53	29	5.37	10	
Short call	105	100	0.45	0.68	29	8.14	−20	
Long call	105	95	0.45	0.81	29	11.64	10	730

The exact option prices are included for completeness; however, they are not required to predict the performance of the trade.

8. A butterfly spread can be decomposed into two common trade structures, a bull vertical spread and a bear vertical spread. The following table contains a relevant example.

Original Structure	First Component (Bull Spread)	Second Component (Bear Spread)
10 long $95 calls	10 long $95 calls	
20 short $100 calls	10 short $100 calls	10 short $100 calls
10 long $105 calls		10 long $105 calls

Traders sometimes adapt to large unanticipated moves of the underlying stock by closing part of a butterfly spread and leaving just one of the components. The following table outlines such a trade.

Comments	Position	Stock Price ($)	Strike ($)	Days Remaining	Contracts Price ($)	Contracts	Position Value ($)
Initial trade—stock	Long call	100	95	29	7.90	10	
Trading at center strike	Short call	100	100	29	5.11	-20	
	Long call	100	105	29	3.10	10	780
3 days later	Long call	90	95	26	2.40	10	
Stock falls to $90	Short call	90	100	26	1.21	-20	
	Long call	90	105	26	0.56	10	540
Adjust trade and create	Long call	90	95	26	2.40	10	
Simple bull spread	Short call	90	100	26	1.21	-10	1,190

What is the maximum potential profit that can be achieved if the stock changes direction and rallies before expiration? What is the maximum potential loss? Does the new structure have an advantage that would make the cost of the position adjustment worthwhile?

Answer: After 3 days we corrected the position by repurchasing 10 short $100 calls for $1.21 and selling 10 long $105 calls for $0.56 (total cost is $0.65 or $650 for 10 contracts). It is tempting to think of the adjustment as representing a $1.36 profit because the original bear spread was short $2.01 ($5.11 – $3.10). However, this profit is offset by a $1.60 loss in the bull spread that was originally long $2.79 ($7.90 – $5.11) and is now long only $1.19 ($2.40 – $1.21).

At expiration, if the stock closes above $100, the position will be worth $5,000. Subtracting the initial trade cost ($780) and the adjustment cost ($650) leaves a profit of $3,570. If, however, the stock continues falling, we will lose both the initial investment of $780 and the cost of the adjustment ($650). Total loss for the trade will then be $1,430.

It would appear that the adjustment adds no value because it reduces the maximum profit and increases the maximum loss. However, the original trade generates its maximum profit only if the stock closes at $100. Conversely, the adjusted trade generates its maximum profit at any point above $100. This structure has advantages for stocks that trade erratically because it generates the maximum profit at all price points above $100.

Straddles and Strangles
(Problems #9–#16)

9. The following table contains two different trades. The first pair is a long strangle composed of $110 calls and $90 puts. The second is an at-the-money straddle composed of $100 calls and $100 puts.

Position	Stock Price ($)	Strike ($)	Volat.	Days Rem.	Contr. Price($)	Contr.	Position Value ($)
Long call	100	110	0.45	29	1.77	10	
Long put	100	90	0.45	29	1.34	10	3,110
Long call	100	100	0.45	29	5.11	10	
Long put	100	100	0.45	29	4.99	10	10,100

What are the break-even points for each trade at expiration?

Answer: At expiration the stock must close far enough in-the-money for one of the sides—put or call—to be worth more than the original trade. This value is $3.11 for the strangle and $10.10 for the straddle. We can add these amounts to the call strikes and subtract them from the put strikes to determine break-even points, as shown in the next table.

Position	Stock Price ($)	Strike ($)	Initial Price ($)	Break-Even Calculation	Expiration Break-Even ($)
Long call	100	110	1.77	$110 + (1.77 + $1.34)	113.11
Long put	100	90	1.34	$90 − (1.77 + $1.34)	86.89
Long call	100	100	5.11	$100 + ($5.11 + $4.99)	110.10
Long put	100	100	4.99	$100 − ($5.11 + $4.99)	89.90

10. What is the profit or loss for each of the trades outlined in problem #9 with the stock trading at $105, $110, and $115 at expiration?

Answer: The following table contains three pairs of results; each contains expiration prices and profit/loss values for both trades.

Position	Stock Price ($)	Strike ($)	Contr. Price ($)	Contr.	Initial Value($)	Exp. Value($)	Profit/ Loss
Long call	105	110	0.00	10			
Long put	105	90	0.00	10	3,110	0	−100%
Long call	105	100	5.00	10			
Long put	105	100	0.00	10	10,100	5,000	−50%
Long call	110	110	0.00	10			
Long put	110	90	0.00	10	3,110	0	−100%
Long call	110	100	10.00	10			
Long put	110	100	0.00	10	10,100	10,000	0%
Long call	115	110	5.00	10			
Long put	115	90	0.00	10	3,110	5,000	61%
Long call	115	100	15.00	10			
Long put	115	100	0.00	10	10,100	15,000	49%

11. The following table is based on the first trade of the preceding two problems. It contains three pairs of entries. The first pair is the initial trade; the second and third are the same trade after 4 days and at expiration. Without knowing exact option prices for the second pair, can you predict which is most profitable?

Position	Stock Price ($)	Strike ($)	Contract Price ($)	Days Remaining	Contracts
Long call	100	110	1.77	29	10
Long put	100	90	1.34	29	10
Long call	108	110		25	10
Long put	108	90		25	10
Long call	114	110	4.00	0	10
Long put	114	90	0.00	0	10

Answer: The second pair generates the most profit. We previously calculated that the break-even point at expiration is $113.11—a $13.11 increase from the starting price of $100. The second entry reveals an increase of $8 or 61% of the distance to the break-even point after only 4 days (13.8%) of the remaining time has elapsed. Conversely, the expiration price shown in the third entry is only 89¢ above the break-even point (an additional increase of only 6.7%). Because the break-even point follows a linear path over time, we can conclude that the trade is more profitable after 4 days than at expiration.

12. Can you calculate the probability associated with the $8 price change that occurred in the first 4 days of the trade outlined in problem #11? (As before, implied volatility is 45%.)

Answer: As always, we must recast the price change in standard deviations.

Timeframes in 1 year	365 / 4 = 91.25
Annualization factor	Sqrt (91.25) = 9.55
Volatility for 4 days	0.45 / 9.55 = 0.047
1 StdDev change	0.047 × $100 = $4.70
$8 price change	$8 / $4.70 = 1.7 StdDev

We can use a statistical calculator or Excel's NORMSDIST function to calculate the probability of a 1.7 standard deviation change. The spreadsheet function reveals that the probability of a change being larger than +1.7 StdDev is 0.0445, or 4.45%. (This value is given by (1− NORMSDIST (1.7)). Multiplying by 2 gives the portion of the normal distribution curve that lies above +1.7 StdDev and the portion that lies below −1.7 StdDev (2 × 4.45% = 8.9%). Subtracting from 100% identifies the portion of the curve that lies between −1.7 StdDev and +1.7 StdDev (100% − 8.9% = 91.1%). Therefore, 91% of all price changes can be expected to fall within a range bounded by $8 in either direction. The probability of an $8 price change occurring in only 4 days is approximately 9%.

13. Option values after the $8 increase of the previous two problems were $4.23 for the $110 call and $0.30 for the $90 put. Can you calculate the probability of the trend continuing and generating the same profit at expiration? Would you keep or close the trade after the $8 underlying price increase? (As before, implied volatility is 45%.)

   Answer: To maintain the same total value, the stock must close $4.53 above the $110 strike on expiration Friday ($114.53). Subtracting $108 from $114.53 gives a price change of $6.53. As always, we must recast this price change in standard deviations for the 25 days that remain.

Timeframes in 1 year	365 / 25 = 14.6
Annualization factor	Sqrt (14.6) = 3.82
Volatility for 25 days	0.45 / 3.82 = 0.118
1 StdDev change	0.118 × $108 = $12.74
$6.53 price change	$6.53 / $12.74 = 0.51 StdDev

   We can complete our calculation by determining the probability of a 0.51 standard deviation upward price change. We can calculate the probability of a price change falling in the range below 0.51 StdDev using Excel's NORMSDIST function, a statistical table, or a statistical calculator. In Excel this value is given by (NORMSDIST (0.51)). The calculation gives a result of 69.5%. We can, therefore, conclude that there is a 30% chance of achieving an upward price change large enough to maintain the put+call value of $4.53, which represents a 46% profit over the initial cost of $3.11.

It would be wise to close the trade and realize the full profit associated with the 4-day/$8 price spike because there is only a 30% chance of maintaining this profit at expiration. Many traders would choose to close the calls for $4.23 and keep the long put position that is worth only 30¢. This approach bets on regression toward the mean, which often results in a trend reversal after a significant price spike.

14. Suppose you were to construct a portfolio of 10 trades similar to that of problems #11–#13. How much time decay loss would you experience over a typical weekend?

Answer: We know that the original trade cost $3.11 and had 29 days remaining before expiration. Dividing the two numbers yields an average daily time decay of 11¢, or $110 for a 10-contract straddle. A portfolio of 10 such trades would, therefore, experience $1,100 per day of time loss. Finally, there are 3 days between the market close on Friday and the next close on Monday (Friday 4 PM to Saturday 4 PM, Saturday 4 PM to Sunday 4 PM, Sunday 4 PM to Monday 4 PM). Multiplying by the daily loss gives an average weekend loss value of $3,300 for the portfolio.

We could alter the calculation to give the time decay between the close on Friday and the open on Monday morning. This value is equal to 2.73 days. Multiplying by the daily loss gives a weekend time decay estimate of $3,003 for the portfolio.

15. The following table describes a short strangle composed of $110 calls and $90 puts. The first pair of entries represents the initial trade with the stock trading exactly at the delta-neutral price of $98.08 (deltas are matched at 0.26). The second pair of entries reveals the changes that occurred 3 days later after a $9 upward price spike. (Options for this problem are priced with 50% implied volatility.)

Position	Stock Price ($)	Strike ($)	Contr. Price ($)	Delta	Days Rem.	Contr.
Short call	98.08	110	2.24	0.26	36	−10
Short put	98.08	90	2.66	−0.26	36	−10
Short call	107.00	110	5.17	0.46	33	−10
Short put	107.00	90	0.90	−0.11	33	−10

Which of the options given in the following table can be used to repair the position? What are the transactions required? Can the loss be recovered without increasing the size of the trade? Can we take advantage of the new structure to increase the size of the trade without adding risk?

Position	Stock Price ($)	Strike ($)	Contract Price ($)	Delta	Days Remaining
Short call	107.00	115	3.45	0.35	33
Short call	107.00	120	2.22	0.25	33
Short call	107.00	125	1.38	0.17	33
Short call	107.00	130	0.83	0.11	33

Answer: The fourth entry ($130 strike) exactly matches the delta (−0.11) of the put side of the original trade after the price spike. We would buy back the $110 calls and sell 10 new $130 calls to create a delta-neutral position. The initial trade was short $4.90 ($2.24 for the $110 call and $2.66 for the $90 put). After the price spike, the position was net short $6.07. The total loss was therefore $1.17, or $1,170 for a 10-contract strangle. A new position structured with $130 calls would be worth $1,730 ($0.83 for the calls and $0.90 for the puts). The loss will be recovered if the stock remains between the strikes. All three steps are displayed in the following table.

Position	Stock Price ($)	Strike($)	Contr. Price ($)	Delta	Days Rem.	Contr.	Net	Comments
Short call	98.08	110	2.24	0.26	36	−10		
Short put	98.08	90	2.66	−0.26	36	−10	−4900	Initial
Short call	107.00	110	5.17	0.46	33	−10		
Short put	107.00	90	0.90	−0.11	33	−10	−6070	Spike
Short call	107.00	130	0.83	0.11	33	−10		
Short put	107.00	90	0.90	−0.11	33	−10	−1730	Correction

Inflating the size of the trade, despite the wider strike price spacing, increases the risk. Although the deltas of the new trade are lower than the original, the wider spacing also allows the two sides to decouple more quickly. That is, a relatively small move of the stock will cause the deltas to become imbalanced more quickly than in a more closely spaced trade. The safest course of action, therefore, is to widen the spacing between strikes from $20 to $40 while maintaining the same trade size. A comparison between the effect of a $10 price spike on the original trade and the same price change on the adjusted, but inflated, 30-contract wider trade is shown in the following table. Note that both trades are exactly delta-neutral at initiation. The wider but larger trade suffers approximately twice as much loss. Had the position not been inflated, the loss would have been one-third as large ($1,200).

Position	Stock Price ($)	Strike ($)	Contract Price ($)	Delta	Days Remaining	Contracts	Net ($)	Profit/Loss ($)
Short call	98.08	110	2.24	0.26	36	–10		
Short put	98.08	90	2.66	–0.26	36	–10	–4,900	
Short call	108.08	110	5.98	0.49	36	–10		
Short put	108.08	90	0.91	–0.10	36	–10	–6,890	–1,990
Short call	107.00	130	0.83	0.11	33	–30		
Short put	107.00	90	0.90	–0.11	33	–30	–5,190	
Short call	117.00	130	2.68	0.27	33	–30		
Short put	117.00	90	0.25	–0.03	33	–30	–8,790	–3,600

16. In the preceding problem, why didn't we simply respond to the $9 price increase by selling more puts and re-creating a delta-neutral position?

Answer: Although this approach creates a delta-neutral position, it adds tremendous risk on the put side of the trade. Quadrupling the size of the put side to match deltas causes the trade to be short large amounts of gamma. As a result, small drawdowns cause delta to rise quickly on the put side. The following table illustrates this situation.

Position	Stock Price ($)	Strike ($)	Contr. Price ($)	Delta	Days Rem.	Contr.	Net ($)	Profit/ Loss ($)
Short call	107.00	130	0.83	0.11	33	−10		
Short put	107.00	90	0.90	−0.11	33	−10	−1,730	
Short call	98.08	130	0.20	0.04	33	−10		
Short put	98.08	90	2.45	−0.26	33	−10	−2,650	−920
Short call	107.00	110	5.17	0.46	33	−10		
Short put	107.00	90	0.90	−0.11	33	−40	−8,770	
Short call	98.08	110	2.03	0.25	33	−10		
Short put	98.08	90	2.45	−0.26	33	−40	−11,830	−3,060

The first pair of entries above the gray bar displays the adjusted 10-contract trade from problem #15. The second pair reveals a small loss after the stock reverses direction and falls back to the starting price of $98.08.

The first pair below the gray bar is an alternative adjustment. A ratio of four puts for each call is used to create a delta-neutral position. In this case a price decline to $98.08 (second pair below the gray bar) generates a considerably larger loss (−$3,060) than the trade above the bar.

Four-Part Trades (Problems #17–#22)

Four-part structures provide the flexibility to achieve many different goals. One of the most popular structures, the condor, combines vertical bull and bear credit spreads into a single trade. Four strikes are involved, two on the put side and two on the call side. An investor might, for example, sell a strangle comprised of $90 puts and $100 calls while simultaneously purchasing the outside "wings"—$85 puts and $105 calls. Strictly speaking, condors are structured with four different strike prices. However, similar dynamics apply to trades that are built around three strikes. Our example might be reduced to a short $95 straddle and a long $90/$100 strangle. Both scenarios are designed to profit from time decay. The long outside wings are an effective mechanism for capping potential losses and reducing the collateral requirement that normally accompanies short option positions.

17. What is the maximum potential loss at expiration for the condor trade outlined in the following table? What is the maximum potential gain?

Position	Stock Price ($)	Strike ($)	Volat.	Days Rem.	Contr. Price ($)	Delta	Contr.	Position Value($)
Long call	93.78	110	0.440	36	0.88	0.14	10	880
Short call	93.78	100	0.460	36	3.06	0.36	10	–3,060
Short put	93.78	90	0.480	36	3.78	–0.36	10	–3,780
Long put	93.78	80	0.500	36	1.08	–0.14	10	1,080

Answer: Maximum potential loss for the trade is $5,120 with the stock trading above $110 or below $80 at expiration. Either of these prices maximizes the loss on the short side while causing the long sides to expire worthless. Beyond either of the strikes, the long side will gain value as fast as the short side and no further loss will be incurred. These results are summarized in the next table.

Position	Stock Price ($)	Strike ($)	Days Rem.	Contr. Price ($)	Contr.	Position Value ($)	Net	Profit/ Loss
Long call	93.78	110	36	0.88	10	880		
Short call	93.78	100	36	3.06	10	−3,060		
Short put	93.78	90	36	3.78	10	−3,780		
Long put	93.78	80	36	1.08	10	1,080	−4,880	
Long call	110.00	110	1	0.00	10	0		
Short call	110.00	100	1	10.00	10	−10,000		
Short put	110.00	90	1	0.00	10	0		
Long put	110.00	80	1	0.00	10	0	−10,000	−5,120

The maximum gain occurs at expiration with the stock closing between the short strikes ($90–$100 inclusive). In this scenario all options expire worthless and the original short value of $4,880 is realized as profit. (Note: The table shows 1 day remaining at expiration because equity options expire Saturday afternoon at 5 PM.)

18. The trade in the following table differs from that of problem #17 in that the outside wings have more distant expiration dates, as noted in the position column.

Position	Stock Price ($)	Strike ($)	Volat.	Days Rem.	Contr. Price ($)	Delta	Contr.	Position Value($)
Long call 7/08 exp	93.78	110	0.440	64	2.04	0.22	10	2,040
Short call 6/08 exp	93.78	100	0.460	36	3.06	0.36	10	−3,060
Short put 6/08 exp	93.78	90	0.480	36	3.78	−0.36	10	−3,780
Long put 7/08 exp	93.78	80	0.500	64	2.28	−0.19	10	2,280

Which trade would you expect to generate a smaller loss if the stock closes the near-dated (June) expiration at $110? Is the loss capped at this price? Why? What is the maximum loss for the new trade at June expiration? At what underlying stock price is the maximum gain realized?

Answer: The loss is considerably smaller when the trade is hedged with longer-dated options because, unlike the near-dated $110 calls, which lose 100% of their value ($0.88) at June expiration, the far-dated calls gain significant value. Moreover, the July position only needs to maintain $2.36 of its initial $4.32 long value to equal this performance ($4.32 − $1.96 = $2.36). This being the case, the long July $110 calls would need to gain only 32¢ for this outcome to be assured.

The following facts support these assertions.

1. The stock must rise $18.26 to $112.04 by July expiration, initially 64 days away, for the long calls to maintain their value.

2. At June expiration, after only 36 days have passed, the stock has risen $16.22 or 89% of the required amount. We can, therefore, state that the stock has risen 89% of the break-even amount in only 56% of the contract lifetime. Furthermore, because time decay accelerates in the final days before expiration, we can also conclude that the $110 calls, which are trading at-the-money, are likely to have gained considerably more than the 89/56 ratio would indicate.

3. At-the-money calls with 1 month remaining before expiration have a delta of approximately 0.50. Since the starting delta of the long July $110 calls was only 0.22 (see the table), we can assume that the price at June expiration has more than doubled.

In summary, the trade outlined in problem #18, like its predecessor, loses $3.16 on the short side ($6.94 loss on the short call,

$3.78 gain on the short put), but gains enough value on the long side to outperform the single-month trade of problem #17. The complete trade with actual June expiration values is displayed in the table that follows.

Position	Stock Price ($)	Strike ($)	Days Rem.	Contr. Price ($)	Delta	Contr.	Position Value ($)	Net	Profit/ Loss
Long call	93.78	110	64	2.04	0.22	10	2040		
Short call	93.78	100	36	3.06	0.36	10	−3060		
Short put	93.78	90	36	3.78	−0.36	10	−3780		
Long put	93.78	80	64	2.28	−0.19	10	2280	−2,520	
Long call	110.00	110	29	5.50	0.53	10	5500		
Short call	110.00	100	1	10.00	1.00	10	−10,000		
Short put	110.00	90	1	0.00	0.00	10	0		
Long put	110.00	80	29	0.05	−0.01	10	50	−4,450	−1,930

(Note: The table shows 1 day remaining at June expiration because equity options expire Saturday afternoon at 5 PM.)

Maximum Possible Loss Comparison

With 1 month remaining before expiration and the stock trading at-the-money, the $110 calls will have a delta of approximately 0.5. Conversely, the short $100 calls that are $10 in-the-money have a delta of 1.0. We can, therefore, conclude that the loss is not capped at a stock price of $110. As the stock continues rising, the delta of the long call will also rise. The maximum loss, equal to the difference between the strikes minus the original position value, will ultimately be realized at a very high stock price where both deltas are equal to 1.0. As in problem #17, the overall position will be short $10,000. However, the two trades differ with regard to maximum potential loss because the initial positions have different values. Problem #17 began with a short position of −$4,880, whereas the problem #18 position was initially short only $2,520 ($2,040 long call + $2,280 long put − $3,060 short call − $3,780 short put). The

maximum possible loss at June expiration for the problem #18
trade is, therefore, larger by $2,360 ($5,120 + $2,360 = $7,480).

Maximum Gain Point

At June expiration, the maximum gain will be realized with the
stock trading at one of the short strikes because these price
points maximize the value of the long straddle while still causing the short side to expire worthless. Beyond one of the inside
strikes, the short put or call will gain value with a delta of 1.0,
and the long side will gain at a lower rate. We know from basic
pricing theory that a $10 out-of-the-money call will always be
worth more than a $10 out-of-the-money put (assuming that
other parameters such as remaining time, implied volatility, and
risk-free interest are identical). We can conclude, therefore,
that the largest position value is achieved at June expiration
with the stock trading at the $100 short call strike. Because this
price point falls below the line that extends from the starting
price ($93.78) to the expiration break-even point ($112.04), the
long calls will definitely have lost some value. This loss, in addition to the loss from the long puts, must be subtracted from the
gain on the short side. Exact values are displayed in the next
table for completeness.

Position	Stock Price ($)	Strike ($)	Days Rem.	Contr. Price ($)	Delta	Contr.	Position Value ($)	Net	Profit/ Loss
Long call	93.78	110	64	2.04	0.22	10	2040		
Short call	93.78	100	36	3.06	0.36	10	–3060		
Short put	93.78	90	36	3.78	–0.36	10	–3780		
Long put	93.78	80	64	2.28	–0.19	10	2280	–2,520	
Long call	100.00	110	29	1.68	0.24	10	1680		
Short call	100.00	100	1	0.00	0.78	10	0		
Short put	100.00	90	1	0.00	0.00	10	0		
Long put	100.00	80	29	0.30	–0.05	10	300	1,980	4,500

Summary

Because the loss dynamics are similar on the put side of the trade, we can summarize by stating that the maximum potential loss for problem #18, although larger, is realized only if the stock trades far beyond one of the two strikes at June expiration. Conversely, the losses associated with moderate underlying stock moves are buffered by the far-dated long options that still have 1 month left before expiration. Finally, the maximum gain occurs only at one specific underlying stock price—the strike of the short calls. This gain is comparable, although slightly smaller, than the gain achieved in problem #17, with the stock expiring anywhere between the short strikes. That said, the trade performs best for small underlying price changes when all options expire in the same month.

19. The positions outlined in the preceding two problems included an implied volatility skew of 2% per $10 change in strike price. If the skew steepened, would the overall trade be affected?

Answer: The effect is virtually insignificant because four-part trades include long and short components at both ends of the skew. The following table outlines the trade from problem #18 with two different implied volatility skews—44%, 46%, 48%, 50% and 39%, 43%, 47%, 51%. Despite a significantly steeper skew, the new value of the trade changed by only $10.

Position	Stock Price ($)	Strike ($)	Days Rem.	Volat.	Contr. Price($)	Contr.	Position Value ($)	Net
Long call	93.78	110	64	0.44	2.04	10	2040	
Short call	93.78	100	36	0.46	3.06	10	–3060	
Short put	93.78	90	36	0.48	3.78	10	–3780	
Long put	93.78	80	64	0.50	2.28	10	2280	–2,520
Long call	93.78	110	64	0.39	1.48	10	1480	
Short call	93.78	100	36	0.43	2.73	10	–2730	
Short put	93.78	90	36	0.47	3.67	10	–3670	
Long put	93.78	80	64	0.51	2.39	10	2390	–2,530

The position shown in the following table will form the basis of problems #20–#22. It is composed of short and long strangles built around the same strikes with the short side expiring in 3 months and the long hedge expiring in the current month. The short position ($250 call/$150 put) is exactly delta-neutral with the underlying stock trading at $197.49. Additionally, implied volatility reflects both a skew in the current month (36%–56%), and a term structure that includes a 1% per expiration month increase.

Position	Strike ($)	Volat.	Days Rem.	Contr. Price ($)	Delta	Contr.	Pos. Value($)	Net
Stock @ $197.49								
Long call 7/08 exp	250	0.36	29	0.08	0.01	10	80	
Short call 9/08 exp	250	0.38	92	2.29	0.13	–10	–2,290	
Short put 9/08 exp	150	0.58	92	4.49	–0.13	–10	–4,490	
Long put7/08 exp	150	0.56	29	0.44	–0.03	10	440	–6,260

20. The following table outlines the value of each component with the stock closing July expiration at $210.

Position	Strike ($)	Volat.	Days Rem.	Contr. Price ($)	Delta	Contr.	Pos. Value($)	Net
Stock @ $210								
Long call 7/08 exp	250	0.01	1	0.00	0.00	10	0	
Short call 9/08 exp	250	0.39	64	2.81	0.17	−10	−2,810	
Short put 9/08 exp	150	0.59	64	1.70	−0.07	−10	−1,700	
Long put 7/08 exp	150	0.01	1	0.00	0.00	10	0	−4,510

Which of the three adjustments shown in the next table most closely resembles the original position with regard to risk? Has the trade generated a profit or a loss? Does the adjustment increase or decrease the potential for additional profit?

Position	Strike ($)	Volat.	Days Rem.	Contr. Price ($)	Delta	Contr.	Pos. Value($)	Net
Stock @ $210								
Long call 8/08 exp	250	0.38	29	0.55	0.06	10	550	
Short call 9/08 exp	250	0.39	64	2.81	0.17	−10	−2,810	
Short put 9/08 exp	170	0.55	64	4.12	−0.15	−10	−4,120	
Long put 8/08 exp	170	0.54	29	1.06	−0.07	10	1,060	−5,320
Long call 8/08 exp	240	0.40	29	1.50	0.13	10	1,500	
Short call 9/08 exp	240	0.41	64	4.93	0.25	−10	−4,930	
Short put 9/08 exp	180	0.53	64	6.07	−0.21	−10	−6,070	
Long put 8/08 exp	180	0.52	29	2.11	−0.13	10	2,110	−7,390
Long call 8/08 exp	260	0.36	29	0.16	0.02	10	160	
Short call 9/08 exp	260	0.37	64	1.44	0.10	−10	−1,440	
Short put 9/08 exp	160	0.57	64	2.70	−0.10	−10	−2,700	
Long put 8/08 exp	160	0.56	29	0.49	−0.04	10	490	−3,490

Answer: The first adjustment ($250 calls/$170 puts) creates a new position that is nearly delta-neutral and composed of options that are priced very close to those of the original trade. The change is accomplished by repurchasing the September $150 short puts for $1.70 and selling $170 strike price puts with the same expiration. The new long side has the same strike and a closer expiration. Similarly priced options imply similar risk, and maintaining delta-neutrality is important for multipart trades designed to profit from time decay.

At July expiration the trade is profitable because the position that was originally short $6,260 is now short only $4,510. Closing the position would generate a net profit of $1,750, or 28%. The adjustment increases the position size by $810 to $5,320.

21. The following table outlines the disposition of our adjusted trade at August expiration after an underlying stock price increase of $30. What is the total gain or loss to this point? What is the percent return?

Position	Strike ($)	Volat.	Days Rem.	Contr. Price ($)	Delta	Contr.	Pos. Value($)	Net
Stock @ $240								
Long call 8/08 exp	250	0.01	1	0.00	0.00	10	0	
Short call 9/08 exp	250	0.44	36	9.21	0.41	−10	−9,210	
Short put 9/08 exp	170	0.60	36	0.49	−0.03	−10	−490	
Long put 8/08 exp	170	0.01	1	0.00	0.00	10	0	−9,700

Answer: The most straightforward method for calculating the return is to consider the pre-adjustment and post-adjustment trades separately, and add the results together. As we previously calculated, the first trade gained $1,750. The second position, originally short $5,320, lost $4,380 to close August expiration short $9,700. Adding the results together reveals that the combined trade lost $2,630 ($1,750 − $4,380 = $2,630). Averaging the returns (+28%, −82%) yields a combined loss of −27%.

22. Shown in the next table are three of the many possible adjustments that can be made to the position at August expiration. Two are very aggressive and significantly increase the profit potential. One is less aggressive and more closely parallels the risk profile of the original trade.

Can you calculate the maximum potential profit and loss for each structure? Which is best hedged against a large change in the underlying stock price? How do the two aggressive trades compare for a 1 or 2 standard deviation price change of the underlying stock? If you were to choose one of the more aggressive trades, which would it be?

Position	Strike ($)	Volat.	Days Rem.	Contr. Price ($)	Delta	Contr.	Pos. Value($)	Net
Stock @ $240								
Long call 9/08 exp	300	0.34	36	0.20	0.02	30	600	
Short call 9/08 exp	280	0.38	36	1.47	0.11	−30	−4,410	
Short put 9/08 exp	200	0.54	36	2.62	−0.12	−30	−7,860	
Long put 9/08 exp	180	0.58	36	0.90	−0.05	30	2,700	−8,970
Long call 9/08 exp	290	0.36	36	0.60	0.05	10	600	
Short call 9/08 exp	260	0.42	36	5.59	0.30	−10	−5,590	
Short put 9/08 exp	220	0.50	36	6.44	−0.26	−10	−6,440	
Long put 9/08 exp	190	0.56	36	1.58	−0.08	10	1,580	−9,850
Long call 9/08 exp	290	0.360	36	0.60	0.05	10	600	
Short call 9/08 exp	270	0.400	36	3.06	0.19	−10	−3,060	
Short put 9/08 exp	210	0.520	36	4.19	−0.18	−10	−4,190	
Long put 9/08 exp	190	0.560	36	1.58	−0.08	10	1,580	−5,070

Answer: Maximum profit for each trade is realized with all options expiring out-of-the-money as shown in the following table for each position.

Trade	Max Profit Range	Return ($)
Trade #1	$200–$280	8,970
Trade #2	$220–$260	9,850
Trade #3	$210–$270	5,070

The maximum loss for each trade occurs with the stock closing at or beyond the long put or call strike price. Because in each case the loss is capped by a long option, the trade will ultimately be short an amount equal to the difference between the strike prices multiplied by the number of contracts sold. Adding back the amount received for the original short sale gives the net loss, as shown in the following table.

Trade	Initial Position Value ($)	Long-Short Strike Difference ($)	Contracts	Max Loss ($)	Net Loss ($)
Trade #1	–8,970	20	30	–60,000	–51,030
Trade #2	–9,850	30	10	–30,000	–20,150
Trade #3	–5,070	20	10	–20,000	–14,930

The third trade suffers the smallest loss when the underlying stock experiences a large price change. This characteristic results from wide spacing of the short strikes ($210–$270) and a small space between short and long strikes ($20). Although the first trade has short strikes that are spaced even further ($300–$280), the larger contract size becomes a destructive force if the stock moves beyond one of the short strikes.

Although the first two trades have similar maximum profit values ($8,970 and $9,850), the large contract size of the first creates significantly more risk. In each case the maximum loss point is reasonably close to the starting point in terms of standard deviations (calculated using the average implied volatility of the group—46%).

Timeframes in 1 year	$365 / 36 = 10.14$
Annualization factor	$\text{Sqrt}(10.14) = 3.18$
Volatility for 36 days	$0.46 / 3.18 = 0.145$
1 StdDev change	$0.145 \times \$240 = \$34.80$
	(stock @ \$274.80)
2 StdDev change	$\$34.80 \times 2 = \$69.60$ (stock @ \$309.60)

Using these values, we can predict that each trade will experience the maximum loss after a 2 StdDev change. The results are dramatically different for a 1 StdDev change—the first trade achieves its maximum profit of \$8,970 because all components expire worthless; the second trade loses \$4,950 with the \$260 short calls expiring \$14.80 in-the-money (\$14,800 ITM value − \$9,850 revenue from initial short position = \$4,950 net loss). The results for all three structures are summarized in the following table.

Trade	Initial Position Value ($)	1 StdDev Change ($)	2 StdDev Change ($)
Trade #1	8,970	8,970	−51,030
Trade #2	9,850	−4,950	−20,150
Trade #3	5,070	270	−14,930

Generally speaking, it is wiser to achieve large profits by altering the strike price spacing than by inflating the size of the trade. The inflated trade with wider short strike spacing performs dramatically better than either of the smaller, more closely spaced trades, if the stock moves only 1 standard deviation. It loses more than twice as much as trade #2, and more than three times as much as trade #3 if the stock moves a significant amount. Of the two aggressive trades, the second is the wiser choice because the contract size is not inflated.

Volatility Index (Problems #23–#27)

The Chicago Board Options Exchange Volatility Index (VIX) is a closely followed, widely studied metric of overall market volatility. It is not calculated using the Black-Scholes pricing model; instead, it uses a formula that averages the weighted prices of out-of-the-money puts and calls for S&P 500 stocks. The contribution of a single option to the index value is proportional to its price and inversely proportional to the strike. Calculations generally span the two nearest-term expiration months; however, in the final 8 days before expiration, the window is rolled forward to the second and third contract months to minimize pricing anomalies that occur just before expiration.

Building on historical information contained in its databases, the CBOE has made available calculated values of the index dating back to 1986. These data have become an important research tool for those attempting to understand the behavior of equity markets. They are also valuable to investors seeking a hedge against large market drawdowns. Trading activities are supported by investment products offered by the CBOE; on March 26, 2004, VIX futures began trading on the CBOE futures exchange, and VIX options were launched in February 2006. The CBOE website is an excellent primary source of information about the VIX and other volatility indexes.

Unlike equity options, VIX options are European-style expiration—that is, they can be exercised only on the final day. Additionally, instead of expiring on the same day as equity options, VIX options expire on the Wednesday that is 30 days prior to the third Friday of the month immediately following the expiration month. Furthermore, expiration occurs at the open, and the contracts are valued using opening quotations of S&P 500 index options.

23. Figure 5.1 displays an implied volatility skew for VIX call options with 70 days remaining before expiration and the index at 25. Strike prices are displayed on the x-axis and implied volatility on the y-axis.

Why does the skew appear to be the reverse of a typical stock option skew—that is, rising with increasing strike price?

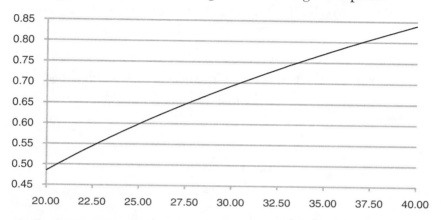

Figure 5.1 **Implied volatility for VIX call options with 70 days remaining and the index at 25. Strike price is displayed on the x-axis, implied volatility on the y-axis.**

Answer: Because falling markets are more unstable than rising markets, the VIX tends to rise sharply when the broad market declines. For example, in the 1987 crash the VIX climbed quickly from 35 to more than 150. The same dynamics that cause out-of-the-money equity puts to be priced with high implied volatility also increase the volatility of out-of-the-money calls on the VIX.

24. The VIX has a history of responding to sudden large drawdowns by spiking sharply for a brief period before returning to a lower, more stable value. For example, on January 22, 2008, a sudden market decline caused the VIX to rise from 24 to a high of 37. One week later, on February 1, the index closed once again at 24. European-style expiration, combined with the index's tendency to rise and fall sharply, often interferes with trade execution by causing bid-ask spreads to widen and reducing the liquidity of in-the-money options. Traders who are short calls are often reluctant to close their positions at inflated prices

because they know the options cannot be exercised and expect the index to fall. These dynamics can make it difficult for an investor to sell DITM calls for the expected value during a price spike.

Figure 5.2 displays closing values for the index during the 40 days that precede this example. This chart should be helpful as a risk-management tool when evaluating trade structures.

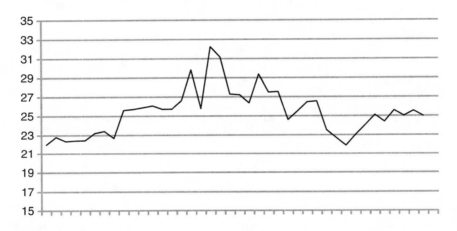

Figure 5.2   Closing values of the VIX for the 40 days that precede problem #24.

With these trading dynamics in mind, which of the structures given in the following table would you choose as a hedge against a market drawdown in a bearish environment with the VIX at 25? Which trade is the most bearish with regard to the overall market? Which is the least bearish?

Position	Strike ($)	Volat.	Days Rem.	Contr. Price ($)	Delta	Contr.	Position Value ($)	Net
1 Short put	20.00	0.55	70	0.50	−0.14	−100	−5,000	
Long call	40.00	0.84	70	0.56	0.14	100	5,600	600
2 Short put	22.50	0.62	70	1.48	−0.30	−100	−14,800	
Long call	30.00	0.69	70	1.40	0.33	100	14,000	−800
3 Short put	25.00	0.68	70	2.92	−0.44	−100	−29,200	
Long call	32.50	0.73	70	1.06	0.26	200	21,200	−8,000
4 Short put	22.50	0.74	42	1.31	−0.29	−100	−13,100	
Long call	30.00	0.75	42	0.97	0.28	100	9,700	−3,400
5 Short put	22.50	0.74	42	1.31	−0.29	−100	−13,100	
Long call	32.50	0.77	42	0.62	0.19	200	12,400	−700

Answer: A certain amount of opinion is always involved in choosing a trade and there is never a perfect choice. However, for several reasons, the final pair (position #5) probably represents the best compromise between risk and potential return under the circumstances described.

Several factors weigh heavily on the decision:

- Risk on the short put side of the trade
- Size of the expected price spike
- Option liquidity during a price spike
- Leverage (effectiveness of the hedge)
- Implied volatilities when the position is established
- Timeframe of the trade

Position #1 is composed of an overly conservative short put and a long call that is likely to present liquidity problems in the event of a modest market decline. Figure 5.2 reveals that the VIX has not closed below 22 for some time, so it is probably not necessary to select the 20 strike for the short sale. Conversely, the 40 strike is 25% above the highest recent peak of the index. This trade, therefore, anticipates a market decline that is significantly larger than the drawdown that caused the peak seen in the figure. With expiration 70 days away, it might prove difficult to close the long side of the trade for a fair price if the VIX spike is generally viewed as temporary. Compounding this problem is the cost of the long 40 strike calls (84% implied volatility). Executing this trade involves selling 55% implied volatility and purchasing 84%—the skew is biased against the trade.

Position #2 is an improvement over position #1. It is less conservative on the short side but very likely too conservative on the long side. Since we know that the index has recently risen above 30, it would be unreasonable to forego the leverage of a slightly higher strike. Position #2 suffers from the same time-frame issues as position #1.

Position #3 has a tremendous advantage over the previous two positions because it is structured with a 2:1 contract size leverage advantage—each short put at the 25 strike pays for 2 calls at the 32.5 strike. This trade is extremely bearish with regard to the overall market because it assumes that the VIX will remain above its current level and is initially net short $8,000. Unlike the other trades, this structure is designed to profit from time decay even if the market does not experience a significant drawdown. Unfortunately, a 2.5-point decline to recent index levels would generate a $17,000 (213%) loss. A 5-point decline would cost $42,000. As in the first two structures, time until expiration might cause a liquidity problem in a brief drawdown. This position, being the most bearish, is likely to be used as a profit engine in a long-term weak market rather than a portfolio hedge.

Position #4 has several advantages, including a conservative short strike and near-dated expiration. As in position #2, the long strike is below the recent peak and probably would not be selected if the goal is to hedge against a significant market decline. This trade is the least bearish because it generates a $3,400 profit even if the market rallies slightly and the VIX falls 2.5 points.

Position #5 is the best portfolio hedge candidate because it combines the leverage characteristics of trade #3 with the more conservative short strike and timeframe of position #4. A modest spike to recent levels would generate a significant profit, and the near-dated options would likely be more liquid than those of the first three positions. Like position #4, this trade can withstand a modest rally that lowers the VIX by 10%. Overall, it is likely the best choice for hedging in a bear market.

25. Problem #24 highlighted pricing problems that sometimes arise when the VIX spikes sharply in response to a short-lived event. As we saw, the market tends to respond with excessively wide bid-ask spreads and reduced liquidity for in-the-money call options.

    VIX option price distortions can also occur if the market's long- and short-term views are significantly different. These differences are almost always mirrored in the prices of VIX futures with different expirations.

    An excellent example occurred during April 2011 when the VIX fell to 16 despite a devastating earthquake and nuclear crisis in Japan, political unrest across the middle East, soaring gasoline prices in the U.S., a sovereign debt crisis in Europe, and a congressional battle over the U.S. debt ceiling. The markets factored in these destabilizing events by raising the price of far-dated VIX futures and out-of-the-money VIX call options. Long-term VIX put contracts that were deep in-the-money mirrored this long-term view by trading for less than their in-the-money amount. As mentioned previously, such distortions can exist because the European-style expiration prevents these options from being exercised.

The pricing anomaly was severe, with September 25 puts trading for only $4.80 even though they were 9 points in-the-money with 6 months remaining before expiration. If they had been exercisable, the market would have extinguished the distortion—investors would have purchased the underpriced puts and immediately exercised them for a $4.20 profit.

An investor who decided to capitalize on the disparity between the actual value of the VIX and the depressed value of the September 25 puts realized that there might be a relationship between the behavior of the broad market and changes in the VIX. While searching for a trade, he discovered that SPY, the exchange traded fund that tracks the S&P 500, tended to rise and fall about half as much as the VIX. His analysis noted that a recent sharp decline had taken SPY down 16 points and the VIX up 32, and that a more modest decline had lowered SPY 7 points while raising the VIX 14.

Can this relationship be used to structure a trade that captures the value contained in the underpriced September VIX 25 puts?

Answer: One way to exploit the pricing anomaly is to sell short 1,000 shares of SPY while purchasing 5 contracts of the underpriced September 25 VIX put. This trade is designed to lock in the statistical arbitrage using the assumption that SPY will fall about half as much as the VIX rises. If nothing happens, meaning that the market stays at its current level and the VIX remains at 16, the 25 put will ultimately rise to a fair value of $9. Conversely, if SPY falls and the VIX rises, the short SPY position will compensate for money lost on the long put (which is initially heavily discounted). Conversely, if the market continues to rally, the loss realized in the short SPY position will be more than compensated for by the correction in the fair value of the long VIX put.

26. What scenario would cause the trade in problem #25 to lose a large amount of money?

   Answer: The greatest danger is a sustained rally because the VIX cannot realistically fall below 10, which limits the level of compensation that can be realized against a loss on the short SPY side of the trade.

27. A second investor who looked at the data from problem #25 decided to pursue a different path by structuring a pure option trade. He noticed two additional distortions. The first involved near-term May options with just 1 month remaining before expiration. Surprisingly, the May 25 put was trading for $5.80—$1 more than the September 25 put. He also noticed that September 20 puts were trading for $1.80, which made them relatively more expensive than the deeper in-the-money September 25 puts trading for $4.80.

   Two possible trades using these options are summarized in the following table.

   VIX = 16   Date = 2011/04/15

Trade	Description	Price ($)	Net ($)	Days Remaining
1	10 long Sep 25 puts	4.80		159
	10 short May 25 puts	–5.80	–1,000	33
2	10 long Sep 25 puts	4.80		159
	10 short Sep 20 puts	–1.80	3,000	159

   - How will each trade perform if the VIX remains at 16 for another month?
   - Which trade will generate the most profit if an unusual event causes the VIX to rise sharply and close May expiration above 25?

- How much profit will trade #2 generate if the VIX closes September expiration at the current level of 16?
- How much profit will trade #2 generate if the VIX closes September expiration at 20?
- What is the greatest risk to each trade?

What can you conclude about the market outlook represented by each of the trades?

Answer: If the VIX remains at 16 until May expiration, the May $25 puts will rise to $9.00 while the longer-term September option prices remain nearly unchanged. Trade #1 is therefore likely to suffer a $3.20 price correction while trade #2 will remain nearly unchanged.

If the VIX experiences a short-term spike to close May expiration above 25, the entire May premium of $5.80 will be retained as profit. This profit will completely cover the cost of the long September 25 puts plus an additional $1.00. The minimum profit of the long-term trade will therefore be $1.00.

If the VIX closes September expiration at 16, the long 25 puts will be worth $9.00 while the short 20 puts will be worth $4.00. The overall position will be worth $5.00 ($5,000 per 10 contracts), which represents a $2.00 profit ($2,000 for 10 contracts).

If the VIX rises to 20 by September expiration, the short 20 puts will expire worthless and the long 25 puts will rise slightly from $4.80 to $5.00. Once again, the overall position will be worth $5.00, which represents a $2.00 profit.

Trade #1 loses substantial amounts of money if the VIX remains at 16 or falls further by May expiration. The break-even point for the short side of this trade is $19.20. At this level, the long side is unlikely to gain or lose substantial value. Below this level, the short side of the trade will gain value faster than the long side, creating progressively larger losses. Trade #1 would be placed by a bearish investor who expects the VIX to rise sharply in the immediate future.

Trade #2 has a break-even point at 22. If the VIX rises above this level by September expiration, the trade will lose money. The maximum loss for the trade is the amount of the initial debit – $3.00 ($3,000 for 10 contracts). This trade would be placed by a bullish investor who believes that the VIX will remain low and that short-term spikes will vanish by September.

Dividend Arbitrage (Problem #28)

28. An impending dividend payment can often be exploited to generate a profit. However, because option prices always comprehend the effect of a dividend payment the moment it is announced, structuring the proper trade can be complex.

   Assume that a $95 stock will pay a $0.50-per-share dividend when the market opens tomorrow. Which of the options in the following table can be used as part of a trade structure that will generate profit after the dividend is paid? How would that trade be structured?

	Position	Strike ($)	Stock ($)	Days Remaining	Contract Price ($)	Theta
1	Call	90	95	14	6.40	–0.10
2	Put	100	95	14	6.00	–0.10

Answer: The $100 put (option #2) can be used as part of a trade consisting of long stock and long puts. Success depends on the

put being underpriced—a signal that the market does not antic-
ipate a drop in the stock equal to the value of the dividend payment. The stock purchase completes the arbitrage by hedging
against a large price increase. We can assume that the put is
underpriced because it has 10¢ per day of time decay with 14
days remaining before expiration. Multiplying these two numbers yields a minimum of $1.40 of time value that must be
added to the amount that the option is in-the-money. We can,
therefore, state that the option should trade for approximately
$6.40, and that the market anticipates an underlying stock price
increase.

If we were to purchase 10 puts along with 1,000 shares of stock
and the underlying price fell to $94.50, the put price would rise
to $6.80 ($5.50 ITM value + $1.30 remaining time). Our trade
would, therefore, generate a loss of $0.50 on the stock side and
a gain of $0.80 on the option side. Since the stock-side loss is
offset by a $0.50 per share dividend, the trade would net $800.

Conversely, if the stock price increased to $95.50, the put price
could be expected to fall $0.20 to $5.80 ($4.50 ITM value +
$1.30 remaining time). The combined trade would experience a
net gain of $0.30. Adding the $0.50 per share dividend once
again yields a profit of $800.

Although these gains are small, they are characteristic of arbitrage trades that are designed to exploit very subtle pricing inefficiencies. In most cases such trades generate returns that are
too small to be exploited by public customers who pay commis-
sions and full bid-ask spreads.

The call version of this trade would involve purchasing underpriced calls and shorting stock. In this scenario, an underlying
price decrease would result in a gain from the short stock that
more than offsets the loss on the originally underpriced calls as

their value resets. A price increase would result in a disproportionate rise in the call price that would more than offset the short stock loss. However, the $90 call price displayed in the table appears not to be discounted, and it is likely that gains or losses on the call side would be offset by the short stock. The call trade also suffers because it does not include long stock and, therefore, does not receive a dividend payment.

Finally, arbitrage trades of this sort can also be structured to exploit overpriced options. The put version would consist of short puts/short stock, and the call version would be composed of short calls/long stock. Most price distortions that arise from a dividend payment involve either underpriced puts or overpriced calls. These anomalies make sense because the market often anticipates that the stock will fall less than the amount of the dividend. Many investors mistakenly believe that in-the-money call prices are guaranteed to fall and in-the-money put prices guaranteed to rise by an amount equal to the dividend. They typically point to a delta of 1.0 and assume that the option will move with the stock. As a result, they often sell calls or buy puts expecting an automatic profit. These scenarios represent a riskless arbitrage that cannot occur because nobody would ever take the other side of the trade. Surprisingly, calls can gain value when the stock falls if they are initially underpriced, and puts can lose value if they are overpriced. It is always better to identify a mispriced option and construct a fully hedged trade than to guess the direction.

Summary

This chapter was designed to explore the trade management dynamics of a representative group of multipart structures. These trades are important because they provide very high levels of flexibility and risk management. As we have seen, it is possible to construct conservative trades that are hedged against large underlying stock price changes but also deliver stable returns. Complex multipart trades are the domain of the conservative investor seeking stability. By combining pricing mathematics with market statistics, knowledgeable investors can take advantage of a myriad of choices regarding strike price and expiration date for each component of a trade. Some investors believe that such trades have too many "moving parts." This view is contradicted by the large number of successful option traders who continually generate predictable income streams using these strategies.

6

Advanced Ratio Trades

Ratio trades are incredibly versatile. They can be structured to capitalize on time decay, rising or falling volatility, or a directional bias that can range from strongly bullish to strongly bearish. Unlike most trade structures, ratios can be precisely tuned to fit almost any environment. These goals are often accomplished with structures that span multiple expirations or several strikes. Not surprisingly, virtually every option trading concept comes into play when structuring and managing these trades. But with complexity comes opportunity, and ratios, more than any other trade structure, allow investors to precisely reflect their view of the market using options. It is possible, for example, to create a ratio structure for a $100 stock that profits between $100 and $110, loses money above $110, but completely protects the investor if the price falls. It would be impossible to achieve these dynamics with any other trade structure.

This section builds on the problems presented at the end of Chapter 4, "Complex Trades—Part 1," with more complex ratios that involve anywhere from 2 to 6 strike prices. These trades can easily become the basis of a complete investment strategy that delivers strong returns in almost any market, ranging from extremely bearish to extremely bullish. In that regard, complexity becomes an option trader's friend. Skilled investors who understand the underlying dynamics will find that they can use these structures to exploit subtle inefficiencies in both the implied volatility skew and the term structure. These concepts also form the foundation for a later section that focuses on expiration trading.

1. The following table contains 4 different ratio trades with 31 days remaining before expiration. Trade #1 is a forward ratio that is long 10 calls at a low strike and short 20 calls at a higher strike. Trade #2 is the reverse-ratio version of the first trade—short 10 calls at the low strike and long 20 at the higher strike. Trades #3 and #4 are the put versions. The forward put ratio, trade #3, is long 10 contracts at the high strike and short 20 at the lower strike. Finally, trade #4 represents the reverse put ratio—short 10 contracts at the high strike and long 20 at the low strike.

Stock = $161.50   Days Remaining = 31   Volatility = 19%

Trade	Position	Strike	Price	Delta	Contr.	Pos. Value	Net
1	long call	165	2.17	0.37	10	2170	
	short call	170	0.90	0.19	−20	−1800	370
2	short call	165	2.17	0.37	−10	−2170	
	long call	170	0.90	0.19	20	1800	−370
3	short put	160	2.79	−0.42	−20	−5580	
	long put	170	9.26	−0.81	10	9260	3680
4	long put	160	2.79	−0.42	20	5580	
	short put	170	9.26	−0.81	−10	−9260	−3680

How would you rank the trades with regard to performance if the stock rises $10 by expiration? How do the rankings change if the stock rises $20 by expiration? Which trade would you consider to be the most bullish? Least bullish? Most bearish? Which trade performs best under both scenarios?

Answer: For modest price increases, the best-performing trade is often a reverse put ratio initiated for a credit. In this example, a 1-month $10 price increase is slightly larger than 1 standard deviation ($161.50 × 0.19 / Sqrt(12) = $8.86). This price change places the position just above the higher strike near the maximum profit point of the forward call ratio (trade #1). It also maximizes the profit for the reverse put ratio (trade #4) by returning 100% of the initial credit with both strikes expiring out-of-the-money. The forward put ratio exhibits the opposite behavior because it was initiated for a debit and the full amount is lost when the stock closes above both strikes (trade #3). The reverse call ratio (trade #2) loses a large amount of money for similar reasons—the long strike is worthless at expiration. Expiration results for the $10 price increase are displayed in the following table, with performance rankings in the final column (1 is the highest, 4 the lowest).

Stock = $171.50   Days Remaining = 0   Volatility = 19%

Trade	Position	Strike	Price	Contr.	Pos. Value	Net	P&L	Perf.
1	long call	165	6.50	10	6500			
	short call	170	1.50	−20	−3000	3500	3130	2
2	short call	165	6.50	−10	−6500			
	long call	170	1.50	20	3000	−3500	−3130	3
3	short put	160	0.00	−20	0			
	long put	170	0.00	10	0	0	−3680	4
4	long put	160	0.00	20	0			
	short put	170	0.00	−10	0	0	3680	1

Results for a large price increase are dramatically different. The reverse call ratio (trade #2) that performed poorly when the stock landed between the strikes delivers a substantial profit when the stock rises far above the high strike. Profit for this trade will continue to rise sharply as the stock price increases because the long side of the trade grows twice as fast as the short side. Conversely, the forward call ratio (trade #1) which delivered a substantial profit when the stock climbed a modest amount is the worst performer in the large-price-increase scenario. As before, the reverse put ratio (trade #4) performs well by delivering 100% of the initial credit, and the forward put ratio (trade #3) loses the initial cost of the trade with both strikes expiring out-of-the-money. Results for the large-price-increase scenario are displayed next.

Stock = $181.50   Days Remaining = 0   Volatility = 19%

Trade	Position	Strike	Price	Contr.	Pos. Value	Net	P&L	Perf.
1	long call	165	16.50	10	16500			
	short call	170	11.50	–20	–23000	–6500	–6870	4
2	short call	165	16.50	–10	–16500			
	long call	170	11.50	20	23000	6500	6870	1
3	short put	160	0.00	–20	0			
	long put	170	0.00	10	0	0	–3680	3
4	long put	160	0.00	20	0			
	short put	170	0.00	–10	0	0	3680	2

The reverse put ratio (trade #4) delivers the most consistent performance and is the wisest choice for a conservative investor who expects a price increase. It will deliver the same profit whether the stock rises, stays at the starting price, or falls $1.50. The trade-off is apparent in the risk involved in a modest price decrease where this trade is the worst performer of the group. However, because large losses of this type can only be realized by holding the trade until expiration, the risk is relatively limited. Trade #4 is, therefore, a surprisingly good choice for a conservative bullish investor. It is also protected against a large price decrease where it will deliver the most profit of any trade in the group.

Most option traders would consider the reverse call ratio (trade #2) to be the most bullish because it has the greatest potential to deliver profit from a large price increase and performs poorly if the price rises a small amount. It should, therefore, only be used in situations where a substantial price increase is anticipated. Many traders would consider the forward put ratio (trade #3) to be the least bullish because it is designed to deliver a large profit from a sharp price decrease. If, however, we draw a distinction between "least bullish" and "most bearish," then the forward call ratio (trade #1) must be labeled "least bullish" because it loses the most money of any trade in the large-price-increase scenario. If we are seeking this distinction, it would be reasonable to label the forward put ratio (trade #3) as "most bearish" and the forward call ratio (trade #1) as "least bullish." The most-least question was actually designed to highlight the fallacy of replacing detailed analysis with simple labels.

2. The following table contains two trades. One is delta-neutral and the other is not. Which trade represents a more bearish view?

Stock = $155   Days Remaining = 31   Volatility = 35%

Trade	Position	Strike	Price	Delta	Contr.	Pos. Value	Net
1	long call	160	4.26	0.40	10	4260	
	short call	170	1.67	0.20	–20	–3340	920
2	long call	160	4.26	0.40	10	4260	
	short call	165	2.73	0.29	–20	–5460	–1200

Answer: Trade #2 is more bearish for two key reasons:

1. Trade #2 is initiated for a credit which is retained as profit if the stock remains below the lower strike. Conversely, trade #1 is initiated for a debit which is lost if the stock declines or remains below the lower strike. With the stock closing expiration below $160, the trades differ by $2,120.

2. Trade #2 reaches its upper break-even point at $171.20 (including the initial credit). The upper break-even point of trade #1 is substantially higher ($179.08). Since both trades begin losing money above their break-even points, trade #1 is substantially safer if the stock rises.

    Trade #2 is also delta short—0.40 for the long side and 0.58 for the short side (0.29 × 2). In general terms, trade #2 can serve as a partial hedge against a long position because it generates profit if the stock declines. Trade #1 cannot be used to hedge a long trade because it loses money if the stock declines.

3. A piece of very bullish news surfaces about the market, and the bearish investor holding trade #2 in the previous problem decides to respond by modifying his original position. The new position is built on the original and contains a second ratio using the $170 and $175 strikes. Its structure—10 long $160 calls / 20 short $165 calls / 10 long $170 calls / 20 short $175 calls—is outlined in the table that follows.

Stock = $155   Days Remaining = 31   Volatility = 35%

Position	Strike	Price	Delta	Contr.	Pos. Value	Net
long call	160	4.26	0.40	10	4260	
short call	165	1.67	0.29	−20	−5460	
long call	170	4.26	0.20	10	1670	
short call	175	2.73	0.13	−20	−1960	−1490

How does the new structure affect the bearishness of the original trade? Does it offer additional protection against a sharp rally? At what expiration price does the new trade begin losing money? How well does the modified trade perform if the stock price falls?

Answer: The new trade raises the expiration break-even point to $176.49 (including the $1,490 initial credit). Stated differently, the original $160/$165 ratio lost money if the stock climbed more than $16.20, but the modified version can tolerate a price increase as large as $21.49—a 33% improvement. The new trade is, therefore, considerably less bearish. However, because the credit is slightly larger ($1,490 versus $1,200), the new trade also delivers a better return if the stock declines.

4. The following table contains two bullish trade structures for a stock trading at $155. The first is a 1:2 call ratio with $10 strike spacing; the second is a 1:3 call ratio with $20 spacing. Both trades are approximately delta-neutral and both have the same expiration. The first trade is initiated for a $920 debit and the second for a $4,090 debit.

How do the positions compare as the stock price rises? How do they compare if the stock falls? At what expiration price are both trades worth $0.00? What are the lower break-even points of the two trades? What does each trade structure suggest about implied volatility? Which is more conservative?

Stock = $155   Days Remaining = 31   Volatility = 35%

Trade	Position	Strike	Price	Delta	Contr.	Pos. Value	Net
1	long call	160	4.26	0.40	10	4260	
	short call	170	1.67	0.20	−20	−3340	920
2	long call	150	9.10	0.65	10	9100	
	short call	170	1.67	0.20	−30	−5010	4090

Answer: Trade #2 generates much more profit for modest price increases. However, as the price rises above $180 where both trades have a net value of $0.00, the destructive effect of the large short ratio causes trade #2 to lose money quickly. Trade #2, because it is initiated for a large debit, also loses more money if the underlying price declines sharply. However, it is important to realize that the lower break-even point of trade #2 is $154.09, while trade #1 loses money below $160.92.

Trade #2 can be considered a large bet that the stock price will remain stable or rise a modest amount. It assumes that implied volatility fairly compensates option sellers for risk without penalizing buyers. Conversely, trade #1 is more effectively hedged against a very large price increase and suffers less if the price declines sharply. It therefore represents a view that volatility is underpriced. A bullish investor would structure trade #1 to bet on an upward move with the expectation that the stock might rise or fall faster than option pricing theory suggests. Trade #1 is more conservative than trade #2. In this regard it is important to remember that a 31-day 1 standard deviation price change for this stock would be equal to $16. Trade #2 loses substantial amounts of money if the stock rises 1.6 standard deviations or falls just 0.3 standard deviations.

The following table reveals both the final value of each trade at various prices and the final profit or loss taking into account the initial cost of the trade.

Expir. Price	Trade 1 Expir. Value	Trade 2 Expir. Value	Trade 1 P&L	Trade 2 P&L
150	0	0	–920	–4,090
155	0	5,000	–920	–910
160	0	10,000	–920	5,910
165	5,000	15,000	4,080	10,910
170	10,000	20,000	9,080	15,910
175	5,000	10,000	4,080	5,910
180	0	0	–920	–4,090
185	–5,000	–10,000	–5,920	–14,090

The relative advantages of trade #2 in modest price increase environments is apparent across the $15 strike range from $160 to $175. The more conservative trade generates much less profit at the $170 peak but, as mentioned previously, is much more resistant to losses at low and high strikes. At $185 the 1:3 ratio loses more than twice as much money as the 1:2 trade.

Most option traders prefer to view these dynamics using the type of chart displayed in Figure 6.1, which traces profit and loss values across various strikes for both positions. Trade #1 is depicted by the solid line and trade #2 by the dashed line.

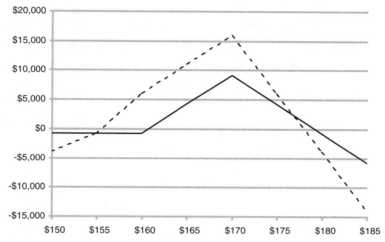

Figure 6.1   Expiration profit and loss values for the trades described in problem #4. The solid line traces the value of trade #1 (1:2 ratio). The dashed line traces the value of trade #2 (1:3 ratio). Strike prices are shown on the x-axis; profit on the y-axis.

Both trades are asymmetric in the sense that they cannot tolerate any decline in the stock price but generate their maximum profit if the stock rises $15 to $170. The maximum loss of trade #1 will be fully realized if the stock does not rise above $160 by expiration. The $910 cap on this loss is reflected in the flat horizontal line near the left side of the chart. Conversely, the low tolerance for large price increases that characterizes trade #2 is apparent in the steep downward slope of the dashed line near the right side of the chart.

5. The following table outlines two structures spanning the same range of strikes. Trade #1 is a 3-part ratio trade consisting of 10 long $150 calls / 30 short $175 calls / 20 long $200 calls. Trade #2 is a more familiar 2-part structure consisting of 10 long $150 calls / 20 short $175 calls.

How do these trades compare with regard to maximum possible gain and loss? What are the upper and lower break-even points for each trade at expiration?

Stock = $158.00   Days Remaining = 100   Volatility = 35%

Trade	Position	Strike	Price	Delta	Contr.	Pos. Value	Net
1	long call	150	15.92	0.65	10	15920	
	short call	175	5.61	0.33	−30	−16830	
	long call	200	1.57	0.12	20	3140	2230
2	long call	150	15.92	0.65	10	15920	
	short call	175	5.61	0.33	−20	−11220	4700

Answer: Trade #1 caps the potential loss as the distance between the strikes ($25) plus the amount paid for the original trade ($2.23). The maximum loss, therefore, is $27.23, or $27,230 for the position outlined in the table. At expiration, both sides of the trade have equal value at a price point halfway between the second pair of strikes ($187.50). At this point the loss would be equal to the debit of the initial position ($2,230). The loss continues to grow beyond this point, reaching its maximum capped value at the third strike ($200).

Trade #2 does not have a maximum loss cap. At expiration, both sides have equal value if the stock is trading at the $200 strike. At this point the net loss would be equal to the debit of the original trade ($4,700). The following two tables reveal expiration P&L detail for each trade at the two key prices just mentioned—$187.50 and $200.00.

Stock = $187.50   Days Remaining = 0

Trade	Position	Strike	Price	Contr.	Pos. Value	Net	P&L
1	long call	150	37.50	10	37,500		
	short call	175	12.50	−30	−37,500		
	long call	200	0.00	20	0	0	−2,230
2	long call	150	37.50	10	37,500		
	short call	175	12.50	−20	−25,000	12,500	7,800

Stock = $200.00   Days Remaining = 0

Trade	Position	Strike	Price	Contr.	Pos. Value	Net	P&L
1	long call	150	50.00	10	50,000		
	short call	175	25.00	−30	−75,000		
	long call	200	0.00	20	0	−25,000	−27,230
2	long call	150	50.00	10	50,000		
	short call	175	25.00	−20	−50,000	0	−4,700

The lower break-even point for each trade is equal to the lower strike ($150) plus the amount paid for the trade. Because trade #1 had an initial debit of $2,230, the stock must end expiration above $152.23 for the 10 long $150 calls to cover the initial cost. Trade #2 can generate the $4,700 initially paid only if the stock ends expiration above $154.70. Both trades lose their entire initial debit below $150.

The capping effect of the 1:3:2 position structure is evident in the following table, which displays values for each trade at a very high expiration price of $250.

Stock = $250.00   Days Remaining = 0

Trade	Position	Strike	Price	Contr.	Pos. Value	Net	P&L
1	long call	150	100.00	10	100,000		
	short call	175	75.00	–30	–225,000		
	long call	200	50.00	20	100,000	–25,000	–27,230
2	long call	150	100.00	10	100,000		
	short call	175	75.00	–20	–150,000	–50,000	–54,700

Trade #1 losses are limited by the space between the second set of strikes. As a result, the 1:3:2 structure loses the same amount at $250 as it does at $200. The simpler 1:2 ratio, however, loses significantly more money because the structure is not capped. For this reason trade #1 can be placed in an individual retirement account (IRA) where positions with unlimited loss potential are generally banned. The amount of collateral required is directly related to the space between the second two strikes.

6. In anticipation of a steep drawdown, an investor structured a put back spread consisting of 10 short $155 puts and 20 long $130 puts for a stock trading at $158. The very next day the stock fell $20 and the trade lost a surprising amount of money. Both parts of the trade before and after the price decline along with implied volatilities for puts at each strike and associated option deltas are displayed in the following tables. The initial position cost $530. After the underlying price decline, it was short $4,660—a loss of $5,190 which is equal to nearly 10 × the original cost.

Stock = \$158.00   Days Remaining = 100

Position	Strike	Price	Impl. Volat.	Delta	Contr.	Pos. Value	Net
	160	15.68	0.45	−0.47			
short put	155	13.33	0.46	−0.42	−10	−13,330	
	150	11.53	0.48	−0.37			
	145	9.94	0.50	−0.32			
	140	8.82	0.53	−0.28			
	135	7.82	0.56	−0.24			
long put	130	6.93	0.59	−0.21	20	13,860	
	125	6.13	0.62	−0.19			530

Stock = \$138.00   Days Remaining = 99

Position	Strike	Price	Impl. Volat.	Delta	Contr.	Pos. Value	Net	P&L
	160	26.73	0.43	−0.70				
short put	155	23.23	0.44	−0.65	−10	−23,230		
	150	19.71	0.44	−0.59				
	145	16.75	0.45	−0.53				
	140	13.77	0.45	−0.47				
	135	11.38	0.46	−0.41				
long put	130	9.55	0.48	−0.35	20	19,100		
	125	7.95	0.50	−0.30			−4,130	−4,660

Can you explain the loss based on the implied volatility skew displayed in the two tables? How are the losses reflected in the starting and ending deltas of the two sides?

Answer: The sharp price decline relocated the long side of the trade (\$130 put) to the flat part of the implied volatility skew. When the trade was initiated, it was long 59% implied volatility and short 46%. Stated differently, we purchased 59% volatility and sold 46%. After the sharp correction, it was long 48% and short 44%. The long side of our trade lost 11% while the short side lost just 2%. The implied volatility collapse overwhelmed the impact of the underlying price movement.

Relocation of the skew is reflected in the surprisingly small change to the position delta. When the trade was initiated, it was exactly delta-neutral (long -0.21×2 / short -0.42). The relative value remained nearly constant despite a $20 (4.6 standard deviation) drop in the stock price. After the collapse the deltas were long -0.35×2 / short -0.65, a net change of just $-.05$.

The implied volatility collapse along with the relevant part of the skew is depicted in Figure 6.2.

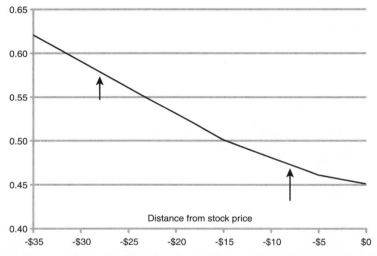

Figure 6.2   Implied volatility skew for problem #6. Arrows mark the relative location of the long $130 put before and after the collapse. Distance to the trading price of the stock is measured on the x-axis. Implied volatility is displayed on the y-axis.

7. Suppose we replaced the trade in problem #6 with a 1:3:2 ratio consisting of 10 short $155 puts / 30 long $145 puts / 20 short $135 puts. How would the performance of this trade have compared to the original described in problem #6? Is the performance of the new trade related to its initial delta?

Answer: The new trade would have an initial cost of $850, which is $320 more than the trade described in problem #6. Initial prices before the large price decline are displayed next.

Position	Option Price	Net Cost
10 short $155 puts	13.33	−13,330
30 long $145 puts	9.94	29,820
20 short $135 puts	7.82	−15,640
Position net cost		850

In sharp contrast to the 1:2 ratio that lost a substantial amount of money, the new trade generates a large profit ($4,260). Exact prices can be obtained from the second table in problem #6.

Position	Option Price	Net Cost
10 short $155 puts	23.23	−23,230
30 long $145 puts	16.75	50,250
20 short $135 puts	11.38	−22,760
Position net cost		4,260

The new trade was very slightly short when it was initiated with a net delta of −0.06. After the large price decline, the 1:3:2 ratio would have had a net delta of −0.12, which represents a very minor increase. Dramatic differences between the outcomes of the two trades, therefore, cannot be rationalized using position deltas (recall that the net delta of the 1:2 ratio was initially zero and barely climbed to −0.05 after the price decline). These dynamics are important because they highlight the difficulty in using simple measures to predict the performance of a trade placed against a steep implied volatility skew.

8. It is reasonable to assume that an investor who structures a trade using options with 100 days remaining until expiration does not expect that it will be closed immediately. Time decay is, therefore, an important consideration.

How would the two trades of problems #6 and #7 compare with regard to daily time decay? What does the difference mean with regard to risk?

Answer: The combination of a relatively long period of time remaining before expiration and a steep implied volatility skew tends to equalize time decay across the out-of-the-money strikes used in problems #6 and #7. If there were only a few days remaining before expiration, options with strikes close to the trading price of the stock would have significant value and exhibit rapid time decay while options at distant strikes would have very little or no value and, consequently, suffer very little time decay. For example, with the stock trading at $158 and 10 days remaining before expiration, a $155 put priced with 46% implied volatility would be worth $3.38 and have a daily theta equal to 23¢. Under the same scenario, a $140 put would be worth just $0.27 and have a theta equal to 6¢.

The dynamics are considerably different for options that have a significant amount of time remaining before expiration. With 100 days remaining, a $155 put at 46% implied volatility would be worth $13.33 and have a theta of 7.7¢; the $140 put would be worth $6.90 and have a theta of 6.3¢. A steep implied volatility skew would increase both the value and the daily time decay of the far strike. These dynamics are displayed in the following table, which lists the price and theta for the four strikes used in problems #6 and #7 with and without an implied volatility skew with 10 and 100 days remaining before expiration. The upper portion of the table (above the gray bar) displays data with 100 days remaining and the lower portion is set at 10 days.

Put Strike	Days Remaining	Impl. Volat.	Option Price	Theta
155	100	0.46	13.33	−0.077
145	100	0.46	8.77	−0.071
135	100	0.46	5.30	−0.053
130	100	0.46	3.97	−0.047
155	100	0.46	13.33	−0.077
145	100	0.50	9.94	−0.070
135	100	0.56	7.82	−0.071
130	100	0.59	6.93	−0.069
155	10	0.46	3.38	−0.229
145	10	0.46	0.74	−0.117
135	10	0.46	0.08	−0.026
130	10	0.46	0.02	−0.009
155	10	0.46	3.38	−0.229
145	10	0.50	0.96	−0.140
135	10	0.56	0.25	−0.063
130	10	0.59	0.12	−0.036

The data reveal that theta varies considerably less across the range with 100 days remaining than it does when expiration is near. A steeper volatility skew further equalizes values across the range. Consequently, the strikes used in the 1:3:2 ratio example of problem #7 have nearly identical theta values. Calculated against the ratio, the position is short $0.219 and long $0.210 of daily time decay—the net ($0.009) very slightly favors the long side of the trade.

By comparison, the 1:2 ratio was initially long $0.138 and short $0.077 of time decay. The net value ($0.061) is the amount that the trade will lose each day if the underlying stock remains at the starting price. Stated differently, the 1:2 ratio initially suffers more than 6¢ of daily time decay while the 1:3:2 ratio has none.

Time decay risk is a significant factor for portfolios containing option positions that exhibit time decay. Long straddles and reverse ratios are notable examples. However, as problems #6–#8 reveal, it is possible to restructure a long-term reverse-ratio trade so that it becomes more sensitive to underlying moves of the stock and less sensitive to the effects of time decay. The additional cost is negligible and the only downside is a cap on the maximum profit that can be realized.

9. The following table contains information that will be used to structure a complex two-sided ratio trade designed to capitalize on a modest move of the underlying stock in either direction.

Stock = $157.50   Days Remaining = 30

Option	Strike	Price	Impl. Volat.	Delta
put	130	0.78	0.49	−0.07
put	135	1.39	0.49	−0.12
put	140	2.20	0.48	−0.18
put	145	3.32	0.47	−0.25
put	150	4.83	0.46	−0.33
put	155	6.79	0.45	−0.42
put	160	9.40	0.45	−0.52
call	160	7.03	0.45	0.48
call	165	4.95	0.44	0.38
call	170	3.48	0.44	0.30
call	175	2.26	0.43	0.22
call	180	1.49	0.43	0.16
call	185	0.88	0.42	0.10

This information was used to construct the following trade consisting of put and call 1:3:2 ratios.

Stock = $157.50   Days Remaining = 30

Position	Strike	Price	Impl. Volat.	Contr.	Pos. Value	Net
20 long puts	135	1.39	0.49	20	2,780	
30 short puts	145	3.32	0.47	−30	−9,960	
10 long puts	155	6.79	0.45	10	6,790	−390
10 long calls	160	7.03	0.45	10	7,030	
30 short calls	170	3.48	0.44	−30	−10,440	
20 long calls	180	1.49	0.43	20	2,980	−430
					total	−820

What is the maximum profit? What is the maximum loss? If the underlying stock falls 1 standard deviation, would this trade outperform a simple long strangle consisting of 10 long $155 puts and 10 long $160 calls? How does the ratio trade perform at the break-even point of the strangle?

Would restructuring the trade by widening the space between the nearest strikes improve the overall dynamics? (The new trade would use the following strikes: $130/$140/$150–$165/$175/$185.)

Answer: The maximum profit occurs with the stock ending expiration at one of the middle strikes ($145 or $170). At either of these points, the profit would be equal to $10,000 plus the initial credit of $820. For example, if the stock falls to $145, all options will expire worthless with the exception of the long $155 puts, which will be worth $10. Those conditions would generate a profit of $10,820.

The maximum loss occurs beyond the third strike in either direction—that is, below $135 or above $180. Maximum loss for this trade structure is $10,000 minus the initial $820 credit.

We can calculate the value of a 30-day 1 standard deviation price change using the initial underlying price and implied volatility of the near strikes: $157.50 × 0.45 / Sqrt(365/30) = $20.32. A 1 StdDev decline would, therefore, take the stock to $137.18.

At $137.18, the ratio trade would lose $5.64 minus the initial $0.82 credit—a total loss of $4,820. The long $155 puts would be worth $17.82 and the short $145 puts would be worth $7.82. Referring to the ratio of the trade, the position value would be $17.82 − $7.82 × 3 = ($5.64). Conversely, the $155/$160 strangle would be worth $17.82. Subtracting the initial position cost ($7.03 + $6.79) yields a net profit of $4.00 or $4,000 for the actual 10-contract trade.

The break-even points for the strangle are $173.82 and $141.18. The ratio trade is profitable at each of these levels. For example, at $173.82 the long side of the call ratio is worth $2.36 ($13.82 for the long $160 call minus $3.82 × 3 for the short $170 call). The ratio, therefore, will generate a profit of $3,180 ($2,360 plus the initial $820 credit).

A wider trade structure provides significant improvement by generating a profit across a larger range of underlying expiration prices. The original trade lost $4,820 if the stock fell 1 standard deviation to $137.18; the new trade would generate a $4,640 profit under the same set of conditions. The long $150 put would be worth $12.82 and the short $140 put would be worth $2.82 × 3. All other options would expire worthless. The final profit would be equal to $12,820 minus the value of the short side ($8,460) plus the initial position credit of $280. Initial and final trade parameters are displayed in the following two tables.

Stock = $157.50   Days Remaining = 30

Position	Strike	Price	Impl. Volat.	Contr.	Pos. Value	Net
20 long puts	130	0.78	0.49	20	1,560	
30 short puts	140	2.20	0.48	−30	−6,600	
10 long puts	150	4.83	0.46	10	4,830	−210
10 long calls	165	4.95	0.44	10	4,950	
30 short calls	175	2.26	0.43	−30	−6,780	
20 long calls	185	0.88	0.42	20	1,760	−70
					total	−280

Stock = $137.18   Days Remaining = 0

Position	Strike	Price	Impl. Volat.	Contr.	Pos. Value	Net
20 long puts	130	0.00	0.49	20	0	
30 short puts	140	2.82	0.48	−30	−8,460	
10 long puts	150	12.82	0.46	10	12,820	4,360
10 long calls	165	0.00	0.44	10	0	
30 short calls	175	0.00	0.43	−30	0	
20 long calls	185	0.00	0.42	20	0	0
					total	4,360
					credit	280
					final	4,640

10. The following table contains information that will be used to evaluate a complex ratio trade spanning two different expirations.

Stock = $157.00   Implied Vol. = 30%

Call Strike	Days Rem.	Price	Delta	Gamma
150	20	8.74	0.76	0.028
155	20	5.49	0.59	0.035
160	20	3.13	0.41	0.035
165	20	1.61	0.25	0.029
170	20	0.75	0.14	0.020
175	20	0.31	0.07	0.012
180	20	0.12	0.03	0.006
150	48	10.86	0.69	0.021
155	48	7.92	0.57	0.023
160	48	5.57	0.46	0.023
165	48	3.77	0.35	0.022
170	48	2.45	0.25	0.019
175	48	1.54	0.18	0.015
180	48	0.93	0.12	0.012

An investor structures a position using near-term options (20 days remaining before expiration) consisting of 10 long $150 calls and 30 short $165 calls. Realizing that the trade will lose a large amount of money if the stock rallies sharply, he decides to hedge with a second ratio trade in the following month. Both trades are displayed in the following table.

Stock = \$157.00   Implied Vol. = 30%

Position	Strike	Days Rem.	Price	Contr.	Pos. Value	Net
10 long calls	150	20	8.74	10	8,740	
30 short calls	165	20	1.61	−30	−4,830	3,910
10 short calls	155	48	7.92	−10	−7,920	
30 long calls	175	48	1.54	30	4,620	−3,300
					total	610

The first trade is designed to profit from a relatively modest price increase over the remaining 20 days. The hedge generates a large return if the stock rallies sharply or falls.

Is the hedge effective? Can you explain the behavior of the combined trade in terms of position gamma? What is the predominant reason for the difference in gamma between the trade and the hedge? Why is delta alone a poor measure of risk?

Answer: The hedge is ineffective and relatively small price increases will lose money. Relative position gamma reveals the problem. Multiplying the gamma of each option by the number of contracts allows us to make a direct comparison.

Stock = \$157.00   Implied Vol. = 30%

Call Strike	Days Rem.	Price	Ratio	Gamma	Position Gamma	Net Gamma
150	20	8.74	1	0.028	0.028	
165	20	1.61	−3	0.029	−0.087	−0.059
155	48	7.92	−1	0.023	−0.023	
175	48	1.54	3	0.015	0.045	0.022

The $150/$165 forward ratio has a net gamma of –0.059 while the offsetting hedge has a gamma of only 0.022. Since gamma determines the rate of change of delta, the overall position will continue to become more delta negative as the price rises— exactly opposite the desired effect of the hedge. Stated differently, the initial trade is short large amounts of gamma.

Delta by itself is a poor measure because the initial trade is almost exactly delta-neutral. Details are displayed in the following table.

Stock = $157.00   Implied Vol. = 30%

Call Strike	Days Rem.	Price	Ratio	Delta	Position Delta	Net Delta
150	20	8.74	1	0.76	0.76	
165	20	1.61	–3	0.25	–0.75	0.01
155	48	7.92	–1	0.57	–0.57	
175	48	1.54	3	0.18	0.54	–0.03

The relative difference in gamma is a result of the trade structure that attempts to hedge near-term options with a later expiration. These differences become more extreme as expiration approaches. For example, an at-the-money option that expires in 1 day will often have a gamma that is nearly 5× higher than the same option with 1 month remaining before expiration. On expiration day the distortion will rise to more than 50×. The effect will rapidly imbalance a delta-neutral position spanning different expirations if the stock moves beyond the strike price (into-the-money).

The complete failure of the hedge is evident in the following table, which depicts both sides of the trade after a 20-day 2 standard deviation rise of the underlying stock.

Stock = $180.00   Implied Vol. = 30%

Position	Strike	Days Rem.	Price	Contr.	Pos. Value	Net
10 long calls	150	0	30.00	10	30,000	
30 short calls	165	0	15.00	−30	−45,000	−15,000
10 short calls	155	28	25.31	−10	−25,310	
30 long calls	175	28	8.80	30	26,400	1,090
					total	−13,910
					initial cost	610
					final	−14,520

Near-term option prices are equal to their in-the-money values. The same is true for the longer-term deep in-the-money $155 calls. Significant time value is only present in the $175 calls which are $5 in-the-money with 28 days remaining before expiration. This value can be derived using an options calculator. The hedge gains a relatively modest $4,390 while the near-term trade loses $18,910, yielding a total loss of $14,520.

11. Problem #10 illustrates the failure of a poorly structured hedge. Following are two alternative trade structures with more effective hedges. The first structure contains a hedge consisting of 10 short $150 calls/30 long $165 calls; the second is 10 short $150 calls/100 long $180 calls. By referring to the delta and gamma values listed in the first table of problem #10, can you determine which structure provides the most protection against a near-term sharp upward move of the stock? Does the wide strike spacing of structure #2 create additional risk? How would you quantify the risk in terms of the daily cost of owning the trade?

Structure #1   Stock = $157.00   Implied Vol. = 30%

Position	Strike	Days Rem.	Price	Contr.	Theta	Pos. Value	Net
10 long calls	150	20	8.74	10	−0.095	8,740	
30 short calls	165	20	1.61	−30	−0.086	−4,830	3,910
10 short calls	150	48	10.86	−10	−0.064	−10,860	
30 long calls	165	48	3.77	30	−0.071	11,310	450
						total	4,360

Structure #2   Stock = $157.00   Implied Vol. = 30%

Position	Strike	Days Rem.	Price	Contr.	Theta	Pos. Value	Net
10 long calls	150	20	8.74	10	−0.095	8,740	
30 short calls	165	20	1.61	−30	−0.086	−4,830	3,910
10 short calls	150	48	10.86	−10	−0.064	−10,860	
100 long calls	180	48	0.93	100	−0.031	9,300	−1560
						total	2,350

Answer: Structure #2 (1:10 ratio hedge) provides better protection. Delta and Gamma values for both trades are listed in the following two tables. Totals appear at the bottom.

Structure #1   Stock = $157.00   Implied Vol. = 30%

Strike	Days Rem.	Ratio	Delta	Position Delta	Gamma	Position Gamma	Price	Position Price
150	20	1	0.76	0.76	0.028	0.028	8.74	8.74
165	20	−3	0.25	−0.75	0.029	−0.087	1.61	−4.83
150	48	−1	0.69	−0.69	0.021	−0.021	10.86	−10.86
165	48	3	0.35	1.05	0.022	0.066	3.77	11.31
		totals		0.37		−0.014		4.36

Structure #2   Stock = $157.00   Implied Vol. = 30%

Strike	Days Rem.	Ratio	Delta	Position Delta	Gamma	Position Gamma	Price	Position Price
150	20	1	0.76	0.76	0.028	0.028	8.74	8.74
165	20	−3	0.25	−0.75	0.029	−0.087	1.61	−4.83
150	48	−1	0.69	−0.69	0.021	−0.021	10.86	−10.86
180	48	10	0.12	1.20	0.012	0.120	0.93	9.30
			totals	0.52		0.040		2.35

Structure #2 has a higher net delta (0.52 versus 0.37) and, more important, a much higher net gamma (0.040 versus −0.014). Simply stated, the 1:3 structure is short gamma while the 1:10 structure is long gamma. As the underlying price rises, position delta will rise for structure #2 but not for structure #1. Repeating the analysis of problem #10 reveals that structure #2 is considerably more profitable. Result tables for the near-term upward price spike are displayed next.

Structure #1   Stock = $180.00   Implied Vol. = 30%

Position	Call Strike	Days Rem.	Price	Contr.	Position Value	Net
10 long calls	150	0	30.00	10	30,000	
30 short calls	165	0	15.00	−30	−45,000	−15,000
10 short calls	150	28	30.18	−10	−30,180	
30 long calls	165	28	16.20	30	48,600	18,420
					total	3,420
					initial cost	4,360
					loss	−940

Structure #2   Stock = $180.00   Implied Vol. = 30%

Position	Call Strike	Days Rem.	Price	Contr.	Position Value	Net
10 long calls	150	0	30.00	10	30,000	
30 short calls	165	0	15.00	−30	−45,000	−15,000
10 short calls	150	28	30.18	−10	−30,180	
100 long calls	180	28	6.03	100	60,300	30,120
					total	15,120
					initial cost	2,350
					gain	12,770

Structure #2 gains $12,770 while structure #1 loses $940. Surprisingly, structure #2 also has an initially lower cost ($2,350 versus $3,420). However, greater profit with a lower initial cost implies greater risk. That risk manifests itself as a high rate of time decay in the trade with the wider strike spacing. Theta parameters for the two trades are displayed in the following tables.

Structure #1   Stock = $157.00   Implied Vol. = 30%

Position	Strike	Days Rem.	Contr.	Theta	Realized Theta ($)
10 long calls	150	20	10	−0.095	−95.00
30 short calls	165	20	−30	−0.086	258.00
10 short calls	150	48	−10	−0.064	64.00
30 long calls	165	48	30	−0.071	−213.00
				total	14.00

Structure #2   Stock = $157.00   Implied Vol. = 30%

Position	Strike	Days Rem.	Contr.	Theta	Realized Theta ($)
10 long calls	150	20	10	−0.095	−95.00
30 short calls	165	20	−30	−0.086	258.00
10 short calls	150	48	−10	−0.064	64.00
100 long calls	180	48	100	−0.031	−310.00
				total	−83.00

Realized theta (rightmost column) refers to the actual daily cost, in dollars, of each position. Since 10 contracts represents 1,000 shares, realized theta for a 10-contract position is equal to theta multiplied by 1,000.

The calculations reveal that net realized theta is positive for structure #1 and negative for structure #2. Stated differently, structure #1 gains $14 each day while structure #2 loses $83. The culprit is the excessive time decay realized in 100 long $180 calls which are $23 out-of-the-money. In percentage terms, structure #2 has a daily time decay cost equal to 3.5% ($83 / $2,350) of its initial cost. These dynamics make sense because excessively wide strike spacing will cause the long side of the hedge to expire worthless unless the stock rises above $180 by expiration. The maximum potential loss for the 1:10 hedge is $30 plus the initial trade cost, while the maximum potential loss of the 1:3 hedge is just $15 plus the initial cost. The hedge contained in structure #2 represents a trade-off between a very large long gamma position and excessive time decay.

12. The following table contains two 1:2 ratio trades. Trade #1 is composed of 10 long $345 calls/20 short $355 calls, both with the same expiration. Trade #2 is also a 1:2 ratio, but the two sides expire in different months. Because implied volatility in the second month is higher (26% versus 22%), the delta-neutral

trade structure has a long strike that is higher than the short strike. Trade #2 is composed of 10 long $360 calls/20 short $355 calls.

Stock = $326.59   Days Remaining = 32/67   Imp. Vol. = .22/.26

Trade	Position	Days Rem.	Strike	Price	Impl. Vol.	Contr.	Delta	Gamma	Pos. Value	Net
1	long call	32	345	2.50	0.22	10	0.21	0.014	2500	
	short call	32	355	1.08	0.22	−20	0.11	0.009	−2160	340
2	long call	67	360	4.13	0.26	10	0.21	0.008	4130	
	short call	32	355	1.08	0.22	−20	0.11	0.009	−2160	1970

Which trade will lose more money if the underlying stock immediately climbs 3 standard deviations? Both trades are almost exactly delta-neutral, so how can the relative risk be identified? What circumstances would support a forward ratio trade structure that spans different months?

Answer: Trade #2 is more dangerous and will lose significantly more money than trade #1 if the stock rallies sharply. Once again, net position gamma is the best metric. The first trade has a net gamma of −0.004; the second trade has a gamma of −0.01, which is 2.5× larger. Stated differently, the position delta of trade #2 rises 2.5× faster than the delta of trade #1. The rate also accelerates and, in the case of a 3 standard deviation increase, the difference becomes significant.

The following table displays relevant parameters for both trades after a 1-day 3 standard deviation upward move. P&L values are listed in the final column.

Stock = $340.00   Days Remaining = 31/66   Imp. Vol. = .22/.26

Trade	Position	Days Rem.	Strike	Price	Impl. Vol.	Contr.	Delta	Gamma	Pos. Value	Net
1	long call	31	345	6.60	0.22	10	0.43	0.018	6600	
	short call	31	355	3.40	0.22	−20	0.26	0.015	−6800	−200
									P&L	−540
2	long call	66	360	7.63	0.26	10	0.33	0.010	7630	
	short call	31	355	3.40	0.22	−20	0.26	0.015	−6800	830
									P&L	−1140

Trade #2 loses more than twice as much money as trade #1. If implied volatility had been equal across expirations or—even better—lower in the second month, we would have been able to structure a delta-neutral trade without inverting the strikes. Being long the far strike and short twice as many options at the near strike creates a high-risk position that is very sensitive to a sharp move of the underlying stock. These dynamics illustrate the important role played by term structure in positions that span different expirations. In the case of trade #2, we purchased 26% implied volatility but sold only 22%.

It is also important to note that trade #2 was initially much more expensive than trade #1. This additional expense creates a second risk because the full value of the trade will be lost if the stock falls sharply. Adjustments in such situations are difficult because the choices all involve taking on more risk by selling lower strikes, more options, or both.

7

Stock and Option Trades

From an option trader's perspective, pure stock investing is relatively dangerous. That view results from an understanding that there are many different ways to structure bullish or bearish positions on a stock using options. In some sense, this entire book is about alternatives to trading stocks.

Option traders know, for example, that buying a stock is mathematically equivalent to simultaneously selling a put and buying a call. They also recognize that there are many safer ways to create a bullish stock position. For example, an option trader who decides to purchase a stock might also sell puts and buy calls to create a more conservative position that caps both the maximum gain and the maximum loss. A more aggressive investor might opt for a covered call where the distance between the spot price of the stock and the strike price of the option can be fine-tuned to manage risk.

As we have seen, there are many other approaches to creating short or long positions—some that involve stock and options and some that only use options. Many option traders with a bullish view simply sell in-the-money puts. Others buy in-the-money calls. The possibilities are almost endless. But there are many situations where it makes sense to structure trades that contain both stock and options.

This chapter is about those situations. It is designed to build on Chapter 3, "Covered Puts and Calls," which explores the dynamics of covered puts and calls. In this regard, the problems in this chapter are fundamentally equivalent to trade structures that have an option component with a delta of 1.

251

The simplest way to protect a stock position is by purchasing a put. Both the level of protection and the cost are determined by the strike price. Far out-of-the-money puts provide less protection; near-the-money puts provide more.

Unfortunately, purchasing protective puts can be an expensive proposition. Not surprisingly, there is a better way. The simple answer is to pay for the long puts by selling similarly priced out-of-the-money calls. The complete position is called a collar.

Collars can obviously be used to protect both short and long stock positions. A short collar is composed of short stock hedged with long calls that are paid for by selling puts. In both cases the concept is simple but the variety of choices is tremendous. Collars can span different expirations and they can be asymmetrical with regard to strike price spacing. Some investors rebracket the stock each month with new options, whereas others use long-term structures.

1. The following table contains two different collars for a stock initially trading at $100. Which of the trades is more bullish?

Trade	Position	Days Rem.	Impl. Volat.	Price	Net
1	100 shares long Stock @ $100			10,000.00	
	1 short $110 call	60	0.45	−3.70	
	1 long $90 put	60	0.45	2.98	9,999.28
2	100 shares long Stock @ $100			10,000.00	
	1 short $120 call	90	0.45	−2.90	
	1 long $80 put	90	0.45	1.63	9,998.73

Answer: Trade #2 is more bullish. Measured in standard deviations, its maximum profit is capped at a greater distance from the trading price of the stock. Trade #2 is capped at 0.89 StdDev while trade #1 is capped at only 0.55 StdDev. The calculations appear in the following table.

Trade	Description	1 StdDev	Dist. StdDev	Calculation
1	60 days / $10	$18.24	0.55	0.45 × $100 / Sqrt(365/60)
2	90 days / $20	$22.35	0.89	0.45 × $100 / Sqrt(365/90)

2. The following table defines a new skew and option prices for the 90-day expiration of problem #1. What effect does the steep skew have on the cost of the trade? How would the change be reflected in annual profit if the trade was repeated each quarter?

Stock = $100   Days Remaining = 90

Option	Strike	Impl. Volat.	Price
call	120	0.45	2.90
call	115	0.46	4.10
call	110	0.47	5.63
call	105	0.48	7.52
call	100	0.50	9.99
put	100	0.50	9.74
put	95	0.52	7.60
put	90	0.55	5.98
put	85	0.59	4.80
put	80	0.64	3.96
put	75	0.70	3.37
put	70	0.77	2.95

Answer: It is no longer possible to use equally spaced options to structure a trade with a credit. (The 90-day trade in problem #1 had a $1.27 credit.) Using the same strikes (short $120 call / long $80 put), the new trade would cost $1.06.

The new trade represents an annual debit of $4.24 or 4.2% of the trading price of the underlying stock. The previous trade delivered a $5.08 (5.1%) annual credit. The difference (9%) represents a large performance gap between the two trades that is comparable to giving up $9 of annual profit. This difference is realized in all scenarios, including those where the trade was consistently profitable.

3. The implied volatility skew of problem #2 reveals a simple trade-off between a collar that is structured with evenly spaced options and one that is asymmetric. We can still create a trade where the short call pays for the long put if we sell $120 calls and purchase $70 puts. This structure, however, trades more favorable pricing for more exposure on the downside. Alternatively, we might choose to accept the relatively large $1.06 debit associated with evenly spaced strikes.

How would you quantify the trade-off in terms of risk versus cost? Is there a way to estimate the fair additional cost of structuring the trade with equally spaced strikes?

Answer: In the most basic terms we are purchasing a $10 improvement in the maximum loss for $1.06. However, because implied volatility varies substantially across strikes, it is relatively difficult to precisely calculate the risk in percentage terms. One reasonable approach is to use the average across the range (63.5%) to calculate the percentage chance of a decline to $70 versus a decline to $80. For a $100 stock with 63.5% volatility, a 90-day 1 StdDev price change is equal to $31.53 ($100 × 0.635 / Sqrt[365/90]). A decline to $80 represents 0.63 StdDev and a decline to $70 represents 0.95 StdDev.

Using the normal distribution, we can calculate the percent chance of each of these declines based on standard option pricing theory. The simplest way is to use the normal distribution (NORM.S.DIST) function in Excel. Results are shown in the table that follows. The results reveal that 73.6% of all price changes can be expected to result in the stock trading above $80 at the end of 90 days; 82.9% of price changes will result in a final stock price above $70. Subtracting from 100% (final column) yields the relative chance of a price change that moves the stock beyond each of these thresholds—26.4% for a decline beyond $80 and 17.1% for a decline beyond $70.

StdDev	New Price	Normal Distribution	% Chance
−0.63	$80	0.736	0.264
−0.95	$70	0.829	0.171

The extra $10 loss, therefore, has a statistical risk of just over 9.3% (26.4%–17.1%). The $1.06 premium is very close to this value since 9.3% × $10 is equal to $0.93. So our decision to purchase the insurance must depend on our view of the stock's likely performance and our own personal tolerance for losses.

4. Can we solve the pricing issue of problem #3 by selling calls with 90 days remaining before expiration and purchasing new puts each month with just 30 days? In what way does this trade structure introduce additional risk?

Answer: Shorter-term deep out-of-the-money puts are proportionately less expensive, so a series of these options will normally add up to less than the value of the single long-term option. Actual values for the $80 put of problem #3 (64% implied volatility / underlying stock @ $100) are $0.88 with 30 days remaining and $3.96 with 90 days remaining. A series consisting of 3 consecutive 30-day puts would cost only $2.64, which is less than the price of the 90-day $120 call ($2.90).

Structuring the trade this way initially reduces the price of the long protective put but can add significant cost to the trade if the stock declines and the price of the long put rises. If, for example, the stock fell to $90 at the end of the first 30-day expiration, the cost of purchasing a new 30-day put would rise to

$1.74. (This price was calculated using the implied volatility skew, which gives a value of 55% for a put that is $10 out-of-the-money.) The total cost of the new trade would then be $0.88 for the first month and $1.74 for the second. With another month left to purchase, the put side of the trade has already cost $2.62 and only $2.90 was realized from the sale of the 90-day $120 call.

5. Assume that the situation described in problem #4 materialized (i.e., the stock fell to $90) and we decided to adjust our trade by selling a $100 call with 60 days remaining and buying another 30-day put at the $80 strike. The new trade would, therefore, be long stock at $90, long an $80 put with 30 days remaining, and short a $100 call with 60 days remaining. Price data for this adjustment is available in the following table. These prices are built on the same implied volatility skew as problems #2, #3, and #4.

Stock = $90

Option	Strike	Days Rem.	Impl. Volat.	Price
call	120	60	0.45	0.47
call	100	60	0.47	3.32
put	80	30	0.55	1.74

What would the cost of this adjustment be? Will the adjustment to the call side of the trade cover the cost of the put side?

Answer: The adjustment is easiest to understand in individual steps. The first step involves buying back the far out-of-the-money $120 calls that still have 60 days remaining before expiration. This trade has a $0.47 debit. The next step is simply the purchase of $100 calls that also have 60 days remaining. This trade has a $3.32 credit. The net credit is, therefore, $2.85.

The final step is the purchase of the 30-day $80 protective put for $1.74.

The call-side adjustment will completely offset the cost of the $80 puts by converting $0.47 of residual value into $2.85. If the underlying price remains at $90, we will be able to repeat the $80 put purchase for another $1.74 and the total for 2 months will be $3.48. The 3 months will have a total cost of $0.88 + $1.74 + $1.74 = $4.36. This expense will be offset by the sale of the first call for $2.90 plus the second call for $3.32 minus the cost to repurchase the first call with 60 days remaining for $0.47 ($2.90 + $3.32 – $0.47 = $5.75). The net credit of all the trades will be $5.75 – $4.36 = $1.39.

6. Investors often generate revenue through sequential sales of near-dated call options against an underlying stock that they already own. Weekly options have ratcheted up the level of interest in this type of covered call strategy because the amount of premium that can be captured is far larger. For example, a 7-day $100 call priced with 30% implied volatility on a $100 stock would be worth $1.67, while a 1-month option (28 days) with the same parameters would be worth only $3.35. Four successive weekly options would, therefore, generate twice as much revenue if the stock remained at this price. These dynamics make sense because time decay accelerates exponentially as options approach expiration.

The following table includes both weekly and monthly prices for 8 weeks of call option sales against a stock that opens the first week trading at $94.45 and closes week #8 at $107.36. All options are priced with 26% implied volatility. Our trade involves purchasing the stock at the beginning of week 1 and selling weekly call options at the nearest out-of-the-money strike each week for the next 8 weeks. We will completely unwind the position by selling the stock and settling the final option trade at the end of week #8 (beginning of week #9).

Comments	Opening Stock Price	Strike	Weekly Call	Monthly Call
week 1/month 1	94.45	95	1.11	2.49
week 2	93.66	95	0.80	
week 3	93.73	95	0.82	
week 4	94.01	95	0.93	
week 5/month 2	92.75	95	0.52	1.75
week 6	95.68	95	1.75	
week 7	99.59	100	1.25	
week 8	103.54	105	0.89	
week 9/month 3	107.36	—	—	—

It is important to note that the closing price for each week is the opening price for the next. For example, the opening price for week #5 ($92.75) is the closing price for week #4. Weeks #1, #5, and #9 also mark monthly expirations.

Does the weekly covered call strategy outlined in the table outperform simply owning the stock? What is the profit/loss with and without the weekly option trades?

Answer: The strategy performed poorly and it would have been better to own the stock without selling options. Overall, we sold options worth $8.07 and spent $11.17 to close in-the-money trades at expiration. Option trades, therefore, subtracted $3.10 from the profit gained by owning the stock. The following table provides details.

Comments	Opening Stock Price	Strike	Weekly Call	Cost to Close Trade
week 1/month 1	94.45	95	1.11	0.00
week 2	93.66	95	0.80	0.00
week 3	93.73	95	0.82	0.00
week 4	94.01	95	0.93	0.00
week 5/month 2	92.75	95	0.52	0.68
week 6	95.68	95	1.75	4.59
week 7	99.59	100	1.25	3.54
week 8	103.54	105	0.89	2.36
week 9/month 3	107.36	—	—	—

The stock traded for $94.45 at the opening of week #1 and closed week #8 at $107.36, generating a profit of $12.91. Subtracting the loss from the option trades yields a net profit of $9.81. Selling weekly calls reduced the net profit by 24%.

7. Would our trade have performed better in problem #6 if we sold monthly options? What is the final P&L for the monthly covered call trade after 2 months?

Answer: The monthly option trade performed much worse than the weekly trades by losing $8.12. Although the two call sales generated $4.24 of option premium, the second trade had to be closed for a loss of $12.36. Details are outlined in the table that follows.

Comments	Opening Stock Price	Strike	Monthly Call	Cost to Close Trade
month 1	94.45	95	2.49	0.00
month 2	92.75	95	1.75	12.36
month 3	107.36	—	—	—

As before, the stock traded for $94.45 at the opening of month #1 and closed month #2 at $107.36, generating a profit of $12.91. Subtracting the loss of the option trades yields a net profit of $4.79. Selling monthly calls, therefore, reduced the net profit by 63%.

8. Can you verify that selling at-the-money naked puts is mathematically identical to selling a covered call using at-the-money options?

Answer: Suppose we own a stock trading for $100 and sell a $100 call for $2.00. If the stock rises $5.00, we will lose $3.00 on the call, leaving a total profit of $2.00. If instead of a covered call, we sell an at-the-money put for $2.00 and the stock rises, our profit will be equal to the value of the put. Both trades yield the same profit.

Conversely if the stock were to fall $5.00, our covered call trade would generate a $3.00 net loss (a $2.00 profit from the short call and a $5.00 loss in the stock). The naked short put would lose the exact same amount of money because we would keep $2.00 premium from the original sale and spend $5.00 to close the position.

8

Trading the Weekly Options Expiration

Expiration provides unusual trading opportunities because traditional option pricing methods are unreliable when the amount of
time remaining is very short. For example, the fair value at 4:00 PM
Thursday for an at-the-money call on a $100 stock trading with 45%
implied volatility is $0.94 if the next day is expiration. The same
option, however, would be worth just $0.49 the next morning when
the market opens at 9:30 AM. A trader purchasing this option on
Thursday must be aware that overnight time decay will destroy nearly
half the remaining value while a seller must somehow protect himself
against the large impact of a relatively small overnight price change—
if the underlying price rises to $101, the option will be worth $1.15.
The effect of this small change appears even more dramatic when
one considers that a 1-day 1 standard deviation price change for this
stock is $2.84.

The appearance of weekly options for popular stocks and ETFs
has created new opportunities in the form of unusual trade structures. It is now possible, for example, to structure a calendar spread
using options that expire one week apart or to buy monthly contracts
and sell new options each week to offset the cost. Conversely, you
might choose to buy weekly options, and offset part of the time decay
by selling options that expire later in the same month. Weekly expirations also overlap because new contracts having 8 days remaining
before expiration become available each Thursday morning when the
current week still has 2 trading days left. The new trading dynamics,

therefore, include back-to-back overlapping expirations coupled with more traditional monthly options.

The enormous popularity of weekly options has created a new set of price distortions because thousands of retail investors flood into the market each week attempting to sell time premium for contracts that have just a few days, or even a few hours, before expiration. The selling pressure manifests itself as depressed implied volatility that tends to undercompensate sellers for the risk they are taking.

Superimposed on these distortions is the "pinning" effect that tends to cause many stocks to gravitate to a strike price on expiration day as traders unwind a variety of complex positions using options at that particular strike. Traders have been trading the pinning effect for many years, and the popularity of this type of trade has exploded since weekly options became available. Unfortunately, pinning effect trades can be very dangerous when a stock suddenly drifts away from a strike price. In the worst cases a stock will jump from one strike to another, causing spectacular losses for trades that depend on stable time decay.

This chapter presents several problems designed to highlight these price distortions and the trading opportunities they create. It is meant to serve as a springboard for investors who are new to options expiration and are interested in testing and understanding a variety of expiration-related trade structures.

1. The following table describes a ratio trade consisting of 10 short $95 calls and 20 long $100 calls for a stock trading at $100. The trade was placed at the market open on expiration day.

Stock = $100   Imp. Vol. = 45%   Time = 9:30

Description	Strike	Price	Delta	Contr.	Value	Net
10 short calls	95	5.00	1.00	−10	−5,000	
20 long calls	100	0.49	0.50	20	980	−4,020

What are the break-even points for this trade structure? What is the maximum profit if the stock rises? What is the maximum profit if the stock falls?

Answer: The upper break-even point is $100.98; the lower break-even is $99.02. Maximum profit if the stock rises is unlimited. Maximum profit if the stock falls is limited to the credit of the trade—$4.02 or $4,020 for the 10-contract trade described in the table.

2. Suppose in problem #1 we had purchased a $100 straddle for $0.98 in place of the ratio trade. How do the two trades compare if the stock rises? How do they compare if the price falls?

Answer: The two trades yield identical results unless the stock falls below the lower break-even point. The following table verifies these results for several different closing prices above and below the initial trading price.

Initial Ratio = –$4.02   Initial Strdl. = $0.98

Stock	Ratio	Ratio P&L	Straddle	Strdl. P&L
100.00	–5.00	–0.98	0.00	–0.98
100.50	–4.50	–0.48	0.50	–0.48
101.00	–4.00	0.02	1.00	0.02
105.00	0.00	4.02	5.00	4.02
110.00	5.00	9.02	10.00	9.02
99.50	–4.50	–0.48	0.50	–0.48
99.00	–4.00	0.02	1.00	0.02
95.00	0.00	4.02	5.00	4.02
90.00	0.00	4.02	10.00	9.02

Note: If the in-the-money $95 calls had additional time pre-mium, the credit of the ratio trade would be larger and the break-even points would be farther away from the $100 strike. Such distortions often occur at expiration when traders become aggressive about unwinding large in-the-money positions. However, the same dynamics would likely affect at-the-money options, inflating prices for the $100 strike. Pricing for both trades would be skewed. It therefore makes sense to compare the break-even points before selecting a trade. The asymmetry of the ratio must also be taken into account because one side of the trade has unlimited profit potential while the other is capped by the value of the initial credit.

3. The following table contains two different trades that were each initiated on Monday at 9:30 AM using options that expire on Friday—that is, 4.27 days before expiration. Which trade would make the most sense in a strongly bearish market characterized by sharp downward corrections?

Stock = $102.50   Imp. Vol. = 50%   Remaining = 4.27 Days

Trade	Description	Strike	Price	Delta	Contr.	Value	Net
1	10 short calls	100	3.67	0.69	−10	−3,670	
	20 long calls	105	1.21	0.34	20	2,420	−1,250
2	10 short puts	105	3.70	−0.66	−10	−3,700	
	20 long puts	100	1.15	−0.31	20	2,300	−1,400

Answer: Trade #2 is more bearish than trade #1. If the stock falls, trade #1 can generate only its initial $1.25 credit. Trade #2, however, does not cap the profit of a move to the downside. Moreover, trade #2 reflects the view that the stock will either rise slightly or fall sharply; its break-even points are $93.60 and $106.40, which translates into down $8.90 or up $3.90.

4. Option traders often take advantage of the rapidly accelerating time decay of expiration week. Especially significant is the decay that occurs over the final weekend. Theoretically, a trade placed on Friday morning will experience 3 full days (72 hours) of time decay before the market reopens at 9:30 AM on Monday. These 3 days represent a major portion of the time remaining before the contracts expire the following Friday at 4:00 PM (174.5 hours).

The following table outlines a four-part short condor trade for a stock trading at $100.00. The trade is placed when the market opens at 9:30 AM on Friday. It consists of a short $100 straddle and a long $105/$95 strangle that caps off both the maximum loss and the collateral requirement. The table displays bid and ask prices for each of the options.

Stock = $100.00   Remaining = 7.27 Days

Description	Strike	Bid (44%)	Ask (46%)
10 long calls	105	0.79	0.87
10 short calls	100	2.49	2.60
10 short puts	100	2.47	2.58
10 long puts	95	0.69	0.77

What is the overall bid-ask spread for the trade? How much net time decay must the trade achieve to break even at the market open on Monday?

Answer: The following tables reveal final prices for the two extremes.

Sell @ Bid/Buy @ Ask

Description	Strike	Price	Net
10 long calls	105	0.87	
10 short calls	100	−2.49	
10 short puts	100	−2.47	
10 long puts	95	0.77	−3.32

Buy @ Bid/Sell @ Ask

Description	Strike	Price	Net
10 long calls	105	0.79	
10 short calls	100	−2.60	
10 short puts	100	−2.58	
10 long puts	95	0.69	−3.70

The net difference of $0.38 represents the slippage of the trade that must be covered by time decay.

5. Projected values for the position outlined in problem #4 are displayed in the following table. The entries are calculated at 9:30 AM on successive days (column 1) using the midpoint implied volatility of the initial position (45%).

Stock = $100
Impl. Vol. = 45%

Day	Pos. Value ($)
Fri	−3.50
Sat	−3.39
Sun	−3.27
Mon	−3.12
Tues	−2.89
Wed	−2.58
Thurs	−2.05
Fri	−0.98

When does time decay finally overwhelm the bid-ask spread cost of the trade? Which day provides the most time decay? When does time decay proceed at the fastest rate?

Answer: Sometime after the open on Monday. We can fill out the table with theta values by subtracting each day's position value from the next.

Day	Pos. Value ($)	Pos. Theta
Fri	−3.50	0.11
Sat	−3.39	0.12
Sun	−3.27	0.15
Mon	−3.12	0.23
Tues	−2.89	0.31
Wed	−2.58	0.53
Thurs	−2.05	1.07
Fri	−0.98	0.98

Time decay values are $0.11 for the time frame from Friday morning to Saturday morning; $0.12 from Saturday to Sunday; and $0.15 from Sunday to Monday when the market opens. In total, therefore, we would expect the trade to experience $0.38 of time decay before the market opens on Monday. Decay accelerates to $0.23 on Monday so we would expect to gain $0.61 by Tuesday if the stock remained exactly at $100.

The overnight time-decay effect can be optimized by placing the trade on Thursday morning when the market opens with $2.05 of time premium remaining and only 30.5 hours left before expiration. The fastest rate of decay occurs on expiration Friday at a rate of $0.98 in 6.5 hours ($0.16 per hour). The absolute fastest rate occurs in the final hour where $0.38 of remaining value vanishes from at-the-money options (data not shown in the table).

6. The following table contains a trade that consists of long and short straddles with different expirations. Both sides of the trade were placed at 9:30 AM on Thursday. The short side expires the next day while the long side has another week remaining before expiration. The trader who placed the trade assumed that the long side would provide protection against a large move of the underlying stock.

Stock = $100   Impl. Vol. = 45%

Days	Option	Price	Delta	Gamma	Contr.	Net	Total
1.27	100 call	1.06	0.51	0.150	−10		
1.27	100 put	1.06	−0.49	0.150	−10	−2,120	
8.27	100 call	2.71	0.51	0.059	10		
8.27	100 put	2.69	−0.49	0.059	10	5,400	3,280

Why does a small move of the underlying stock generate a relatively large loss?

Answer: The large gamma of the near-expiration options makes the short side of the trade sensitive to small moves of the underlying stock. Stated differently, the overall trade is short large amounts of gamma. A relatively small price change has the capacity to imbalance the near-expiration deltas. Once the deltas are imbalanced, the in-the-money side will rise quickly and the out-of-the-money side will stop falling. The near-expiration will, therefore, become equivalent to a long or short stock position.

The distant expiration is much less sensitive to small moves of the underlying stock. The difference is apparent in the gamma values which are barely more than 1/3 of the near-expiration options. Small moves of the underlying will, therefore, generate much less imbalance in the deltas of the two sides, and the gain on one side will be partly offset by the loss on the other. The following table depicts the effect of an immediate $3.00 upward move of the underlying stock.

Stock = $103   Impl. Vol. = 45%

Days	Option	Price	Delta	Gamma	Contr.	Net	Total
1.27	100 call	3.18	0.87	0.077	−10		
1.27	100 put	0.18	−0.13	0.077	−10	−3,360	
8.27	100 call	4.51	0.68	0.051	10		
8.27	100 put	1.49	−0.32	0.051	10	6,000	2,640

The value of the position fell 19.5%, from $3,280 to $2,640.

7. Is the maximum loss capped in problem #6? If so, what is the maximum loss? Why do gamma values fall when the stock rises? How does the change in gamma relate to the maximum loss?

Answer: The maximum loss is capped when the stock moves far into-the-money because the deltas of the in-the-money options eventually rise to 1.0. Once this point is reached, the far-dated expiration will gain value as fast as the near-dated expiration. The maximum loss is equal to the initial value of the trade—in this case $3,280 for a 10-contract calendar spread straddle.

As one side of a straddle moves far into-the-money, its delta approaches 1.0 while the delta of the losing side falls to zero. Once these extremes are reached, gamma falls to zero on both sides. The $3 move depicted in problem #6 reduced the near-expiration gamma values by approximately half. Further movement of the stock in the same direction will cause the gammas of the near and far expirations to equalize as the deltas approach their limits. For large underlying price changes the gammas will all fall to zero and the maximum loss will be capped.

For example, a $10 underlying move will set the near-dated expiration gammas to 0.00 and the far-dated expiration gammas to 0.019. At this point, 84% of the maximum loss has been realized, with the position retaining just $530 of its initial $3,280 value.

Stock = $110   Impl. Vol. = 45%

Days	Option	Price	Delta	Gamma	Contr.	Net	Total
1.27	100 call	10.00	1.00	0.000	−10		
1.27	100 put	0.00	0.00	0.000	−10	−10,000	
8.27	100 call	10.28	0.93	0.019	10		
8.27	100 put	0.25	−0.07	0.019	10	10,530	530

8. Would it make sense to take the other side of the trade described in problems #6–7 by purchasing the near-dated straddle and selling the far-dated straddle? Can you describe the results in terms of price changes measured in standard deviations?

Answer: The $3 price increase of problem #6 resulted in a loss of 19.5%. Taking the other side of this trade would, therefore, have resulted in a 19.5% gain. Since a 1-day 1 StdDev price change for this stock is equal to $100 × .45 / Sqrt(252) = $2.84, the price change in question is equal to 1.05 StdDev. Trades that generate 19.5% profit from a 1 StdDev underlying price change in either direction are very rare.

Glossary

American-Style Option   An option that can be exercised at any time prior to expiration.

Arbitrage   Simultaneous purchase and sale of the same or equivalent security on the same or different markets in order to profit from price discrepancies. Many authors mistakenly define arbitrage as buying in one market and selling in another to take advantage of a price disparity. However, more often than not, arbitrage trading occurs across equivalent financial instruments in the same market. For example, the simultaneous purchase of stock and an equivalent number of mispriced put options can often be used to structure an arbitrage prior to a dividend payment. This trade, properly executed, is riskless. Merger arbitrage involving the exchange of stock between companies and arbitrages that are related to put-call parity violations are also common variations. In all cases the trade must be riskless to be considered an arbitrage.

At-the-Money   An option whose exercise (strike) price is equal to the current trading price of the underlying security. The term is sometimes used to refer to the option whose strike price is closest to the current trading price of the underlying.

Backspread A structure in which more options are purchased than sold but at a less favorable strike. A call backspread is established by selling calls at a lower strike and purchasing more at a higher strike.

Bear Spread A trade consisting of long and short contracts having different strike prices and/or expiration dates that increase in value when the price of the underlying security declines.

Bull Spread A trade consisting of long and short contracts having different strike prices and/or expiration dates that increases in value when the price of the underlying security rises.

Butterfly The sale (purchase) of two options with the same strike price along with the purchase (sale) of one option at a lower strike and one option with a higher strike. All options must be the same type (call or put) and have the same expiration date. Exercise prices must be symmetrically spaced. For example, the structure 10 long $100 calls/20 short $110 calls/10 long $120 calls is a long butterfly.

Calendar Spread A position consisting of long and short components that spans different expirations—a time spread.

Condor The sale (purchase) of two options with different exercise prices along with the purchase (sale) of one option at a lower strike and one with a higher strike. All options must be the same type (call or put) and have the same expiration date. Exercise prices must be symmetrically spaced. For example, the structure 10 long $100 calls/10 short $110 calls/10 short $120 calls/10 long $130 calls is a long condor. Such trades are designed to profit from time decay; the outside long positions, also known as "wings," are hedges against large price changes. Short condors in which the inside strikes are purchased are designed to generate profit when the underlying security moves a substantial amount. In this case the wings are used to offset time decay costs.

Covered Call   A structure consisting of long stock and an equivalent number of short calls. Covered call positions can also be established using long calls instead of stock. In the pure option case, the long option must have more favorable terms—that is, the same or later expiration and the same or lower strike.

Covered Put   A structure consisting of short stock and an equivalent number of long puts. Covered put positions can also be established using long puts instead of short stock. In the pure option case, the long option must have more favorable terms—that is, the same or later expiration and the same or higher strike.

Delta   The sensitivity of an option price to a change in the price of the underlying security. For equity options, delta is measured as the effect of a $1 increase in the underlying. Call options have positive deltas and put options have negative deltas.

Delta-Neutral   A position in which the sum of all deltas—long and short—is approximately zero.

Diagonal Spread   A structure consisting of long and short options having different strike prices and expiration dates. Both sides of the trade must be the same type (call or put).

European-Style Option   An option that can be exercised only at expiration.

Gamma   The sensitivity of an option delta to a change in the price of the underlying security. For equity options gamma is measured as change in delta that accompanies a $1 increase in the underlying. Gamma can also be used to refer to an overall position or a portfolio. Hedge funds often track portfolio gamma because it is an important measure of risk. Generally speaking, it is dangerous to be short large amounts of gamma. The value is always positive regardless of the type of option because delta increases for both puts and calls when the underlying price rises—put delta becomes less negative and call delta becomes more positive.

Implied Volatility   The volatility derived from a known option price using associated parameters—underlying security price, time left before expiration, and risk-free interest rate.

In-the-Money   A term used to describe an option with intrinsic value. A call option is described as in-the-money when the underlying security trades below the strike price. The reverse is true for a put option, which is in-the-money when the underlying trades above the strike.

Intrinsic Value   The value of an option with all time premium removed—that is, the value if it were to expire immediately. For calls in which the strike is below the stock price, this value is equal to the stock price minus the strike price. For puts in which the strike is above the stock price, this value is equal to the strike price minus the stock price.

Out-of-the-Money   A term used to describe an option with no intrinsic value. A call option is described as out-of-the-money when the underlying security trades above the strike price. The reverse is true for a put option, which is out-of-the-money when the underlying trades below the strike.

Ratio Strategy   Any strategy built around unequal numbers of long and short securities.

Ratio Vertical Spread   A trade consisting of long and short options (calls or puts) in which a greater number are sold at the more distant strike and all contracts have the same expiration date. In most cases the initial position is structured so as to be delta-neutral.

Rho   The change in value of an option price that results from a 1% increase in the risk-free interest rate. Rho is larger for long-term or in-the-money options.

Straddle   A position consisting of equal numbers of long (short) calls and long (short) puts having the same expiration date and strike price.

Strangle   A position consisting of equal numbers of long (short) calls and long (short) puts having the same expiration date and different strike prices.

Synthetic Stock   A structure composed of a long (short) call and a short (long) put in which both options have the same expiration date and strike price. The long call/short put combination is equivalent to long stock; short call/long put is equivalent to short stock.

Term Structure   Measures the effect of time on implied volatility. Term structure can be visualized in a plot of implied volatility for at-the-money options versus expiration month. Its behavior tends to compress the shape of the smile curve as the maturity date increases. (See *Volatility Skew.*)

Theta   The amount of value that an option loses for each day of time that passes. Theta increases as expiration approaches, causing option values to fall more quickly near expiration. The Black-Scholes pricing formulas can be used to derive an accurate value for theta at any point in the expiration cycle if the underlying price, strike price, implied volatility or option price, and risk-free rate of return are known.

Time Value   The price of an option minus its intrinsic value. The value of an out-of-the-money option is equal to its time value.

Vega   The change in value of an option price that results from a 1% increase in implied volatility.

Vertical Spread   A structure composed of long and short options of the same type (calls or puts) expiring on the same date with different strike prices.

Volatility Skew   Describes the phenomenon in which implied volatility varies with strike price in the same month. The best-known skew is the "volatility smile," which causes out-of-the-money puts to be more expensive than option pricing theory would normally predict. The volatility smile became much more pronounced after the stock market crash of October 1987. Since then, implied volatility profiles for equity and index options have taken on a distinctly negative skew—that is, implied volatility tends to rise as the strike price decreases. Additionally, because put-call parity dictates that the relationship between strike price and implied volatility is the same for both types of contracts, in-the-money calls are also more expensive. The complete smile takes the form of an asymmetric curve that rises slightly above the trading price of the underlying security—that is, out-of-the-money calls also exhibit implied volatility increases. In a family of volatility smile curves containing one curve per month, the steepness of each successive curve becomes less pronounced.

INDEX

Numbers

FT Press
FINANCIAL TIMES

In an increasingly competitive world, it is quality
of thinking that gives an edge—an idea that opens new
doors, a technique that solves a problem, or an insight
that simply helps make sense of it all.

We work with leading authors in the various arenas
of business and finance to bring cutting-edge thinking
and best-learning practices to a global market.

It is our goal to create world-class print publications
and electronic products that give readers
knowledge and understanding that can then be
applied, whether studying or at work.

To find out more about our business
products, you can visit us at www.ftpress.com.